CLASSIC
VEGETARIAN
COOKING

from the
MIDDLE EAST
& NORTH AFRICA

CLASSIC
VEGETARIAN
COOKING

from the
MIDDLE EAST
& NORTH AFRICA

HABEEB SALLOUM

Interlink Books

An imprint of Interlink Publishing Group, Inc.
New York • Northampton

First published 2000 by

INTERLINK BOOKS
An imprint of Interlink Publishing Group, Inc.
99 Seventh Avenue • Brooklyn, New York 11215 and
46 Crosby Street • Northampton, Massachusetts 01060
www.interlinkbooks.com

Library of Congress Cataloging-in-Publication Data

Salloum, Habeeb.
    Classic vegetarian cooking from the Middle East and North Africa/by Habeeb
Salloum.
        p. cm.
    ISBN 1-56656-335-6 (hbk)
    1. Vegetarian cookery. 2. Cookery, Middle Eastern. 3. Cookery, North African.
    I. Title.

TX837 .S243 1999
641.5'636'0956--dc21

99-052103

Printed and bound in Canada

CONTENTS

ACKNOWLEDGEMENTS

I wish to especially thank my daughter Muna Salloum for her valuable advice in the organization of the book, for providing the historical background to some of the foods, and for her help in testing a number of the recipes. I also wish to thank my wife Fareeda Salloum and my daughter Leila Elias for their assistance in testing and tasting some of the recipes. In addition, I wish to thank those authors whose books provided interesting material, which I have quoted.

METRIC CONVERSION CHART

WEIGHT

1 ounce (oz) = 437.5 grains = 28.35 g
1 pound (lb) = 16 oz = .4536 kg
1 gram (g) = 1000 mg = .0353 oz
1 kilogram (kg) = 1000 g = 2.2046 lb

TEMPERATURE

Celsius° = 5/9 (F° - 32°)
Fahrenheit°= 9/5 C° + 32°

VOLUME

1 fluid ounce (fl oz) = 2.957 cl
1 pint (pt) = 16 fl oz = .4732 l
1 quart (qt) = 2 pt = .946 l
1 gallon (gal) = 4 qt = 3.7854 l
1 liter (l) = .2642 gal

INTRODUCTION

Walking through the streets of Baghdad, Damascus or any other city in the Middle East, engulfed in the smoke of barbecuing kebabs, the traveler is not apt to guess that behind these tempting aromas hides a world of vegetarian delights. Yet, in the historic Middle Eastern lands, which include the modern-day countries of the Arabian Peninsula, Egypt, Iraq, Syria, Lebanon, Jordan and the Palestine area, including Israel, meatless dishes have been the food of the masses since time immemorial.

For millennia the peasants and laborers in that part of the world have sustained themselves on these simple but tasty victuals. Rich, wholesome, economical, and full of flavor, these dishes have stood the test of centuries. Broad beans, *burghul,* chickpeas, eggs, grains, lentils, rice, yogurt and all types of cultivated and wild greens, flavored with just the right amount of seasoning, produce hearty and scrumptious appetizers, salads, soups, stews and vegetable patties, with a mouthwatering, delightful quality.

The skillful cook's use of herbs and spices creates a combination of tempting aromas that stimulate and invigorate the senses of taste and smell. This heady fragrance whets the appetite and heightens the anticipation of the meal to come. The aromatic and tasty patties, sauces and soup stocks, permeated with seasonings, are a gourmet's delight.

Be assured, however, that condiments are employed in moderation—just enough to give taste and enticement. You won't find the hot spicy dishes of the mysterious Orient in the cuisine of the Middle East.

Vegetable and yogurt appetizers, salads, bean patties and omelets can be served as main courses or as side dishes with stews and stuffed leaves. Stuffed vegetables—prepared most often with greens, such as cabbage, kohlrabi, Swiss chard and vine leaves—make excellent main courses for both ordinary meals and special occasions.

The herbs and spices used in the stuffings blend with the vegetables and enhance their taste. For lovers of vegetarian foods, stuffed leaves are perhaps the most toothsome of meatless dishes.

The Middle Eastern kitchen rarely uses canned vegetables, thus avoiding the preservatives that pose a constant and serious threat to human health. Only fresh or sun-dried grains and vegetables are utilized, and the water in which they are cooked is not discarded, preserving their nutrients.

From the simplest appetizer to the most elaborate stuffed vegetables, all dishes are prepared with attention to detail and presented with pride to family and guests. A meal that includes a half-dozen of these vegetarian dishes is an amazing gastronomic feast. The never-ending storehouse of Middle Eastern vegetarian cuisine contains a world of nutritious and satisfying foods.

Meat in Middle Eastern Culture

In these historical lands, vegetarian dishes have been the staff of life for farmers and laborers since the beginning of civilization. For the aristocrats it was a different story. The wealthy and powerful, through the centuries, disdained vegetarian dishes as the food of the lowly. For them, meat on the table meant food for their pride.

Even if they envied their servants' tasty vegetable dishes, their status required them to reject such simple food. The tantalizing aromas rising from the simmering pots of their servants were not for their tables.

Today, the status implied by meat still permeates Middle Eastern society. A farmer or factory worker subsists on a daily menu consisting almost entirely of fresh and dried vegetables and some milk products. But when a guest arrives, meat dishes are always served, even if the host can barely afford the expense. The simple vegetable stews and other meatless dishes that have kept their peasant ancestors healthy since recorded history, are not considered suitable for honored guests.

Middle Eastern restaurants, too, have fallen into this trap. According to culinary historians, the Arab kitchen includes, perhaps, 40,000 dishes. Yet, most public eating places in the Middle East, especially those catering to the upper and middle classes, offer a meager dozen dishes on their daily menu, all of them with meat. With the exception of falafel and hummus, the vegetarianism of the toiling masses is rarely reflected on restaurant tables.

In my youth, my parents, who had emigrated from Syria to Canada, homesteaded in southern Saskatchewan. During the Depression era they struggled to make a living in the thirst-starved soil of the Canadian West. The drought that forced many farmers to leave their land did not affect our family as severely, because my parents' background came to their aid. The vegetables they had grown in their semi-desert homeland kept us well fed and healthy. Still, when guests arrived, my mother would scurry to kill a chicken, disdaining to serve our usual delicious vegetable stews or the chickpea and lentil patties.

In later years, when I traveled to the Middle East, I searched in vain for quality restaurants that served the exquisite vegetarian dishes of my youth. These tasty vegetable delights, with their mouth-watering blend of smells, were nowhere to be found. I got the impression that in the Arab countries all meals were cooked with meat. I could not comprehend why the savory vegetarian foods were rejected. Apparently the codes of the affluent had not been discarded. Rather, they are guidelines by which all classes of Middle East society live, even in the furthest corners of these lands.

Unbroken Tradition

On the southern edge of the Arabian Peninsula lies Yemen. Once, on a visit, I was elated to receive an invitation to an authentic Yemeni feast in Sana'a, Yemen's capital. "At last I'm going to sample this country's cuisine at its best," I told my friend. My appetite for Yemeni food had been whetted a long time before when I read that Ibn Rusta, an Arab traveler who visited Sana'a in the tenth century, had written in his *Book of Useful Notes* that the city was unrivaled in its many tasty foods. At last, I was to test his culinary observation.

The invitation came from a former Yemeni Consul General who had been posted to Detroit, a city that has a large Yemeni community. His family was hosting a magnificent meal for business colleagues and friends. Knowing that my brother and I were visiting Sana'a with a group of American Yemeni immigrants, he included us among his guests.

His hospitality, typically Arab, is very common in the Yemen of our times. It is said that in the remote districts of the country, a Yemeni farmer or tribesman will aim threatening shots over the heads of travelers if they pass without stopping to sample his hospitality.

A cover had been spread on the carpeted floor, with cushions all around. Plates and bowls of attractively presented foods covered every inch of space. Again I thought of Ibn Rusta's words as our host and about fifty guests, including a number of foreign women—Yemeni women do not usually dine with strangers—sat down on the floor around the steaming dishes.

Among us were high government officials and businessmen who, along with peasants and workers, continue to eat in the ways of their ancestors. Yemenis, even the wealthy and the highly educated, have not adapted the Western fashion—they still eat with their hands while seated on the floor.

Silently we dipped our right hands, which we had washed in an adjoining room, into the savory foods. The mouth-watering aroma floating around us enhanced the atmosphere as we feasted on the foods of this ancient land—the land of the Queen of Sheba. As we supped on endless succulent dishes, it seemed to us North Americans that we had entered one of the stories found in the *Arabian Nights*.

Of course, this feast, offered by a wealthy host, consisted mostly of meat dishes. On the other hand, in that country, it is a different story for the poor.

The Yemeni kitchen, however, offers its poorer folk an equally tasty vegetarian cuisine. Leafy greens, *burghul,* dried beans, lentils, rice, eggplants, okra, tomatoes, and sorghum, along with a number of other vegetables and cereals, are the ingredients used in daily meals—always accompanied by bread, served hot out of the oven. Very little fat is employed in Yemeni cooking, contributing to the country's good record when it comes to heart ailments.

An Affinity for Spices

Cardamom, caraway, coriander, cumin, fenugreek, saffron, turmeric and, after the discovery of the Americas, fiery chilies, have always been the favored flavorings. Yemenis love hot spicy foods prepared with these seasonings, plus garlic and a good number of herbs, especially fresh cilantro and mint leaves. Relatively unknown to the outside world for centuries, Yemen's spiced foods have emerged from hiding. Yemeni Jews emigrating to Israel and Yemeni workers settling in Europe and North America have introduced their food to the outer world.

Long ago, the cuisine of the Arabian Gulf countries was dominated by the simple bedouin and pearl diver's foods. The choice of ingredients was limited: a few vegetables, seafood, and rice brought by Arab dhows that traded along the coasts of East Africa and the Indian subcontinent. In time, these renowned ships of commerce also brought back the spices of India and the Indonesian archipelago, and the people of the Arabian Gulf developed their own cuisine dominated by the aromatic essence of these spices.

The perfumes of these spices must have softened the once harsh life lived by most of the people of the Gulf area. Afnan R. Zayani writes in her *Taste of the Arabian Gulf:*

> In those days, [before the discovery of oil] women would daily decorate their simple homes with fragrant flowers and constantly burn *oud* (incense). This love for aromatic smells found its way to their taste in food to the extent of using the word *khaneen*— literally meaning perfumed—to pay a compliment to a particularly delicious dish.

The Arab association with spices goes back a long time. Even before the birth of Christ, Arab merchants dominated the spice trade. Acting as middlemen, they transported exotic herbs and spices to the Mediterranean region and beyond. The Arab dominance of commerce, which continued until the sixteenth century when the Portuguese captured the Arab-controlled ports and trade routes, was so strong that in the middle ages Arabic was considered to be the language of traders. When Columbus attempted to reach India by sailing westward, he took an Arabic-speaking interpreter with him.

In the past few decades, the newly discovered oil wealth in the Arabian Gulf countries has lured millions of workers from around the world. The foods brought by these migrants from the Indian subcontinent, Iran, and the Far East, have enriched the cuisine of this part of the Arabian Peninsula with an array of mouth-watering meatless dishes.

Despite the Middle East's emphasis on the prestige of meat consumption, the undeniable fact is that the health, vitality and strength of the majority of inhabitants of these lands are sustained by delicious vegetarian foods. From the time of the ancient Egyptians, believed to be the first people to appreciate food plants, seasoned vegetable dishes have been the pillars of life in these lands. Though hidden for centuries in the kitchens of the poor, these delectable dishes can be enjoyed today by anyone who wishes to visit the culinary world of the Middle East.

North African Parallels

In the North African countries, a similar pattern exists. No one who has enjoyed couscous, the national dish of these southern Mediterranean lands, in all its meaty variations, would dream that in many peasant homes this delicacy is prepared solely from vegetables and semolina. The toilers of the soil, who don't taste meat for weeks at a time, prepare not only couscous, but almost all their dishes from grains and vegetables only. With the right amount of herbs and spices, they create incredibly tasty meals. Their age-old recipes are an important part of the North African kitchen—a cuisine with an illustrious history.

A great number of North Africans firmly believe that no other place in the world has achieved a culinary art that reaches the exalted heights of their own cooking. In confirmation, a number of travelers have stated that the foods of the North African countries near the top—if not the greatest—of the world's eminent cuisines.

These spellbinding North African nations, with their long sandy coasts, rich plains, towering mountains and endless deserts, have seen many civilizations come and go. Phoenicians, Greeks, Romans, Arabs, French, Italians, Spanish and the Berbers, the original inhabitants of that part of the world, all had their day. They ruled for a while, then faded into history. All these peoples, with a touch of Portuguese, Turkish and Jewish influence, contributed to the creation of the North African kitchen as we know it today.

There is no doubt that Morocco has created the most well known of the North African cuisines. Culinary experts have written that great food and glorious civilizations complement each other. These food connoisseurs say that the factors that create a noteworthy cuisine are an abundance of ingredients, outside influences, a noble civilization, and refined palace life. These conditions were all present in the elegant palaces of the rich in Fez and Marrakesh. Here the superb Arab-Islamic civilization of Spain had its highest expression, and here the culinary art of Morocco flourished. In the homes of the wealthy, especially in Fez, a reception is still full of color and romance. The rich foods, the opulence of the surroundings, the elegance of the costumes, the Andalusian music, the dances of the *shikhaf,* the conversation and the courtesy of the hosts all create a sublime dining atmosphere.

In her book, *Couscous and the Other Good Foods from Morocco,* Paula Wolfert writes that Moroccan cooking is the last of the great undiscovered cuisines. Included in this relatively unknown kitchen with a distinguished past are the savory dishes of the workers and peasants. As in all foods prepared by the toiling masses in non-affluent lands, little meat is utilized. Grains and vegetables are combined with numerous herbs and spices to produce a savory taste, more satisfying than that produced with any kind of meat.

The herbs of the Moroccan kitchen—chervil, garlic, fresh cilantro, mint, parsley and *za'tar* (a mixture of thyme, marjoram and oregano)—are blended with a variety of spices: aniseed, cayenne, cinnamon, cumin, ginger, paprika, pepper, saffron, turmeric and *ras el-hanout* (a mixture of spices). The mouth-watering dishes are enlivened with the addition of onions, olives, pickled lemons, almonds and sesame seeds. The resulting dishes are succulent and appetizing.

Moroccan salads are somewhat different from other Middle Eastern salads. They are, in most cases, prepared from cooked vegetables and are somewhat zesty but not spicy hot. In the homes of the well-off they are served at the beginning of meals as appetizers. In poor households, they are usually the main course.

The Moroccan kitchen is enriched by its delectable vegetable stews, or *tajins.* Fragrant, tart, spicy or sweet, they are always delicious and inviting. As the tasty sauces of the *tajin* simmer, their aromas entice even one who is sated to sample the simmering dish. So perfectly are they prepared that even meat eaters will be hard put to find anything wanting.

Couscous, perhaps more than any other food has been adapted by the peasants to meet their needs. A Berber fare embellished by the Arabs and Spanish Muslims, it is prepared in endless varieties. Known as the king of the Moroccan kitchen, it is served at the end of *diffas* (great feasts) to sate the hunger of guests. This satisfying dish amply fulfills the Arab host's obligation to send his guests home well filled.

Pleasing to the eye, couscous is served on a platter, heaped in a pyramid with a hollow in the peak filled with stew. In the mansions of the wealthy, couscous dishes are prepared with meat; in the abodes of the poor they are simply made with vegetables. Couscous alone is often sweetened with sugar and served as a dessert. For other sweets, the Moroccans make creations based on honey, almonds, sugar and the flaky dough we know as filo. Honey and almonds have always been utilized in Moroccan pastry. The sugar and filo, however, were introduced to North Africa and Spain by the eastern Arabs. Most Moroccan sweets were developed in Arab Spain and brought to North Africa by Muslims expelled from the Iberian Peninsula. A number of the desserts, as well as many of the other dishes prepared in Morocco today, can be found in a cookbook entitled *Fadaalat al-Khiwaan fi Tayyibaat at-Ta'aam wal-Alwaan* written in the thirteenth century by Ibn Razeen at-Tujeebee, an Andalusian Arab from Murcia.

This food author from antiquity is famous not only for his cookbook but also because he introduced the art of decorating food dishes with fresh vegetables. The recipes in his book are rich and varied, reflecting the affluence of the upper classes of his era and their taste for rich dishes. From among these are a number of vegetarian foods that can match the most tasty dishes prepared today. Long before the Spaniards became renowned for their use of saffron in cooking, Ibn Razeen employed it in many of his dishes.

The illustrious background and centuries of evolution of Moroccan and other North African cuisines have earned them a place among the highly developed world cuisines. Regardless of her social rank, the housewife prepares her dishes with such care that it is considered vulgar to place salt on the table. Usually, she keeps her recipes secret and improves them with the passing years until they reach perfection.

I remember traveling in the 1960s across the Middle Atlas Mountains of Morocco and being invited to dinner by a Berber farmer. While waiting for the meal, we talked about North America and its foods. My host, M'hamid, was intrigued when I described one of North America's favorite meals, roast beef and mashed potatoes, but my mind was on the enticing odor coming from his primitive kitchen. Little by little, the North American cuisine faded into oblivion as I imagined the meal to come. Notwithstanding the protests of M'hamid that he would have liked to butcher a lamb in my honor, the ensuing feast, cooked from the products of his fields, put the meals of the opulent to shame.

Another time I was dining in Tunis at the home of a driver whom I had hired for the week. Habib, who had become like a brother after our few days together, had insisted that I have at least one meal with his family. Being familiar with his modest way of life, I had been reluctant to put him to any unneeded expense. Nevertheless, after he promised that we would be eating only the family's daily vegetarian fare, I agreed. As we nibbled on nuts, delighting in the aromas wafting from the kitchen, I suddenly was reminded of the Middle Atlas meal.

Now the mouth-watering aroma made it hard to wait for the food that was arousing my hunger pangs. When I ate, I was not disappointed. Every morsel was a delight. With my host urging me on, I savored dish after dish of vegetarian delights, each more tasty than the one before. It was like a dream.

During my many travels to the far corners of the lands bordering the southern edge of the Mediterranean, I have often sampled delectable traditional vegetarian fare. Roaming through the villages on the edge of the Sahara or exploring the ancient North African coastal cities, I have never been disappointed when dining in the people's eating places or the homes of the ordinary inhabitants.

With limited means, the toiling masses have created a savory and nourishing cuisine, encompassing a large repertoire of exotic and delightful dishes. Unfortunately, visitors rarely have a chance to sample these vegetarian meals. If one is fortunate enough to be invited to a North African home, meat is usually on the menu even if the host or hostess has to borrow money to buy it. Tradition demands that a guest be fed the best the land has to offer, which means meat.

A determined traveler can find, hidden in the souks of the older part of the cities, exquisite tiny restaurants and food stalls that cater to the working class. In these eating places, unknown to most tourists, some of the finest North African dishes can be found. Visitors who are fortunate enough to stumble upon such food outlets will recall with nostalgia the meatless victuals they discover.

Although most visitors to North Africa will not chance upon local eating places or be invited to feast on home-cooked meals, there is another food experience that shouldn't be missed. Nearly every large city in Morocco has a restaurant set in a converted Moorish-Andalusian palace. In these settings, with haunting Arab music in the background, one can enjoy a sumptuous Moroccan repast—always including a number of tempting vegetarian dishes. Such a meal will linger in the memory long after the visitor has returned home.

Middle Eastern Cooking at Home

After returning from trips (or mental excursions) to the exotic lands of the Arabs, a gourmet traveler may be inspired to recreate some of these amazing vegetarian dishes. The variety of Middle Eastern and North African vegetable foods makes many savory feasts possible.

For the Arabs, good eating has had a long, recorded history. Excellent, usable cookbooks were compiled during the golden age from the eighth to the thirteenth centuries. Of these, the work of the tenth-century Sayyar al-Warraq, who wrote *Kitab al-Tabikh wa Asl al-Aghdiya al-Ma'kulut* (The book of cookery and the origin of nourishing foodstuffs) refers to numerous cookbooks, now lost, compiled long before his time. The most important cookbook that has survived, also titled *Kitab al-Tabikh*, was written by Muhammad Hassan al-Baghdadi in 1239 AD. He divided pleasures into seven classes: clothing, drink, food, scent, sex, sound, and wit. For him, food was the noblest of these pleasures, and for that reason, he composed this book of hundreds of recipes.

Because he wrote his book for the wealthy, who of course considered meat the most desirable of foods, most of his dishes include meat. Nevertheless, dishes made only from vegetables and fruits are also included.

The world has come a long way since al-Baghdadi's time. Today, millions of people, both those who live on diets of garden greens and those who eat meat, are seduced by the toothsome and nutritious vegetarian dishes of the Middle East. Those who have tried them have discovered in the rich heritage of Middle Eastern and North African meatless dishes a cuisine of exciting and delicious culinary delights. For those who have yet to try these dishes, the vegetarian kitchen of the Arab lands is a world waiting to be discovered.

—Habeeb Salloum

SPICES, HERBS,

and Other

ARABIAN DELIGHTS

allspice (*bahaar*): The dried berry of the pimento tree. The name derives from its taste, resembling a combination of cinnamon, cloves, and nutmeg.

aniseed (*yaansoon*): The seed of a small annual plant which has a licorice taste. It is used to flavor pastries and drinks, especially the Arab brandy *arak*.

baklawa or **baklava dough**: A fine, thin dough known in the West as *filo* (also *phylo* or *phyllo*) dough. Sold in all stores stocking Mediterranean foods, including many large supermarkets, often as a frozen product.

bamiya or **bamya**: *See* okra.

basil (*rayhan*): The dried or fresh leaf of an annual plant native to the Mediterranean, employed in flavoring soups and salads.

bay leaf (*ghar*): The aromatic leaf of the sweet bay or laurel tree. It gives flavor to soups and stews.

brochette: The French word for shish kababs.

burghul or **bulghur**: Whole wheat kernels that are boiled, then dried and broken into fragments. It is always soaked before used in a dish.

butter, clarified: To make, melt butter in a saucepan over medium-low heat; then raise heat until butter boils and becomes foamy. Skim the foam from the surface; then set the pan aside for 15 minutes. Pour the now clarified butter into a covered container, being careful to omit the residue at the bottom of the saucepan.

caraway (*karawya*): The fruit of a biennial plant used to flavor bread, pastries, and other types of dishes.

cardamom (*haal*): An aromatic dried pod of the cardamom plant which is used to flavor Arabic coffee and pastries.

cayenne (*fulful ahmar*): The dried and powdered fruit of the hot red pepper belonging to the *capsicum* family.

chickpeas: *See* hummus.

chili powder: Dried and powdered red peppers; can be fairly mild or hot.

chives: A herb allied to the leek and the onion; the thin green leaves of the plant are used.

cilantro: *See* coriander.

cinnamon (*qurfa*): The dried bark of the caccia tree, available in stick form or ground. Widely used in foods and beverages.

clarified butter: *See* butter, clarified.

cloves (*kurunful*): The dried unopened bud of an evergreen tree. It has a wide variety of uses as a spice.

coriander (*kouzbara*): A herb whose seed and leaf are used in a variety of stews and salads. The leaves are also known as cilantro or Chinese parsley. A mixture of half chives and half parsley can be substituted for cilantro. The seed is used as a spice, either whole or ground.

couscous: Strictly speaking, couscous is a cereal dish prepared by rolling moistened semolina into small pellets that are dried for storage. When served as a dish, it is steamed. The term couscous, however, is also applied to the great variety of *tajins* (stews) and desserts made with it.

cumin (*kammoon*): A small, dried, slightly bitter fruit of the parsley family, used as a spice in many dishes.

dibs rumman: *See* pomegranate concentrate.

dill (*shummar*): An annual yellow-flowered herb employed chiefly as an ingredient in pickling. The classical Arabic name for this herb is *shabath*, but, in the Syrian–Lebanese colloquial it is *shummar*.

fava beans: *See* fool.

fennel (*shammar*): The dried fruit of a plant belonging to the parsley family.

fenugreek (*hulbah*): An Old World herb with strong-scented leaves and mucilaginous seeds, belonging to the pea family.

filo dough: *See* baklawa.

fool: The Arabic word for fava or broad beans, used both dried and fresh.

ginger root (*zinjabeel*): A spice in root form, used fresh, preserved, or dried and powdered.

hareesa, hreesa or **harisa**: A Tunisian hot sauce.

hummus: A legume known in English as chickpea. (*Garbanzos* in Spanish, *chiches* in French and *cecci* in Italian). The root word "chick" comes from the Latin *cicer*. To split: soak chickpeas overnight. Drain and spread on one half of a towel, fold over the other half to cover; then roll with a rolling pin. The chickpeas will split into two and the skin will loosen. Discard the skins.

ibzar: A mixture of Arabian Gulf spices.

kama, kamaieh: *See* truffles.

kishk: A type of powdered cheese. See recipe on page 16.

knafa: a shredded wheat-like dough used in making pastries. It is sold in Middle Eastern stores.

koosa: A green squash, similar to zucchini. Favored by the Arabs for stuffing with rice, meat, and tomato sauce.

laban: Known commonly in the West as yogurt. This is the universal sauce of the Arabs.

labana: The cheese-like paste derived from yogurt or *laban* when most of the watery whey has been extracted by drainage through a cloth. Also known as yogurt spread.

leeks (*kurath*): A culinary green plant related to the onion and belonging to the lily family.

lentils (*'adas*): The edible seed of a plant belonging to the pea family. There are red, green, and brown lentils, used interchangeably in these recipes. Middle Eastern cooks usually use a greenish variety.

mace (*khoolinjaan*): The ground outer shell of the nutmeg.

mahlab: The seeds of the black cherry, found in most Middle Eastern food outlets, have a somewhat vanilla aroma. *Mahlab* should be purchased whole and ground just before use; once ground, it quickly loses its fragrance.

maza or **mezze**: An array of Arabic appetizers, usually served in small dishes.

mazahar: Orange-flower water.

mint (*na'na*): This fragrant herb comes in many varieties. Arabs prefer spearmint. Used in many dishes and particularly favored as a tea.

molokhia or **melkhia**: Jew's mallow. An edible plant resembling spinach.

mung beans (*maash*): Small green beans much favored in northern India. When the skin is removed, the bean inside is yellow. Both the green and yellow varieties are sold in Indian shops and health food stores.

nutmeg (*jawz at-teeb*): The dried seed,

or nut, of the tropical nutmeg tree.

okra *(bamiya)*: The edible pods of an annual belonging to the mallow family.

orange-flower water *(mazahar)*: *See* mazahar.

oregano *(anrar)*: A fragrant herb used to flavor a wide variety of dishes in Arabic and Italian cuisine. There are many varieties—some mild, others bitter.

orzo *(sha'reeya)*: Rice-shaped pasta.

paprika *(fulful hiloo)*: A sweet red pepper that is dried and powdered, used to flavor and color dishes.

peppercorn *(habb al-fulful)*: The berry of the tropical vine *Piper nigrum* which, when ground, is used as a spice.

pimiento: A sweet pepper used as a relish and for stuffing olives.

pine nuts *(sanawbar)*: White, rice-shaped seeds from the cones of certain pine trees that grow on the shores of the Mediterranean.

pomegranate *(rumman)*: A tropical fruit favored in the Middle East. To prepare, press and roll the pomegranate on a hard surface, then remove the stem. With a sharp knife, score the outer skin from top to bottom at one-inch intervals. After this, the fruit can be easily broken into pieces with the fingers and the seeds removed.

pomegranate concentrate *(dibs rumman)*: A concentrated syrup distilled from the pomegranate fruit. Available in Middle Eastern grocery stores.

ras el hanout: A mixture of Moroccan spices.

rawba: Part of the prepared yogurt to be used as a starter for the next batch of yogurt.

ricotta: A fresh, white cheese similar to cottage cheese. Often used as a filling for pastry.

rose water *(maward)*: The water obtained from the distillation of rose petals.

rosemary *(ikleel al-jabal)*: The leaf of an evergreen shrub used as a flavoring in a great variety of dishes.

saffron *(za'faran)*: The dried stigma of the yellow crocus native to the Mediterranean. Its strong yellow color and delicate flavor are used in many dishes.

sage *(maryamiya)*: A shrub of the mint family used for flavoring.

sauté: To fry quickly and superficially in fat or oil.

savory *(naghd)*: A herb of the mint family. It is mild in flavor and can be used fresh or dried.

scallions *(qufloot)*: Also called green onions. Young onion plants often used raw for their mild taste.

semolina *(smeed)*: The gritty grain-like portions of wheat.

sesame butter: *See* tahini.

sesame seed *(simsim)*: The seeds of the sesame plant, used whole, and also as a source of *tahini*. When finely ground, sesame seeds are used in pastries.

strudel dough: *See* baklawa.

sumac *(summaaq)*: The dried seeds of the fruit of the Mediterranean sumac (also spelled sumak). When ground, the powder is sprinkled on food as a spice.

Swiss chard: A vegetable of the beet family whose large leaves are used in salads and as a cooked vegetable.

tahini, taheena or **tahina**: An oil-rich paste of ground sesame seeds. Best known for its use in hummus. Americans often use the word *tahini* to refer to the sauce made with the paste;

see recipe on page 18.

tajin: The name applied to North African stews often served with couscous. *Tajin* is also the name of the earthenware vessel in which they are cooked.

terfez: *See* truffles.

thyme *(za'tar):* A herb of the mint family. Very aromatic and widely used.

truffles *(faqa'a, kama, kamaieh, terfez):* An edible subterranean fungus. There are two types: the European, very aromatic and highly valued by connoisseurs of fine foods; and Arab (Middle Eastern and North African), with a meaty-mushroom taste but milder than the European type.

turmeric *(kurkum):* This yellow spice is often substituted for the very expensive saffron. It is much used in pickling and in curries.

vermicelli: A very thin spaghetti-type pasta.

za'tar *(see also* thyme): A mixture of thyme, marjoram and oregano.

SPECIAL EQUIPMENT

None of the Arabic equipment included in the following list is absolutely necessary; suggestions are included for appropriate substitutions.

blender or **food processor:** For pureeing food.

corer: For removing pulp from zucchini, small eggplants, etc.

couscousière: Two-compartment steamer pot used for cooking couscous. Substitute a colander over a saucepan.

falafel mold: A mold for shaping falafel patties. They can also be shaped by hand.

garlic press: A small, hand-operated press for crushing garlic.

grater: For shredding and grating various ingredients.

ibreeq: An open-topped metal pot with a long handle for making and serving Arabic coffee. Substitute a small saucepan.

meat grinder or **food processor:** For chopping or grinding meat, vegetables, etc.

mortar and pestle: A wooden, metal, or porcelain bowl and rounded hammer for crushing garlic, spices, etc. A rolling pin or blender can sometimes be substituted, but a mortar and pestle can be purchased cheaply, and once you are accustomed to using them, you will find there is really no good substitute. By far the best tool for grinding and crushing spices.

raqwa: *See* ibreeq.

sieve or strainer: Vessels with holes or mesh for draining foods.

skewers: Sharpened metal rods used in barbecuing meat, etc.

ESSENTIAL
RECIPES

THE
following   recipes
comprise foods basic to
Arabic cuisine. Some are eaten
as dishes in their own right, but
most supplement other dishes, for
example, yogurt as a sauce, or rice
as a base for vegetables. A number
of recipes throughout the
book will refer to these
basic items.

ARABIC PLAIN RICE

Rizz Mufalfal
Middle East
Serves 4

4 tablespoons butter
1 cup long grain rice, rinsed
2 cups boiling water
salt to taste

Melt butter in a saucepan; then add the rice and stir-fry on high heat for a few minutes until rice is well coated with butter.

Stir in water and salt; then reduce heat to medium and bring to boil. Lower heat to medium low and cover; cook for about 25 minutes. Turn off heat and allow rice to finish cooking in its own steam—about 30 minutes.

ARABIC BREAD, PITA

Khubz 'Arabee
Middle East
Makes about a dozen medium-sized loaves, or 24 small loaves

Arabs eat bread with every meal, claiming that they cannot taste other foods without bread. It is used for picking up meat, vegetables, and salads, and serves as a scoop for sauces, dips, yogurt, and other semi-liquids. When the loaf is cut into two, the top and bottom of the loaf separate easily and the halves form pockets which can be filled with hot falafel, and/or salads. In tradition, and in daily life, bread is held to be a divine gift from God.

2 packages dried yeast
1 teaspoon sugar
3 cups lukewarm water
8 cups flour (white, whole wheat, or a mixture of the two)
2 teaspoons salt
1 tablespoon oil

Dissolve yeast and sugar in 1 cup of the water and set aside for about 5 minutes.

Mix flour, salt, and oil in a large bowl; then add yeast mixture and remaining warm water. Knead until smooth and elastic, adding more water or flour if necessary. Place in a warm, oiled bowl, turning dough over to coat surface with oil. Cover bowl with a dry cloth and set in a warm place, allowing dough to rise until double in volume (about 2 to 3 hours).

Punch dough down and knead for about 2 minutes. Form into smooth balls the size of small oranges, rolling them gently between the hands. Place balls on dry cloth in warm place, cover with another cloth and let rise for about 30 minutes.

Preheat oven to 500°F. On lightly floured board, roll balls one at a time into circles about ¼-inch thick. Bake the loaves 5 to 8 minutes on a preheated baking sheet with the oven rack at the center notch.

Note: The bread will puff up like a balloon during baking and will collapse when cooled. Loaves can be eaten immediately or frozen for long-term storage. For short-term storage, the loaves should be sealed in plastic wrap or a plastic bag. The loaves can be quickly warmed in the oven before being served.

Bread, Yemeni-Style

Khubz Yemeni
Makes about 8 loaves

To truly appreciate the cuisine of the Queen of Sheba's land, one must dine in a Yemeni home. Dipping this warm bread in Yemeni fenugreek paste, then scooping up the vegetable morsels was, for me, an exotic way of enjoying the foods of that ancient part of the world.

2 cups flour
½ teaspoon salt
1 package dried yeast, dissolved in ½ cup warm water
2 cups water

Combine all ingredients; then cover and allow to rest for 1 hour.
Thinly spread 4 to 6 tablespoons of the soft dough on a heated griddle. Cook for about 4 minutes or until bread begins to brown (on one side only). Remove and keep warm until ready to serve.

Cucumber and Pepper Relish

Falfal bil-Labid
Tunisia
Serves 4 to 6

Unknown in the Old World before Columbus's travels, both hot and sweet peppers were brought back to Europe by the Spaniards. And despite the fact that many believe peppers are native to India, it was the Portuguese in the seventeenth century who introduced them to the subcontinent.

3 tablespoons lemon juice
salt and pepper to taste
2 medium sweet red peppers, seeded and cut into 1-inch squares
2 medium cucumbers peeled, sliced in half lengthwise, and cut into 1-inch-long
    pieces

In a serving bowl, combine lemon juice, salt and pepper; add peppers and cucumbers and stir until they are thoroughly coated. Cover bowl and marinate at room temperature for at least 8 hours before serving.

Note: This relish is traditionally served with couscous in Tunisia, but it can be served with all types of stews.

BASIC DOUGH FOR SAVORY PIES

'Ajeenat al-Fatayar
Syria and Lebanon
Makes about 18 pies

This recipe is designed for spinach, cheese, leek and all other types of pies.

1 tablespoon sugar
¼ cup lukewarm water
1 package dry yeast
3 cups flour
2 tablespoons butter, melted
½ teaspoon salt
⅛ teaspoon ground ginger
¼ cup warm milk
1 tablespoon olive oil

Dissolve sugar in water, then sprinkle in yeast and stir. Allow to sit in warm place until yeast begins to foam.

Meanwhile, combine flour, butter, salt, and ginger in a large mixing bowl. Make well in flour; then add milk and yeast mixture. Knead well, adding more warm milk or flour if necessary. Do not allow dough to become sticky.

Shape into ball. Brush the ball with oil and place in a floured pan. Cover with a dampened cloth, place in warm spot, and allow to rise until double in bulk.

Note: The dough can be frozen at this point. Defrost thoroughly before using as directed in the pie recipes.

FENUGREEK PASTE

Hulbah
Yemen
Makes about ¾ cup

In Yemen, fenugreek is the most commonly used spice, forming the basis of an everyday paste or sauce called hulbah. *It goes well with* zhug—*another food enhancer. These are present at all meals and are added to almost every nonsweet food that is eaten. Hulbah, flavored with* zhug, *is employed by Yemenis as a dressing for salads, a sauce for vegetables and other foods, and a dip.*

2 tablespoons ground fenugreek
1½ cups water, plus extra as needed

In a bowl, mix fenugreek and 1½ cups water; allow to stand for at least 2 hours. Drain; then, adding a little water at a time, stir until bubbly. Refrigerate and use as needed—it will keep up to a week.

GARLIC SAUCE

Taratoor
Syria and Lebanon
Makes about ¾ cup

There is no place in the world where garlic is more used and enjoyed, especially in sauces, than in the eastern Arab lands. This simple garlic sauce called taratoor *is a common dish of the peasants in Syria and Lebanon. It is used as a condiment with all types of vegetables. It serves extremely well as a dip with boiled, baked, fried, or barbecued potatoes.*

2 heads of garlic, peeled
salt to taste
⅓ cup olive or vegetable oil
⅓ cup lemon juice

Place all ingredients in a blender and purée until a creamy sauce is produced. Store in a container with a tight-fitting lid; refrigerate until ready to use.

GULF SPICES

Ibzar
Arabian Gulf
Makes about 1 cup

The Arabian Gulf cuisine is characterized by the tantalizing aroma of foods seasoned with the spice mixture called ibzar—*an aroma that has infatuated the inhabitants of that part of the Arab world for centuries.*

4 tablespoons cumin
4 tablespoons black pepper
4 tablespoons ground coriander seeds
1 tablespoon cinnamon
1 tablespoon ground ginger
1 teaspoon ground cloves
1 teaspoon cayenne
1 teaspoon turmeric
½ teaspoon nutmeg
½ teaspoon ground mace

Combine all ingredients and store in a tightly covered container.

HOT SPICE SAUCE

Shatta
Sudan
Serves 4 to 6

In the Sudan, a main meal usually consists of five dishes: soup, salad, a meat or fish entrée, shatta, *and dessert, accompanied by cinnamon tea.*

½ cup lemon juice
2 tablespoons olive oil
4 cloves garlic, crushed
1 tablespoon ground chili pepper
½ teaspoon pepper
salt to taste

In a bowl, thoroughly combine all ingredients. Serve with the entrées in tiny dishes and set before each person.

Lemon and Oil Salad Dressing

Maraq Tawaabil bil Laymoon wa Zayt
Syria and Lebanon
For a salad that serves 6 to 8

It is believed that lemons originated in India. Around 1100 AD, Arabs brought them to the Iberian Peninsula, from whence their cultivation spread to the remainder of southern Europe. In Italian, Portuguese, Spanish, and English the word for lemon is derived from the Arabic laymoon, originally a Persian word.

The lemon tree was brought to the New World by Columbus on his second voyage, and a few centuries thereafter they were to be found in many parts of the Western Hemisphere. Today, the United States grows a large part of the world's lemon crop—three-quarters of it in California. This, with Italy's production, accounts for most of the world's supply.

4 tablespoons olive oil
4 tablespoons lemon juice
2 tablespoons finely chopped fresh cilantro
1 clove garlic, crushed
salt and pepper to taste

Thoroughly combine all ingredients; then stir and pour over salad. Toss and serve immediately.

Moroccan Spice Mixture

Ras El Hanout
Morocco
Makes about ⅓ cup

In Morocco ras el hanout (the head of the shop) is employed in everyday cooking. The mixture of spices given here is a simpler version of the original. Often up to a hundred ingredients—including cantharis (an aphrodisiac), fruit of the ash tree, belladonna berries, lavender flowers, gouza el asnab (a type of nut), monk's pepper, and grains of paradise—are combined. Ras el hanout is not as much used today as in former times when people believed it heated the body and rendered it virile.

1 tablespoon ground coriander seeds
1 tablespoon cumin
1 tablespoon ground ginger
1 tablespoon pepper

½ teaspoon mace
½ teaspoon nutmeg
½ teaspoon allspice
½ teaspoon cardamom
½ teaspoon turmeric
½ teaspoon cinnamon
¼ teaspoon ground cloves
¼ teaspoon cayenne

Combine all ingredients; then store for use in a tightly covered container.

POMEGRANATE SALAD DRESSING

Maraq Tawaabil bil Dibs Rummaan
Syria and Lebanon
For a salad that serves 6 to 8

In a number of countries in Asia and North Africa, numerous healing qualities are attributed to the products of the pomegranate tree. The roots, skin, and seeds relieve liver congestion and arthritis, purify the blood, ease heart pain and coughs, and serve as an antibacterial agent in relieving stomach ailments, especially dysentery. Whether or not these claims are true, the pomegranate's cleansing and cooling effects on the body are uncontestable.

2 tablespoons pomegranate concentrate, diluted in 1 tablespoon of water
4 tablespoons olive oil
1 tablespoon vinegar
2 cloves garlic, crushed
½ teaspoon powdered mustard
¼ teaspoon pepper
pinch of cayenne
salt to taste

Thoroughly combine all ingredients and add to salad.

Note: This dressing can be used with all types of salads.

POWDERED CHEESE

Kishk
Syria and Lebanon
Makes about 4 pounds

Kishk, a type of powdered cheese, is considered to be one of the oldest cheeses known to humankind. Perhaps only the bone-dry yogurt produced by the bedouin of the desert goes back to remoter times. It is believed that kishk was discovered in the Fertile Crescent when people started domesticating animals instead of hunting them. Kishk can be bought from Middle Eastern specialty stores, or you can make your own, as follows.

2 quarts *laban* (yogurt, see recipe, p. 22)
3 pounds coarse *burghul*, rinsed, drained, and allowed to stand for ½ hour
4 pounds *labana* (yogurt cheese, see recipe, p. 22)
2 tablespoons salt

Mix *laban* with *burghul* and let stand for 6 hours.

Add 2 pounds of the *labana* and salt, mix well, and place in a warm place to ferment. Every day for the next 9 days, add a little of the remaining 2 pounds of *labana* and stir. Make sure the *labana* lasts for the 9 days.

On the tenth day, form the cheese into small balls and spread on a white sheet in the sun to dry. How long this takes depends on the weather. With no humidity and a temperature of about 75°, it would take 5 to 6 hours for the balls to partially dry. They are ready when they no longer stick to your fingers. To speed dry, though the taste will not be the same, place in a 150° oven for about 3 hours.

When the cheese has dried halfway, put through a grinder twice, then return to dry in sun, spreading out thinly on a white sheet. Rub between palms of hands once in a while to break up balls.

When *kishk* is bone dry, divide into fine and coarse grades by rubbing through a sieve.

Note: Kishk does not need to be refrigerated, but it should be stored in a cool, dry place.

PRESERVED LEMONS

Hamid Msyiar
Morocco

In Egypt and Morocco, marinated lemons are highly prized as food enhancers in a good number of dishes. After being pickled, the lemons will keep for about one year. Hence, only a few lemons should be prepared at one time.

6 lemons
4 tablespoons salt
4 peppercorns
4 coriander seeds

Deeply score the rind of the lemons from top to bottom, but do not cut apart. Using 2 tablespoons of the salt, rub salt heavily into the scores. Place lemons in a sterilized wide-mouthed jar and cover with cold water; then close tightly. Allow to stand for about 2 weeks, at which point remove the mold from the top and change water. Add the peppercorns, coriander seeds and the remaining salt and reseal. In another week, the lemons will be ready. To use, discard the inner flesh. Use the rind to flavor *tajins* or to garnish foods.

RED PEPPER SPICE

Hreesa
Tunisia
Makes about 1½ cups

Unlike most Middle Eastern and North African foods, the food of Tunisia is noted for its spicy hotness. It is said that a husband will judge his wife by the amount of hreesa *she uses to prepare his food. Some even believe that if a wife's cooking becomes bland, it means her love for her husband is fading. On the other hand, when food is prepared for visitors, the amount of* hreesa *is decreased to suit the more delicate palates of the guests.*

2 tablespoons ground caraway seeds
5 cloves garlic, crushed
½ cup ground fresh cayenne
¼ cup cumin
2 tablespoons salt
½ cup olive oil

In a bowl, thoroughly mix all ingredients. Store in a jar with a tight fitting lid in a cool place, to use as needed.

SESAME TAHINI SAUCE

Taheena
Palestine and Jordan
Makes about 1 cup

Versatile in all types of cooking, this sauce is utilized in a wide variety of everyday dishes. However, it is chiefly used as a basis for many sauces and dips, and as a healthy substitute for butter on bread.

Serve this sauce as an appetizer with pita bread. It also makes an excellent sauce for other foods.

1½ small head of garlic, peeled and crushed
salt to taste
½ cup tahini (sesame seed paste)
¼ cup cold water, extra as desired
3 tablespoons lemon juice
1 tablespoon hot pepper, finely chopped
¼ cup finely chopped parsley
1 tablespoon olive oil

Place garlic, salt, tahini, water, lemon juice, and hot pepper in a blender and blend for a few moments. If a thinner sauce is desired, add more water, a little at a time, while blending further until sauce becomes light in color and the same consistency as mayonnaise.

Place on a serving platter, garnish with parsley, and sprinkle with olive oil. Refrigerate for at least ½ hour before serving.

SPICY RELISH

Zhug
Yemen
Makes about 1 cup

The origin of Yemeni cuisine goes back to the ancient civilizations of Awsan, Hadramout, Ma'in, and Qataban and the two important powers in the ancient world: Saba and Himyar. Controlling frankincense, myrrh, and the spices brought from India and beyond and selling them to the kingdoms of the north, these south Arabian countries prospered. Through the centuries, a number of the priceless condiments in which these South Arabians traded, entered their cuisines, including this tasty relish, which is used to flavor many types of foods.

10 tablespoons tomato paste
6 cloves garlic, crushed
1 teaspoon salt
1 teaspoon pepper
1 teaspoon ground caraway seeds
1 teaspoon ground coriander seeds
1 teaspoon ground cardamom seeds
½ teaspoon cayenne

Thoroughly combine all ingredients, then refrigerate and use as needed.

Sumac and Thyme Seasoning

Za'tar
Syria and Lebanon
Makes about 2⅔ cups

Sumac, a condiment almost unique to the Middle East, gives bread, olives, and yogurt an exquisite taste. Za'tar can be found mixed and ready to use in almost all Middle Eastern markets located in every large city in North America. If it cannot be found, this simple recipe can be followed.

1 cup dried thyme, pulverized
1 cup sumac
¼ cup cooked, roasted unsalted chickpeas (*qadaama*), finely pulverized
3 tablespoons sesame seeds, toasted
1 tablespoon marjoram
2 tablespoons salt

Combine all ingredients together and store in a jar to use as needed.

SYRUP

Qater
Middle East
Makes 2 cups

This recipe is responsible for the divine sweetness of baklawa and many other Arab pastries.

2 cups sugar
1 cup water
2 tablespoons lemon juice
2 tablespoons orange-flower water (*mazahar*)

Place sugar and water in a pot; cook over medium heat, stirring constantly for 10 minutes or until the sugar is thoroughly dissolved.

Remove from heat and stir in lemon juice. Return to heat and bring to boil; again remove from heat. Stir in *mazahar* (orange-flower water) and allow to cool somewhat, but it should be poured on the pastry still warm.

Note: If a less sweet syrup is desired, use only half the sugar.

TAMARIND BUTTER

Zibda Tamar Hindi
Arabian Gulf
Makes about ½ cup

The tamarind tree produces an exotic, spicy fruit with a reddish pulp and small shiny seeds resembling peas in the pod. The major edible part, the pulp, inside the 4- to 5-inch-long pod is very fruity, strongly acidic, slightly sugary, and heavily scented. The sticky pulp is employed extensively in the cuisines of many lands; in addition, the tree's attractive fern-like foliage and fresh yellow flowers are sometimes utilized in cooking.

6 tablespoons butter
1½ tablespoons tamarind paste, dissolved in a little hot water
⅛ teaspoon salt
⅛ teaspoon cayenne

Place all ingredients in a small saucepan and heat. Stir for a few moments; then serve with cooked vegetables.

Tamarind Relish

Salsa bi Tamar Hindi
Arabian Gulf
Makes about ⅔ cup

For centuries the tamarind has been included in a great number of dishes throughout much of Asia. It is believed that the Arabs brought it to the Iberian Peninsula, from whence its use as a condiment and souring agent spread to the remainder of Europe and later the Americas.

4 tablespoons tamarind paste diluted in 4 tablespoons hot water
1 tablespoon finely chopped fresh ginger
4 cloves garlic, crushed
1 teaspoon paprika
½ teaspoon nutmeg
⅛ teaspoon cayenne
salt and pepper to taste

Place all ingredients in a blender and blend for a few moments; then serve with all types of baked vegetables.

Tomato Hot Sauce

Salsat Banadoora Harra
Arabian Gulf
Makes about 1¼ cups

In the modern Arabian Gulf countries, this sauce is served with all types of rice dishes. In the past, however, when most of the people were poor, it was served as a replacement for meat to give rice a delicious flavor.

4 tablespoons tomato paste
1 cup water
4 cloves garlic, crushed
½ teaspoon cumin
¼ teaspoon cayenne
1 tablespoon vinegar
2 tablespoons olive oil
salt to taste

Thoroughly combine all ingredients in a saucepan and bring to boil. Cover and cook over medium heat for 10 minutes; then allow to cool. If sauce is too thick, add a little water. Store in a covered container in the refrigerator and use as needed.

YOGURT

Middle East
Laban
Makes about 1 quart

The history of yogurt goes back perhaps 8,000 years, to the dawn of civilization. It is believed to have been discovered by the bedouins of the Arabian Peninsula. The story goes that when a family of nomads had stored milk in bags made from goat stomachs in preparation for a long journey, the hot sun, the movements of the pack animal, and the bacteria from the goat's stomach combined to ferment the milk, producing yogurt.

1 quart milk, preferably homogenized whole milk
2 tablespoons plain yogurt

Heat milk in a saucepan over medium heat until it begins to rise and bubbles form around the edges; then allow milk to cool to the point at which you can insert your little finger and count to ten (110°F).

Pour into an earthenware jar/pyrex bowl with a tight-fitting lid. Stir in the yogurt until thoroughly mixed; then place in a warm spot away from drafts. Cover with a wool blanket to keep warm. Alternatively, place container in an oven heated to 150°F. After five minutes, turn the heat off, and let the container sit for 6 hours undisturbed; then uncover or remove from oven, and refrigerate until the following day.

Remove about 2 tablespoons of yogurt and place in a small, covered glass jar; then store in refrigerator. This will be your starter (or *rawba*) for the next yogurt preparation.

YOGURT CHEESE

Middle East
Labana

Pour a quart of yogurt (see preceding recipe) into a bag made of fine white cotton. Stir in 1 teaspoon of salt. Suspend the tied bag from a faucet over a sink, allowing the water to drip out, overnight or until contents are firm.

When the yogurt is firm, remove contents from the bag and place in a deep bowl. Taste to see if *labana* requires more salt; then stir. Cover, refrigerate, and use as needed.

To serve, remove required amount and spread it evenly on a small plate. Sprinkle with a little olive oil just before serving.

Note: Sometimes called yogurt spread, *labana* is available ready-made in Middle Eastern specialty stores.

Yogurt Cheese Balls

Zanakeel Laban
Syria and Lebanon

To preserve the *labana* or yogurt cheese for long periods, follow these steps:

Place 1 heaping tablespoon of *labana* in the palm of the hand; roll into a ball and place on a tray. Repeat, using as much as you wish to preserve.

Allow to stand overnight, then place in sterilized jars and cover with olive oil. Seal and store for future use. They will keep indefinitely, especially if stored in the refrigerator or a cool place.

Serve balls with a little of the olive oil.

Note: Both forms, *labana* and *zanakeel laban,* are excellent for appetizers, sandwiches, and as a toast spread.

Yogurt Sauce

Labaniyya
Syria and Lebanon
Serves 6

Milk, both fresh and sour, and particularly in the form of laban *(yogurt), is a very ancient ingredient in the cooking of the Arabs. In some soups,* laban *is added at the end of the cooking and allowed to become hot, without boiling. In this case, there is little danger of it curdling. When* laban *is called for in the actual cooking, however, precautions must be taken in order that it does not curdle or separate. This is done by gently stirring over low heat until it comes to a gentle boil.*

2 eggs, beaten
3 cups *laban* (plain yogurt)
3 cups cold water
2 tablespoons butter
2 cloves garlic, crushed
salt to taste
2 tablespoons dried mint

Place eggs and yogurt in a saucepan and stir until well blended. Add cold water and stir well. Place over medium heat and, with a wooden spoon, stir gently in one direction until mixture comes to a boil; then reduce heat to very low.

Melt butter in a small saucepan and add to it the garlic, salt, and mint. Sauté over medium heat until garlic turns golden brown; then stir garlic mixture into yogurt sauce and taste for seasoning. Remove from heat; serve hot as soup or as a sauce for other foods.

APPETIZERS

Appetizers, called *mazas* in Arabic, are one of the glories of Middle Eastern cuisine. Suggestions of the delights to come in the meal, *mazas* are served in small dishes, the number of which reflects the formality and importance of the meal to follow.

The impressive variety of these appetizers ranges from the simple—small dishes of olives, various cheeses, sliced tomatoes, fresh broad beans, seasoned diced potatoes—to the more complex—chickpea and eggplant purées or tabouli.

Served both in restaurants and homes, these *mazas* entice unsuspecting guests into eating too much before the main courses are brought out. After sampling two or three dozen *mazas* out of a total, at times, of a hundred or more, guests may find that they are unable to eat the main course. Moreover, the code of hospitality forbids warning guests not to partake too much of the appetizers. Foreigners especially tend to eat so many of the delicious *mazas* that they have no room left for the main meal. Even experienced visitors will have trouble confining themselves to a reasonable number of appetizers. Meals in which *mazas* play a large role are usually those to which guests are invited.

Beginning the meal with *mazas* is a great way to eat. Sitting around a table covered with plates of *mazas*, guests nibble on whatever foods they fancy, chatting between mouthfuls. The *maza* course of the meal can continue for hours.

Serving these tidbits of food before a meal is believed to have been carried by the Arabs to the Iberian Peninsula during the 900 years they were in that part of Europe. The Spanish tradition of gathering before a meal for a drink and for the sampling of endless appetizers, called *tapas*, matches the Arab custom. To a large extent, this pleasant precursor to an elaborate meal is found only in the Middle East and in Spain.

Once in Cordoba, a Spanish friend invited me to dinner in one of that city's fine restaurants. As we enjoyed dish after dish of succulent *tapas*, I remarked to my friend, "It's as if we are dining in one of the Syrian–Lebanese resorts. *Tapas* are like the *mazas* of the Middle East." He smiled. "Are we not the same people? Many of our ancestors came from that part of the world."

ARTICHOKE HEARTS IN VINEGAR

Maazat Khurshoof
Syria and Lebanon
Serves 4 to 6

In the past, artichokes acquired a reputation as an aphrodisiac. According to R. Hendrickson in Lewd Food, there is an old French saying advising that this vegetable, like wine, is good for the ladies when gentlemen partake of them. He goes on to state that Paris street vendors used to hawk artichokes with the cry "Artichokes! Artichokes! Heat the body and spirit! Heat the genitals!"

2 14-oz cans artichokes
3 tablespoons olive oil
2 tablespoons vinegar
1 clove garlic, crushed
2 tablespoons finely chopped fresh cilantro
1 teaspoon thyme
pinch of cayenne
salt and pepper to taste

Drain and quarter the artichokes, place in a serving bowl, and set aside.
Thoroughly combine remaining ingredients; then pour over the artichokes. Toss and serve.

ASPARAGUS APPETIZER
Maazat Halyoon
Syria and Lebanon
Serves 8

A universal favorite, asparagus is a delicious and nutritious vegetable, first cultivated in the eastern Mediterranean lands. The ancient Egyptians considered it a food fit for the gods and, after the Greeks introduced this delicacy to the Romans, asparagus became a must on any feast table. However, after the downfall of the Roman empire, except in Arab Spain, it was neglected for hundreds of years until the late middle ages.

1 pound asparagus (about 12 spears), each about the thickness of a finger
4 tablespoons crumbled feta cheese
salt to taste
8 slices buttered toast

    Place asparagus and salt in a saucepan and cover with water. Bring to boil, cover, and cook over medium heat for 8 minutes. Drain and allow to cool.
    Cut off and discard tough ends; then cut each spear into two pieces.
    Cut each toast slice into 3 pieces. Arrange toast on a platter and place 2 pieces of asparagus on each piece of toast. Sprinkle with the cheese and serve.

Note: In the eastern Arab world, where toast is not usually available, Arabic bread (pita) is used instead.

AVOCADO APPETIZER
Abakadoo ma' Taheena
Syria and Lebanon
Makes 1 cup

Avocados are believed to be native to Mexico and were first grown in that country some 7,000 years ago. They were very important in the kitchens of both the Aztecs and Incas. According to R. Henrickson in Lewd Food, *the first Europeans to taste avocados were Cortez and his conquistadors—they were served this vegetable/fruit at a feast to which they were invited by the Aztec leader, Montezuma.*
    In the Middle East, it has been only in the last half century that avocados have become popular.
    Often thought of as a rich food, avocados, when ripe, are soft as butter and high in fat content. Their fat, however, is free of cholesterol and easily digestible. In addition, avocados have a high carbohydrate and protein content, making them extremely nutritious.

4 tablespoons lemon juice
3 tablespoons tahini
1 large or 2 medium avocados
¼ cup finely chopped parsley
2 tablespoons olive oil
1 clove garlic, crushed
¼ teaspoon salt
¼ teaspoon pepper
pinch cayenne
½ teaspoon paprika

Place lemon juice and tahini in a blender or food processor and blend for a moment; set aside.

Pit and peel avocados and cut into pieces. Add, with remaining ingredients, except paprika, to the lemon juice–tahini mixture; then blend to a smooth paste. Place on a flat serving platter, sprinkle with paprika, and serve as is or chilled.

BURGHUL AND YOGURT APPETIZER

Kishkeh
Syria and Lebanon
Serves 4 to 6

Modern medicine has confirmed what the ancient civilizations in the Middle East have long known about yogurt—it is a healthy food. This simple dish, which is a favorite food of both the rich and poor in Damascus, is not only healthy but also tasty.

½ cup medium *burghul*
4 tablespoons finely chopped cucumbers
¾ cup plain yogurt
1 teaspoon dried mint, finely crumpled
salt and pepper to taste
2 tablespoons finely chopped fresh cilantro

Soak the *burghul* in warm water for 15 minutes, then put in a strainer and press out all excess water.

Combine all ingredients except cilantro; place on a serving platter. Chill; then decorate with the cilantro and serve.

CHICKPEA APPETIZER

Hummus Habb
Palestine and Jordan
Serves 4 to 6

This simple appetizer does not need any great effort to make, yet it is very tasty.

2 cups cooked chickpeas (or canned)
¼ cup olive oil
¼ cup lemon juice
6 cloves of garlic, crushed
1 teaspoon salt
2 tablespoons finely chopped scallions
2 tablespoons finely chopped fresh cilantro
1 tablespoon finely chopped fresh mint

Thoroughly mix all ingredients except the mint; then place in a serving bowl and refrigerate for 1 hour. Just before serving, garnish with mint.

Note: Chives may be substituted for the cilantro and ½ teaspoon of dried mint for the fresh mint.

CHICKPEA DIP

Hummus bi Taheena Filasteeniya
Palestine and Jordan
Serves 6 to 8

Chickpeas are used extensively in Middle Eastern and North African cooking and are credited with more than mere nutritional value. Many believe that chickpeas increase the energy and sexual desires of both men and women. Shaykh 'Umar Abu Muhammad Nefzawi, a sixteenth-century North African Arab writer, in his book The Perfumed Garden, *suggests chickpeas as a cure for impotence and as a first-rate sexual stimulant.*

In the eastern Arab lands, those who labor on the land are convinced that chickpeas provide the energy necessary for their lives of toil. As is often the case with folk wisdom, modern science supports such claims, at least partially: chickpeas are a valuable source of both muscle-building proteins and energy-rich carbohydrates.

2 cups cooked chickpeas
¼ cup of water
½ cup tahini
6 tablespoons lemon juice
pinch of cayenne
salt to taste
2 tablespoons olive oil
1 tablespoon finely chopped fresh mint

Place chickpeas, water, tahini, lemon juice, cayenne, and salt in a blender or food processor and blend until a smooth paste is formed. The paste should be of an easily spreadable consistency. If too thick, thin with water.

Spread on a serving plate, sprinkle with oil, and garnish with mint. Serve with raw vegetables, bread sticks, or cut pieces of Arabic bread (pita).

CHICKPEA AND OLIVE APPETIZER
Maazat Hummus wa Zaytoon
Palestine and Jordan
Serves 6 to 8

Chickpeas have been, since the beginning of civilization, one of the favorite foods around the Mediterranean basin. They are consumed in great quantities—alone or with other foods.

1 cup dried chickpeas, washed and soaked overnight in 8 cups water
½ cup black olives, chopped
¼ cup green onions, finely chopped
1 clove garlic, crushed
salt to taste
½ teaspoon paprika
⅛ teaspoon chili powder
2 tablespoons finely chopped fresh cilantro
1 tablespoon olive oil
2 tablespoons lemon juice

Place chickpeas with their water in a saucepan and bring to boil. Cook over medium heat for about 2½ hours, or until chickpeas are tender. Drain; then place chickpeas in a salad bowl and allow to cool. Add the remaining ingredients, combine thoroughly, and serve immediately.

CHICKPEAS AND POMEGRANATE

Hummus bi Dibs Rumman
Syria and Lebanon
Serves 6 to 8

The outer skin of the pomegranate is rich in tannin and is employed in Middle Eastern countries in the preparation of dyes. In fact, the ruby-red color of woolen handmade fabrics and rugs, admired by tourists in these historic lands, frequently comes from dyes made with the rind of this fruit.

1 19-oz can chickpeas, drained
1 tablespoon pomegranate concentrate (*dibs rumman*)
2 cloves garlic, crushed
¼ teaspoon pepper
4 tablespoons olive oil
2 tablespoons chopped parsley
1 tablespoon pomegranate seeds

Place chickpeas, pomegranate concentrate, garlic, pepper, and 2 tablespoons of the oil in a blender or food processor and purée until mixture is the consistency of peanut butter.

Spread on a serving platter; then garnish with parsley and pomegranate seeds. Sprinkle with remaining oil just before serving.

CHICKPEA PURÉE

Hummus bi Taheena
Syria and Lebanon
Serves 6 to 8

In the Arab lands along the eastern Mediterranean, one usually starts the day by breakfasting on hummus bi taheena. *This delightful dish is also on the menu when appetizers are served, and almost always accompanies a normal Middle Eastern family meal.*

2 cups cooked chickpeas
¼ cup water
4 tablespoons tahini
4 tablespoons lemon juice
2 cloves garlic, crushed

salt to taste
pinch of cayenne
1 tablespoon finely chopped parsley
2 tablespoons olive oil

Place chickpeas, water, tahini, lemon juice, garlic, salt, and cayenne in a blender or food processor and blend to a thick paste. (If a thinner consistency is desired, add more water.) Place on a shallow platter and refrigerate for at least 1 hour. Just before serving, decorate with parsley and sprinkle with oil.

CHICKPEA PURÉE, MOROCCAN STYLE
Serrooda
Morocco
Serves 6 to 8

Made a little differently from the chickpea purées of the Middle East, this Moroccan dish is simple to make yet has a subtle and enticing taste.

1 medium onion
1 19-oz can chickpeas, drained
3 tablespoons melted butter
2 tablespoons water
½ teaspoon cumin
salt and pepper to taste
pinch of cayenne
a large pinch of saffron
1 clove garlic, crushed
1 tablespoon olive oil

Place onion in a saucepan, cover with water, and bring to a boil. Cover and cook over medium heat for 10 minutes. Drain and allow to cool.

Place onion and remaining ingredients, except olive oil, in a food processor and blend to a fine paste, adding a little water if necessary. Place on a serving platter, sprinkle with oil and serve.

CHICKPEA AND TAMARIND APPETIZER

Hummus bi Tamar Hindi
Arabian Gulf
Serves 6 to 8

In North America, tamarind is available dried and pressed into one-pound bricks or as a paste. When purchased in bricks, the tamarind must be cut into small pieces and soaked overnight in twice as much water. The soaked tamarind with the juice is then repeatedly rubbed through a fine strainer until only seeds and fibrous material remain. (These thick leftovers can be discarded or utilized to polish brass!) Four parts of the pulpy juice are equal to one of the paste.

The paste is much easier to use and, hence, tamarind is usually purchased in this form. Tamarind can be found in specialty food shops, Middle Eastern and Chinese stores, Indian markets under the name imli, and in some Spanish groceries where it is called tamarindo.

This dish is similar to the usual hummus bi taheena, *but with an Indian influence.*

2 cups cooked chickpeas
3 tablespoons tahini
1 tablespoon tamarind paste
1 tablespoon finely chopped fresh ginger
salt and pepper to taste
1 tablespoon finely chopped fresh cilantro
1 tablespoon olive oil

Place all ingredients, except cilantro and oil, in a food processor and process into a somewhat thick paste, adding a little water as necessary. Place on a serving platter and sprinkle with cilantro and oil just before serving.

DAMASCUS GARLIC APPETIZER

Thoom
Syria and Lebanon
Serves 4 to 6

In Damascus, traditional dishes, like this one, prepared in the home, are rarely revealed to outsiders. From ancient times, when new products were introduced—in this case, the potato—the Damascenes have taken them as their own. If you like garlic, this dish is highly addictive. It is a relative of the French aioli, *but simpler to prepare. Thoom goes well with all types of foods and makes a scrumptious dip, especially with Arabic bread (pita).*

1 cup mashed potatoes
6 cloves garlic, crushed
¼ cup olive oil
¼ cup plain yogurt
salt and pepper to taste
8 black olives, pitted and sliced in half
4 medium sliced radishes

Thoroughly combine potatoes, garlic, olive oil, yogurt, salt, and pepper; then place on a platter. Chill, and served garnished with olives and radishes.

DRAINED YOGURT WITH ZA'TAR

Labana ma' Za'tar
Syria and Lebanon
Makes 8 ounces

Much more easily digestible than milk, yogurt is ideal for the aged, pregnant women, children, and the sick. It is believed that people who consume this fermented milk product tend to have clear skin and find no problem in enjoying a good night's sleep.

½ pound *labana* (Yogurt Cheese, see recipe, p. 22), or cream cheese
1 tablespoon olive oil
1 teaspoon *za'tar* (Sumac and Thyme Seasoning, see recipe, p. 19)

Spread *labana* or cream cheese evenly on a serving dish; then sprinkle with olive oil. Sprinkle *za'tar* over top; then serve as a dip or as a spread for toast.

Eggplant Appetizer

Salatat Bathinjan
Palestine and Jordan
Serves 4 to 6

Eggplants, often called poor man's meat or poor man's caviar, are one of the staple foods of the Middle East, valued for their great versatility.

1 large eggplant, peeled and thickly sliced
salt
1 cup olive oil
4 cloves garlic
1 medium hot pepper, finely chopped
3 tablespoons lemon juice

Sprinkle eggplant slices with salt and place in a strainer. Top with a weight and allow to drain for 45 minutes.

Heat oil in a frying pan, add eggplant slices, and fry on both sides until they turn golden brown. Remove and allow to drain in a strainer or on paper towels; then dice and place in a serving bowl.

Mash garlic cloves with a little salt. Stir into diced eggplant along with the hot pepper and lemon juice; then chill slightly and serve.

EGGPLANT DIP

Bathinjan Mfasakh
Syria and Lebanon
Serves 6 to 8

Since the dawn of recorded history eggplants have been an element in the culinary art of Iran and India. It was only after the Arab conquests that the cultivation of the eggplant spread to the Mediterranean basin. In the seventh century AD, Arab armies entering Iran, immediately took to this vegetable and brought it back under the name bathinjan, *an Arabized form of the Persian* badnjan.

After subjugating the Iberian Peninsula, the Arabs introduced the eggplant to Europe. The names for eggplant—Spanish berenjena, *Portuguese* berinjela, *and French* aubergine—*are all derived from the Arabic name. Curiously, even though most European tongues adapted the Arabic name, English speakers came to call it eggplant, because of the species that is egg-shaped.*

1 large eggplant, peeled and sliced ½-inch thick
½ cup olive oil
salt to taste
2 cups yogurt (see recipe, p. 22)
2 cloves garlic, crushed
1 teaspoon crushed dry mint
½ teaspoon pepper
½ cup finely chopped tomatoes
½ cup finely chopped parsley

Sprinkle eggplant slices with salt and place in a strainer. Top with a weight and allow to drain for 45 minutes.

Heat oil in a frying pan; then sauté eggplant slices over moderately high heat until they turn golden brown, adding more oil if necessary.

Remove eggplant from oil and drain in a strainer or on paper towels. Mash; then add salt, yogurt, garlic, mint, and pepper. Mix thoroughly and place on a flat serving dish. Refrigerate until chilled; garnish with tomatoes and parsley just before serving.

EGGPLANT PICKLES

Bathinjan Makboos
Syria and Lebanon
Makes one quart

In the villas and palaces of Muslim Spain, the eggplant often graced the tables of the Moors. Soon its cultivation spread to the remainder of Europe, and with the conquistadors it came to the New World. Nevertheless, in North America, it is only in the last few decades that eggplant has been grown in appreciable quantities, mainly in the southern United States.

1 large eggplant, unpeeled
salt to taste
½ cup vinegar
4 large cloves of garlic, finely chopped
1 teaspoon dried thyme
1 teaspoon peppercorns
1 teaspoon ginger
1 teaspoon ground coriander
1 cup olive oil

Cut eggplant in half lengthwise; then slice across into ½-inch-thick slices. Sprinkle eggplant slices with salt and place in a strainer. Top with a weight and allow to drain for 45 minutes.

Place eggplant slices and vinegar in a pot, cover with water, and bring to boil. Cook from 3 to 5 minutes; then remove, drain, and allow to cool.

Combine garlic, thyme, peppercorns, ginger, coriander, and some salt; set aside.

Pack eggplant slices in a quart jar, sprinkling the seasoning mixture over each layer. Add olive oil and, if needed, extra oil to cover eggplant slices by ½ inch; then store on a shelf in a cool place for two weeks before use.

EGGPLANT PURÉE

Baba Ghannooj
Syria and Lebanon
Serves 6 to 8

Baba Ghannooj *translates as "spoiled old daddy." Its inventor is said to have mashed the eggplant to a pulp in order to pamper her old and toothless father. When properly garnished, it is as pleasing to the eye as it is to the palate—and enjoyed by all ages.*

1 large eggplant
2 cloves garlic
salt to taste
⅓ cup lemon juice
⅓ cup tahini
3 tablespoons olive oil
a few parsley sprigs
1 tablespoon pine nuts, fried
½ small tomato, diced

Place eggplant in a pan and bake in a 425°F oven, turning frequently until tender. Allow to cool; then remove skin and mash pulp well. Set aside.

Mash garlic with salt, add 1 teaspoon of lemon juice and mix until smooth, then stir into eggplant. Place remaining lemon juice and tahini in a blender and blend for a few moments; then stir into eggplant. Spread on a platter; then sprinkle with the oil and garnish with parsley, pine nuts, and tomato pieces.

Note: A simpler way of preparing this dish is to place all ingredients, except garnish, in a food processor and process into paste; then place on a platter and garnish.

Eggplant Purée, Yemeni Style

Mutabbal Yamani
Yemen
Serves 6 to 8

Appealing to the eye, delicious tasting and versatile, eggplants are a vegetarian's dream vegetable. They come in all shades of color, the vast majority ranging from jet black to light purple, and in many shapes, from round or egg-shaped to finger-like and tiny. This attractive vegetable is catching the fancy of an increasing number of people.

2 medium eggplants
1 medium Spanish onion, very finely chopped
3 tablespoons olive oil
1 clove garlic, crushed
salt to taste
½ teaspoon pepper
2 tablespoons lemon juice
¼ cup olives, pitted and sliced
1 small tomato, finely chopped
¼ cup finely chopped parsley

Grill eggplants over an open fire or bake in hot oven, turning often until they become tender.

Peel eggplants while still hot; then mash flesh. Add onion, olive oil, garlic, salt, pepper, and lemon juice and mix well and place on a flat serving platter. Garnish with olives, tomato, and parsley; serve.

Eggplant and Yogurt Paté

Bathinjan ma' Laban
Palestine and Jordan
Serves 6 to 8

Traditionally, in lands where yogurt is on the menu every day, it is considered a health food and labeled the "milk of eternal life." This sobriquet might have some basis. Modern research reveals that yogurt contains a digestive enzyme that appears to prolong life. Humans naturally produce this enzyme in their childhood, but when they reach adulthood production of the enzyme drops off. Hence yogurt is an important part of the diets of the aged.

K. S. Nelson, in Yogurt Cookery, *reports that the bacteriologist Ilya Netchnikoff of*

the Pasteur Institute in Paris, after investigating the longevity of the Bulgarian peasants, asserted in his Prolongation of Life *that "the good health and long life of the Bulgarians was due to the custardy fermented milk that they consumed in great quantity."*

1 large eggplant
2 medium sized tomatoes, finely chopped
1 cup yogurt
2 cloves of garlic, crushed
½ cup very finely chopped fresh cilantro
salt and pepper to taste
⅛ teaspoon cayenne
2 tablespoons pomegranate seeds

Broil eggplant in the oven, turning until the skin blisters. Allow to cool, then peel.
Mash eggplant; then, in a mixing bowl, combine with the remaining ingredients, except the pomegranate seeds. Place on a flat serving dish; garnish with pomegranate seeds just before serving.

GARLIC–MASHED POTATO APPETIZER

Mutabbal Batata
Palestine and Jordan
Serves 8

Due to its odor, some call garlic a destroyer of romance, an enchanted poison, or the fare of the poor. Nevertheless, a great many people are enamored of its food-enhancing qualities. To these lovers of garlic, fresh or cooked, it is a delicious and healthy addition to a myriad of dishes.

3 cups mashed potatoes
½ head garlic, peeled and crushed
½ cup shelled pistachios
4 tablespoons lemon juice
2 tablespoons olive oil
½ teaspoon nutmeg
salt and pepper to taste
6 tablespoons water

Place potatoes in a bowl and set aside.
Place remaining ingredients in a blender and blend for 1 minute. Thoroughly stir the blender's content into the potatoes; then spread on a platter and serve (hot or at room temperature).

GARLIC ZUCCHINI APPETIZER

Mutabbal Koosa
Syria and Lebanon
Serves 6 to 8

Research teams in Japan and other countries have found that methyl allyl trisulphide, a substance extracted from garlic, has been effective in slowing down the formation of blood clots, which trigger strokes and heart attacks.

4 tablespoons olive oil
1 small head of garlic, peeled and sliced
1½ pounds zucchini, cut into ¼-inch thick slices
4 tablespoons vinegar
salt and pepper to taste
2 tablespoons chopped green onions
⅛ teaspoon cayenne
2 tablespoons finely chopped fresh cilantro

Heat oil in a frying pan and sauté garlic slices over medium heat until they turn light brown. Remove garlic slices with a slotted spoon and set aside.

In the same oil, adding more if necessary, sauté zucchini slices over medium heat until they turn light brown, turning them over once. Remove and drain on paper towels.

Combine vinegar with remaining ingredients.

Place zucchini on a serving platter. Sprinkle vinegar mixture over top; then evenly top with garlic slices. Allow to stand for 4 hours or so before serving.

Note: 2 tablespoons of pomegranate concentrate (*dibs rumman*), diluted in 2 tablespoons water, may be substituted for the vinegar.

INSTANT LABANA

Labana 'ala al-'Ajl
Syria and Lebanon
Serves 6 to 8

Cottage cheese and yogurt, closely related, blend well. In fact, when combined together, they become as one.

1 pound dry cottage cheese, also known as farmer's cheese or baker's cheese
6 tablespoons plain yogurt
salt to taste
1 tablespoon oil

Place cheese, yogurt, and salt in a blender or food processor and blend for a minute.

Place on a platter; then refrigerate for at least an hour. Remove and sprinkle with the olive oil just before serving.

KISHK DIP

Kishk Majbool
Syria and Lebanon
Serves 6 to 8

In the nineteenth century, missionaries from the United States traveling through the Syrian mountains, noted that although the peasants were poor, they were as healthy as American farmers. After a number of years of informal research, they concluded that kishk *was at least part of the answer. This ancient food, produced from the two most basic staples of humankind—wheat and milk—contains most of the nourishment people need.*

1 cup fine *kishk* (Powdered Cheese, see recipe, p. 16)
cold water
¼ cup olive oil
1 large onion, finely chopped
2 small tomatoes, finely chopped
a few sprigs of parsley

Place *kishk* in a small bowl; gradually stir in cold water until the *kishk* reaches the consistency of thick cream.

Place on a flat serving dish; then sprinkle with olive oil. Spread onions and tomatoes evenly over top. Garnish with parsley and serve.

Moroccan Fava Bean Purée

Bissara
Morocco
Serves 8

Although frozen or canned green fava beans are, at times, used in cooking, the beans are usually allowed to dry on the plant before harvesting. Dried fava beans, brown in color, are either sold in bulk or packaged in plastic bags.

2 cups large-size dry fava beans, soaked overnight, drained and peeled
3 cloves garlic, crushed
salt to taste
½ cup olive oil
8 cups water
5 tablespoons lemon juice
2 teaspoons cumin
1 teaspoon paprika
⅛ teaspoon chili powder
½ cup chopped parsley

Place fava beans, garlic, salt, 4 tablespoons of the olive oil and water in a saucepan. Cook over medium heat until beans are tender. Drain, reserving 1½ cups of the water. Place beans with reserved water in a food processor and blend until smooth. Return to saucepan; stir in lemon juice and cumin. Cook for 5 minutes over low heat, stirring a few times, then place on a serving platter. Sprinkle remaining olive oil evenly over top; then sprinkle with paprika and chili powder. Garnish with parsley and serve.

Okra and Garlic Appetizer

Bamya ma' Thoom
Syria and Lebanon
Serves 4

Once only soul food in the southern United States, okra is slowly becoming familiar in other parts of North America. Known as bamiya, bamya, *gumbo, and ladies' fingers, it has been a popular vegetable for hundreds of years, especially in Africa, India, and most of the Arab countries.*

With European expansion into the New World, okra's role as an important food spread to the Caribbean, Central America, and the southern United States. Today, thanks to modern methods of food preservation and rapid transportation, this warm-climate vegetable is available on most supermarket shelves, and more North Americans are becoming aware of okra's deliciously unique taste.

4 tablespoons cooking oil
1 11-oz package frozen okra, thawed
½ head garlic, crushed
4 tablespoons olive oil
4 tablespoons lemon juice
⅛ teaspoon cayenne
salt and pepper to taste
2 tablespoons finely chopped fresh cilantro

In a frying pan, heat oil and sauté okra over medium heat for 10 minutes or until pods begin to brown. Remove with a slotted spoon and place on paper towels to drain and cool. Place on a serving platter and set aside.

Prepare a sauce by placing the remaining ingredients in a blender; blend for a minute.

Spread sauce evenly over okra just before serving.

Olive Dip

Maazat Zaytoon
Palestine and Jordan
Serves 6 to 8

Olives are the fruit of an evergreen tree with small silvery green leaves bearing clusters of fragrant white flowers. The plant, started from a cutting, grows in height from 10 to 40 feet and begins to bear fruit when 4 to 8 years old. An olive tree takes about 15 years to mature fully, but will bear fruit for hundreds of years. Some trees in the eastern Mediterranean are believed to be over 2,000 years old.

Table olives are usually picked by hand while the ones for oil are either beaten off the branches or allowed to fall on the ground and then gathered. An orchard will yield about two tons of olives per acre—a ton producing about 50 gallons of oil.

2 cups green olives, pitted and washed
4 tablespoons tahini
2 tablespoons chopped fresh cilantro
1 tablespoon lemon juice
2 cloves garlic, crushed
⅛ teaspoon cayenne
1 small tomato, finely chopped
1 tablespoon olive oil

Place all ingredients except tomatoes and olive oil in a blender and blend until smooth.

Spread on a serving platter and refrigerate for 1 hour. Garnish with tomato pieces, sprinkle with oil, and serve.

Olives with Za'tar

Zaytoon bi Za'tar
Syria and Lebanon
Makes 1 pound

The people of the early civilizations in the Middle East believed that olive oil would cure every illness except the illness of death. A story is related that Adam was suffering with pain and complained to God. Gabriel descended from heaven with an olive tree and presented it to Adam, telling him to plant it, then pick the fruit and extract the oil to use whenever he had pain, assuring him that it would cure all illnesses. In the Arab world, this story is still told.

Some people in the Middle East believe that if they drink half a cup of olive oil

before breakfast, it will clear their system and they will live a long life free from disease. Their cure for an infected ear is several drops of heated olive oil placed into the ear. For sore muscles, the remedy is a massage of olive oil.

1 pound black olives, washed
½ cup olive oil
2 tablespoons *za'tar* (Sumac and Thyme Seasoning, see recipe, p. 19)

Combine all ingredients and store in a covered jar, serving as needed. Stir the olives before each serving.

SESAME SEED STICKS

Asaabi' Simsim
Bahrain
Makes about 2 dozen sticks

"Open Sesame," the magical Arabian Nights phrase that is supposed to open doors to untold riches, is well known in the literature of the West. Not many of us, though, relate this saying from Ali Baba and the Forty Thieves *to sesame seeds—one of the oldest foods known to man. Yet, there is a plausible connection between this phrase and the seeds.*

According to E. A. Weiss in Castor, Sesame and Safflower, *the saying "Open Sesame" could be related to the opening of the sesame capsule; if opened at the right time, it takes only a slight tap to release the seeds.*

From the days of The Arabian Nights, *and even before, sesame seeds have been a part of Arab cuisine. However, this dish probably originated in India.*

1 cup sesame seeds, toasted and pulverized
⅓ cup flour
2 eggs
1 teaspoon baking powder
½ teaspoon paprika
¼ teaspoon ground coriander
⅛ teaspoon cayenne
salt and pepper to taste
water
oil for frying

Place all ingredients, except water and oil, in a bowl and mix thoroughly. Add water gradually, and knead until a dough is formed. Roll into finger sticks and set aside.

Place cooking oil in a saucepan to a depth of a ½ inch and heat. Fry sticks over medium heat until they turn golden brown. Drain on paper towels; serve hot or cold.

Tahini Appetizer

Mutabbalat Taheena
Yemen
Serves 4

The Yemenis have a good number of dishes similar to those of the Fertile Crescent, but they have adapted them somewhat to their own taste.

4 tablespoons tahini
4 tablespoons lemon juice
4 cloves garlic, crushed
¼ cup finely chopped parsley
salt and pepper to taste
6 hard-boiled eggs, mashed
2 tablespoons water
½ teaspoon paprika

Place tahini and lemon juice in a blender and blend for a few moments; then transfer to a bowl. Add garlic, parsley, salt, pepper, eggs, and water and stir gently until well mixed.

Place on a platter, sprinkle with the paprika, and serve.

Note: This dish can be served as a dip or a salad.

Tahini Mix

Salatat Taheena
Palestine and Jordan
Serves 4 to 6

Tahini (also spelled taheeni, taheneh, tahineh, *or* taheena) *derived from the Arabic word tahana (to grind), is a very nutritious food. It has no cholesterol, is relatively sodium free, and contains about 50% fat, 20% protein, 16% carbohydrate, and 5% fiber—and a good amount of calcium, iron, potassium, phosphorus, and vitamins A and E. In the Middle East it has long been believed that, when combined with legumes, tahini becomes the ultimate edible.*

5 medium tomatoes, finely diced
1 medium cucumber, finely diced
½ cup finely chopped parsley

3 tablespoons tahini
¼ cup lemon juice
4 cloves garlic, crushed
salt to taste
1 tablespoon dried mint

Combine tomatoes, cucumber and parsley in a serving bowl; set aside.

In another bowl, thoroughly mix the tahini with the lemon juice, and set aside.

Mash garlic with salt; then stir into tahini–lemon juice mixture. Add to vegetables and toss; then garnish with dried mint and serve.

Turnip Pickles

Lift
Syria and Lebanon
Makes 6 quarts

As a child, I enjoyed the look and the taste of red-colored pickled turnips, served regularly by my mother. They always seemed to add an appetizing touch to the other dishes.

3 small beets (for color)
10 to 12 pounds (6 quarts) small white turnips, peeled and cut into quarters
6 garlic cloves, peeled
6 teaspoons coarse pickling salt
10 cups of water
4 cups white vinegar

Boil beets until tender; then peel and cut in half. Set aside.

Divide turnips evenly among six sterilized quart jars. Add 1 beet half, 1 garlic clove, and 1 teaspoon coarse salt to each jar. Set aside.

Place water and vinegar in a saucepan and bring to a boil. Lower heat and simmer for 5 minutes.

Place a towel under jars; then pour in enough hot vinegar solution to cover contents. Seal jars immediately and allow to cool; then store in a cool, dry place. The pickles should be ready in 2 to 3 weeks.

Note: This measured quantity of vinegar and water, with the coarse salt added to each jar, is suitable for pickling many other vegetables. Some examples: cauliflower florets, carrots, small peppers, green tomatoes, gherkin-size cucumbers.

Yogurt and Basil Appetizer

Laban ma' Habaq
Palestine and Jordan
Serves 6 to 8

All types of milk, from reindeer to cow, can be made into yogurt. The fat and nutrient value of the yogurt will depend on the type of milk used—cream, whole, or part-skim or skim milk—and on any additives included, like fruits or syrups.

This simple appetizer is nourishing as well as tasty.

4 cups yogurt, plain
¼ cup finely chopped fresh basil, or 2 teaspoons dried basil
2 cloves garlic, crushed
salt to taste

Place all ingredients in a blender or food processor and blend for a few moments. Place in a serving bowl and chill. Serve with wedges of pita bread.

Yogurt Ginger Appetizer

Laban ma' Zanjabeel
Arabian Gulf
Serves 4

Treasured for centuries by Chinese and Indian cooks, ginger, in the last few decades, has come to be revered in many European and North American kitchens. A good number of cooks say that the secret of the world-renowned cuisine of China is ginger—called by some the "spice of the ages."

1 cup plain yogurt
4 tablespoons pulverized almonds
2 tablespoons finely chopped green onions
2 tablespoons finely chopped parsley
1 tablespoon finely grated ginger
1 tablespoon olive oil
1 clove garlic, crushed
⅛ teaspoon cayenne
salt and pepper to taste
1 small tomato, finely chopped

Thoroughly combine all ingredients, except tomato, in a mixing bowl. Place in a serving dish; garnish with tomato and serve with pita bread or crackers.

Zucchini and Yogurt Dip

Koosa ma' Zanjabeel
Palestine and Jordan
Serves 6 to 8

For thousands of years, the peasants in Biblical lands have been nourished by the consumption of meatless foods such as this tasty and healthful combination.

1 pound zucchini
1 cup yogurt
2 cloves garlic, crushed
½ cup tahini
2 tablespoons lemon juice
salt to taste
½ teaspoon pepper
2 tablespoons finely chopped parsley

Bake zucchini in oven until soft; then peel and mash. Add remaining ingredients, except parsley, and mix thoroughly. Place on a serving platter and chill for at least one hour.

Garnish with parsley and serve.

SOUPS

Wholesome, tasty, and simple to prepare, vegetarian soups have been on the everyday menu of the Arab kitchen since the dawn of history. At very little cost, the farmers of the Arab world enjoy healthy and nutritious broths developed by their ancestors over the centuries. Generation after generation have been sustained by these peasant soups. And when the people of the countryside in the Arab lands emigrated to other places, they took along their culinary delights.

My parents, who left Syria for western Canada in the early 1920s, were no exception. Through the Great Depression they survived and raised a healthy family, nourished by vegetarian dishes developed in their land of origin. When our neighbors found great difficulties in obtaining enough food to sustain themselves, we always had our stock of dried vegetables. Even in 1937, when a severe drought parched the lands of southwest Saskatchewan, my parents were able to cope, for they had inherited the knowledge of their ancestors. Hardy vegetables that thrived in the arid Arab world kept our family well nourished in Canada.

Broad beans, chickpeas, and lentils were the basic legumes that kept us well fed and healthy. Fresh from our hand-watered garden in summer and dried in winter, they were prepared with herbs and spices and became the substance of our lives. As the basis for many types of savory soups, they graced our table day after day. Even after many years, I can still visualize pots of simmering chickpeas and lentils diffusing their enticing aroma.

These appetizing soups were superb for all types of meals and snacks. Often we relished them as the main course. At other times they whetted our appetite for the meal to come. Or we enjoyed them as snacks, especially as a late evening treat. On cold winter days we consumed them for breakfast, and—strange as it may sound—they were excellent as a recuperative after a night of festivity.

The history of Arab soups goes back to the beginning of civilization when humankind in the Middle East boiled wild vegetables in water to make a hot meal. Later, as people became more sophisticated, herbs and spices were added to enhance the food's appeal. With the passing centuries, delicious soups were concocted with ingredients readily found by the farmers of these historic lands. Even today, soups are at their best when prepared by poor peasants who cannot afford meat, creams and butter.

Vegetarian soups are one of the basic foods of the peasants and working classes in the Arab countries. These succulent broths, made from easily obtainable vegetables, are simple to prepare, inexpensive, filling, and do not require exotic ingredients. Herbs and spices give them their zest and tang. Meat is not essential to a rich and full-bodied stock. Any available vegetable that is slow simmered with condiments produces a tasty delectable soup.

There are Arab vegetarian soups to satisfy all tastes. As they did in our Depression years, broad beans, chickpeas, and lentils form the basis of most of these savory dishes. These legumes have stood the test of ages. Since the days of the Babylonians and ancient Egyptians, they have been utilized in countless types of vegetarian dishes.

The ancients in the Middle East believed that the herbs and spices they added to the broth stimulated the appetite, helped in the circulation of the blood, alleviated rheumatic disorders, and eased diabetic problems. Other attributes were imputed to these legumes as well. The Romans believed the chickpea to be an aphrodisiac and called it a love food. In the same fashion, the Arabs and other Middle Eastern peoples believed that it gave its consumers sexual strength. Even if these claims are only myths, these hearty and nourishing concoctions make appetizing and gratifying meals.

It is ironic that, in the homes of wealthy Arabs, vegetarian soups do not often form part of the daily menu. The smooth and refreshing taste of this poor man's delight are appreciated even by the well-to-do. When there are no guests to impress, vegetarian soups are consumed in their homes with great gusto—despite their public disdain of this food of the poor.

Arab vegetarian soups are easy to make, tasty, and wholesome, and can be served as one-dish meals. To complete the repast, add pita bread, yogurt cheese, and perhaps a salad.

Many of the soups start by sautéing the vegetables with herbs, especially fresh cilantro—a condiment that gives the stock its characteristic richness. For many Westerners, the taste of cilantro is a new experience—if you wish, you can substitute a mixture of green onions and parsley.

There are both hot, hearty Arab soups and cold soups, which, especially in the summer months in the hot lands of the Middle East and North Africa, provide a refreshing midday meal or snack. Both types are simple to prepare and can be gourmet delights. The skilled chef Escoffier could well have been talking about Arab soups when he said, "Soup puts the heart at ease, calms down the violence of hunger, eliminates the tension of the day, and awakens and refines the appetite" (Nelson 48).

The cook who prepares the following Arab vegetarian soups will find that Escoffier's words hold true for the broths of the historic Middle East and North Africa.

ALEPPO LENTIL SOUP

Shawrbat 'Adas Halabiya
Syria and Lebanon
Serves 6 to 8

Lentils are among the most nutritious of legumes, rich in iron, calcium, vitamins A and B, and, above all, protein. Dried lentils have more protein than an equal weight of choice lean sirloin steak. Few legumes can equal their food value.

1 cup split red lentils, washed
6 cups water
¼ cup flour
4 tablespoons lemon juice
salt to taste
2 tablespoons olive oil
4 cloves garlic, crushed
¼ cup finely chopped fresh cilantro
1 teaspoon cumin
pinch of cayenne

Place lentils in a saucepan with 5 cups of the water. Bring to boil; then lower heat and simmer for approximately 10 minutes.

In the meantime, mix flour with remaining water to make smooth paste. Stir into lentils; then add lemon juice and salt. Continue stirring over high heat until soup mixture returns to a boil; add more water if necessary. Lower the heat; then cover and cook for 15 minutes or until the lentils are tender, stirring once in while and adding more water if needed.

While mixture is cooking, heat the oil in a frying pan. Add garlic and cilantro and sauté until garlic turns golden brown, about 3 minutes. Stir contents of frying pan into soup. Simmer for few minutes; then add cumin and cayenne. Stir and serve hot.

BASIL-FLAVORED VEGETABLE SOUP

Shawrbat Habaq
Palestine and Jordan
Serves 8 to 10

Pleasing to the eyes, nose, and tongue, basil has been known for hundreds of years, in a number of Mediterranean countries, as the herb of kings. In these lands, it has long been prized above other herbs and spices. The ancient Greeks gave it the name basileus, *meaning "king." Its essence was used as a royal perfume and its countless joys and benefits have been preserved in ancient writings.*

1 cup navy beans, soaked for 24 hours, and drained
8 cups water
3 medium potatoes, peeled and chopped into small pieces
1 cup fresh or frozen peas
1 cup fresh or frozen lima beans
2 cups stewed tomatoes
1 teaspoon cumin
½ teaspoon savory
¼ teaspoon cayenne
salt and pepper to taste
4 tablespoons finely chopped fresh basil or 2 teaspoons dried basil
4 tablespoons olive oil
2 cloves garlic, crushed

Place beans and water in a saucepan and bring to boil. Cook over medium heat for 2½ hours; then add remaining ingredients, except basil, oil, and garlic, and bring to boil. Cook over medium heat for 30 minutes or until beans are tender, adding more water if necessary. Stir in basil, oil, and garlic and serve immediately.

BEAN AND ALMOND SOUP

Asseeda
Morocco
Serves 6

In North Africa, soups are prepared somewhat differently than they are in the Middle East. Although the ingredients are usually similar, North Africans omit the preliminary sautéing.

½ cup navy beans, soaked overnight in 6 cups of water
¾ cup blanched almonds, ground
2 medium onions, chopped
¼ cup finely chopped fresh cilantro
3 cloves garlic, crushed
salt and pepper to taste
½ cup white grape juice
4 tablespoons slivered almonds, toasted

Place beans with their water in a large saucepan and bring to boil; then cover and cook over medium heat for 1 hour.

Add remaining ingredients, except slivered almonds, and cook for another 45 minutes or until beans are tender, adding more water if necessary.

Purée in a blender, then place in a serving bowl. Garnish with almonds and serve immediately.

Bean Soup

Shawrbat Fasoolya
Syria and Lebanon
Serves 8

For thousands of years in the Greater Syria area, broad beans (favas) were the only beans available for cooking. During the past few centuries, however, many other types of beans were introduced and are now on the daily menu.

½ cups dried navy beans, soaked overnight in 8 cups of water
3 tablespoons olive oil
2 medium onions, chopped
3 cloves garlic, crushed
½ cup finely chopped fresh cilantro
1 medium carrot, finely chopped
1 large potato, diced
3 large tomatoes, chopped
½ cup finely chopped green onions
salt and pepper to taste
¼ teaspoon allspice

Place beans with their water in a large saucepan and cover; cook over medium heat for about 2 hours or until beans are cooked but still firm.

In the meantime, heat oil in a frying pan, and sauté onions, garlic, and cilantro, stirring constantly until they begin to brown.

Add frying pan contents and remaining ingredients to beans; then simmer until beans and vegetables are tender, adding more water if necessary.

Bean and Celery Soup

Hasa Fasoolya
Iraq
Serves 8

There is little doubt that the ancient Babylonians were the first people to write cookbooks. Some 4,000 years ago the princes and priests of ancient Mesopotamia were great gastronomers and, hence, their chefs had to be master cooks. Deciphered from the cuneiform tablets is evidence that they created at least a hundred types of soup, eighteen types of cheese, and three hundred types of bread—in shapes from a heart to a woman's breast, made with all types of flours, and enhanced by spices and fruits. There are today a good number of food historians who believe that the cradle of civilization was also home to the world's first haute cuisine.

The Arab and many other Middle Eastern cuisines are direct descendants of the dishes that originated in the kitchens of the Babylonians two millennia before the birth of Christ.

1 cup white beans, soaked overnight and drained
7 cups water
2 medium onions, chopped
4 large cloves garlic, crushed
4 tablespoons butter
4 tablespoons flour
1 teaspoon cumin
1 teaspoon ground mustard seed
salt and pepper to taste
2 cups finely chopped celery

Place beans, water, onions, and garlic in a saucepan and bring to boil. Cover and cook over medium heat for 2 hours or until the beans are well cooked, adding more water if necessary; then mash or purée in a food processor. Set aside.

Place butter and flour in a clean saucepan and stir-fry for a few moments until flour begins to brown. Add mashed beans, cumin, mustard, salt, and pepper; then bring to boil and cook for 3 to 4 minutes, stirring constantly and adding a little more water if necessary. Serve hot, with each diner adding celery to taste.

CARAWAY SOUP

Hareera Karawiya
Morocco
Serves 6

In North Africa, the pervasive aroma of herbs and spices emanating from a pot of soup simmering on the fire whets the appetite of all returning from their labors. A poet could well have been describing this simple soup when he wrote:

> Let Omar sing of wine and bread,
> But I prefer fine soup instead.

6 cups water
2 tablespoons flour, dissolved in ½ cup water
2 cups very finely chopped fresh mint leaves
1 tablespoon ground caraway seeds
3 tablespoons butter
salt and pepper to taste
¼ cup lemon juice

Heat water in a saucepan and before it comes to the boil, slowly stir in flour and water mixture. Add the remaining ingredients except lemon juice; then bring to a boil, stirring constantly.

Remove from heat and stir in lemon juice. Serve immediately. If the soup is not served at once, it will lose much of its taste.

CHICKPEA SOUP

Leblabi
Tunisia
Serves 8

The Arabs extolled chickpeas for their aphrodisiac values. R. Henrickson in his book Lewd Foods, *quotes these lines by Shaykh Nefzawi in* The Perfumed Garden:

> Abu el-Heidja has deflowered in one night
> Once eighty virgins, and he did not eat or drink between,
> Because he surfeited himself with chickpeas,
> And had drunk camel's milk with honey mixed.

1½ cups dried chickpeas, washed and soaked overnight in 10 cups water
4 cloves garlic, crushed
1 hot pepper, finely chopped
1 teaspoon ground caraway seeds
1 teaspoon oregano
salt and pepper to taste
2 tablespoons lemon juice
3 tablespoons olive oil
2 cups croutons
¼ cup finely chopped fresh cilantro

Place chickpeas with their water in a saucepan and bring to boil; cover and cook over medium heat for 2 hours.

Add remaining ingredients—except lemon juice, olive oil, croutons and cilantro—and cook over medium heat for another 30 minutes or until the chickpeas are tender, adding more water if necessary. Remove from heat; then stir in lemon juice and olive oil.

Place in serving bowls and garnish with chopped cilantro and croutons and serve.

CHICKPEA AND FAVA BEAN SOUP

Shawrbat Hummus wa Fool
Palestine and Jordan
Serves 10 to 12

Fava beans, chickpeas, and lentils were the basis for soups eaten by the Arab families who settled in western Canada and the United States. These tasty soups relieved some of the hardships of the drought-ridden West. They not only satisfied hunger but also gave warmth, pleasure, and excitement at very little expense.

1 cup small fava beans, rinsed
8 cups of water
2 medium potatoes, peeled and diced
¼ cup olive or vegetable oil
2 medium onions, diced
4 cloves garlic, crushed
¼ cup finely chopped fresh cilantro
2 cups stewed tomatoes
2 cups cooked chickpeas
1 teaspoon cumin
1 teaspoon oregano
salt and pepper to taste
pinch of cayenne

Place fava beans and water in a saucepan and bring to boil. Cover and cook over medium heat for 1½ hours; then add potatoes and cook for 25 minutes more.

In the meantime, heat oil in a frying pan; sauté onions until they begin to brown. Add the garlic and cilantro and stir-fry for 3 minutes.

Add frying pan contents along with remaining ingredients to fava beans and bring to boil. Simmer over medium heat for 30 minutes, adding more water if necessary. Serve piping hot.

Note: The fava beans should be the small Egyptian type, about the size of a pea. They can be found in Middle Eastern stores in large cities. Or substitute navy beans, which, though not traditional, make an equally delicious soup.

CHICKPEA AND POTATO SOUP

Shawbrat Hummus wa Batata
Syria and Lebanon
Serves 8

For more than a century the peoples of the Greater Syria area in the Middle East have been emigrating to the Americas. Many of these emigrants, after living for years in the West, return to end their days in the land of their birth. They bring back Arab foods that have been transformed by their stay in the Americas. This dish, Arab in origin, is a fine example.

1 cup chickpeas, soaked overnight and drained
10 cups water
4 medium potatoes, chopped into small pieces
4 tablespoons olive oil
2 medium onions, finely chopped
6 cloves garlic, crushed
4 tablespoons finely chopped fresh cilantro
1 teaspoon paprika
1 teaspoon cumin
½ teaspoon ground caraway seeds
salt and pepper to taste
4 tablespoons, finely chopped green onions

Place chickpeas and water in a saucepan and bring to boil; then cook over medium heat for 1½ hours. Add potatoes and cook for another hour.

In the meantime, heat oil in a frying pan and sauté onions, garlic, and cilantro for 10 minutes. Stir the contents of the frying pan and remaining ingredients, except green onions, into the chickpeas. Cook for a further 30 minutes. Stir in green onions and serve hot.

CHICKPEA AND TOMATO SOUP

Shawrbat An-Nikhi
Arabian Gulf
Serves 8

The first time I enjoyed a version of this soup was in an Indian restaurant in Dubai, the industrial heart of the United Arab Emirates. In this land, which is a mixture of the past and present, men and women from all around the globe are building a country that is quickly becoming a model for other developing lands.

People from the shores of northern Europe, the Americas, the Far East and beyond rub shoulders and converse in a multitude of tongues. The foods they bring with them mingle and evolve, to produce this trading city's succulent, modern cuisine.

1 cup chickpeas, soaked overnight and drained
8 cups water
4 tablespoons olive oil
4 tablespoons finely chopped fresh cilantro
2 medium onions, chopped
2 cups stewed tomatoes
2 teaspoons *ibzar* (Arabian Gulf Spices, see recipe, p. 13)
⅛ teaspoon cayenne
salt to taste

Place chickpeas and water in a saucepan and bring to boil. Cook over medium heat for 2 to 3 hours or until chickpeas are well cooked, adding more water if necessary.

In the meantime, heat oil in a frying pan and sauté cilantro and onions over medium heat for 10 minutes. Stir in remaining ingredients and cook for another 10 minutes. Add frying pan contents to the chickpeas and cook over medium heat for 20 minutes; then remove from heat and allow to cool. Purée; then return to saucepan, adding more water if desired. Heat and serve.

COLD YOGURT AND CUCUMBER SOUP

Hasa Laban Barida
Iraq
Serves 6 to 8

Modern nutritionists have found that yogurt is a medically beneficial food. In addition to the healthful elements found in milk, yogurt contains a teeming load of beneficial bacteria—almost 100 million in one gram. These multiply in the intestines and kill off accumulated germs, thus promoting digestion.

5 cups yogurt
1 small cucumber, peeled and finely chopped
2 cups water
¼ cup finely chopped fresh cilantro
1 clove garlic, crushed
½ cup almonds, pulverized
salt and pepper to taste
pinch of cayenne

Thoroughly mix all ingredients in a serving bowl; then chill for at least two hours before serving.

COLD YOGURT AND TOMATO SOUP -

Hasa Laban ma' Tamata
Iraq
Serves 6 to 8

Cold soups provide a refreshing midday meal or snack in the hot lands of the Middle East and North Africa. They are simple to prepare and often a gourmet's delight.

4 cups tomato juice
2 cups yogurt
¼ cup lemon juice
2 tablespoons olive oil
salt and pepper to taste
⅛ teaspoon chili powder
2 tablespoons finely chopped fresh cilantro

Thoroughly mix all ingredients, except cilantro and chill in a refrigerator for at least two hours. Top with cilantro and serve.

Couscous Soup

Hareera Kuskus
Morocco
Serves 6 to 8

Soups—the mainstay of the poorer peasants in North Africa and at times their only meal of the day—are based mostly on chickpeas and lentils. Occasionally, other ingredients are utilized, as in this delightful soup, infused with herbs and spices.

6 cups warm water
¾ cup couscous
5 tablespoons butter
salt and pepper to taste
pinch of saffron
1½ teaspoons ground aniseed
¼ cup finely chopped fresh cilantro

Place all ingredients, except aniseed and cilantro, in a saucepan and bring to boil. Cook over medium heat for 3 minutes; then stir in aniseed and cilantro and serve immediately.

Note: If soup is not served immediately, the texture and taste will change.

EGYPTIAN LENTIL SOUP

Shawrbat 'Adas Misriya
Egypt
Serves 6

In Egypt, from the days of the Pharaohs until the present time, lentil soup has been on the menu. The Qur'an *mentions that one of the foods the Jews in Sinai asked Moses to provide was lentils. The following lentil soup recipe could possibly have been made, with the exception of the tomato, a New World discovery, in the same fashion at the time of Moses and the Pharaohs.*

5 cups vegetable stock
1 cup split brown lentils, washed and drained
2 large onions, chopped
2 medium tomatoes, finely chopped
4 cloves garlic, crushed
4 tablespoons butter
2 teaspoons cumin
salt and pepper to taste
4 teaspoons lemon juice

Place vegetable stock in a saucepan and bring to boil. Add lentils, two-thirds of the onions, tomatoes, and garlic and bring again to boil. Reduce heat and simmer until lentils become tender, adding more water if necessary.

While lentils are cooking, melt 2 tablespoons of butter in a frying pan and sauté remaining onions over medium heat, stirring frequently until they turn golden brown. Set aside.

Purée lentil mixture in a blender, then return to saucepan and reheat, stirring constantly. Stir in cumin, salt, pepper, lemon juice, and remaining 2 tablespoons of butter. Place soup into soup bowls and top with the fried onions.

Note: For a Bahraini version, omit the fried onion garnish and do not purée the lentils. Add ¼ cup broken vermicelli, ½ teaspoon ground coriander, and a pinch of cayenne toward the end of the cooking time and more water if necessary. Cook until the noodles are done.

Fava Bean Soup

Fool Nabed
Egypt
Serves 8 to 10

Since the beginning of civilization in the Middle East, fava beans have been one of the staffs of life. To the vast majority of Arabs, they are one of the most delectable of foods, in soups, appetizers, or main courses.

2 cups large fava beans, washed and soaked in 6 cups of water
salt and pepper to taste
1 teaspoon cumin
2 cloves garlic, crushed
¼ cup olive oil
¼ cup lemon juice
2 tablespoons finely chopped cilantro

Drain fava beans, reserving water; peel the beans and place in a saucepan. Measure the reserved water, and top up if necessary to make 6 cups; then add to beans and bring to a boil. Cover and cook over low heat for about 1 hour or until the fava beans are tender, adding more water if necessary.

Purée in a blender or food processor; then return to saucepan and stir in remaining ingredients, except cilantro. Bring to boil and cook for about 5 minutes over low heat. Serve in individual bowls garnished with cilantro.

Iraqi Chickpea Soup

Hasa al-Hummus
Iraq
Serves 8

Neither a pea nor a bean, yet combining the best qualities of both, the chickpea is gradually making itself at home in the western kitchen.

1 cup dried chickpeas, washed and soaked overnight in 9 cups of water
2 tablespoons butter
2 medium sized onions, chopped
4 cloves garlic, crushed
½ cup finely chopped fresh cilantro
salt and pepper to taste
½ teaspoon mustard powder
¼ teaspoon cayenne

    Place chickpeas with their water in a saucepan and bring to boil; cook over medium heat for 1½ hours.

    In the meantime, melt butter in a frying pan; stir-fry onions and garlic until they begin to brown. Add cilantro and stir-fry a few minutes longer. Add frying pan contents and remaining ingredients to the chickpeas and stir. Cover and cook over medium heat for 1 hour or until chickpeas are tender, adding more water if necessary.

Iraqi Yogurt Soup

Hasa Laban ma' Rizz
Iraq
Serves 8

In the Middle East, countless varieties of yogurt soup are prepared. Hot, cold, spicy, or sweet, they are all exotic and delectable.

½ cup rice, rinsed
2 cups of water
5 cups yogurt
2 cloves garlic, crushed
salt and pepper to taste
1 cup finely chopped fresh mint

Place rice and water in a saucepan and cook over a medium heat for about 20 minutes or until rice is cooked but still firm.

Remove the saucepan from heat; gradually add yogurt, garlic, salt, and pepper, stirring constantly. Return to heat and continue to stir until the soup begins to boil; immediately remove from heat and stir in the mint just before serving.

KISHK SOUP
Shawrbat Kishk
Syria and Lebanon
Serves 4

As I look back at my childhood years, I believe that this soup, served almost every morning by my mother, had a great hand in keeping our family healthy. Containing almost all the essential food elements, kishk *is one of the most healthful of foods.*

2 tablespoons butter
1 medium onion, finely chopped
2 cloves garlic, crushed
¾ cup *kishk* (Powdered Cheese, see recipe, p. 16), dissolved in ½ cup water
4 cups water
salt and pepper to taste

Melt butter in a saucepan; then add onion and garlic and sauté until they begin to brown.

Stir in *kishk* and sauté for a moment; then add the water and bring to boil. Season with salt and pepper, and cover, allowing to simmer over low heat for 10 minutes. Serve hot with toast.

Note: Makes an excellent breakfast dish, especially on cold winter mornings.

LENTIL & GARLIC SOUP FLAVORED WITH CUMIN

Shawrbat 'Adas bi Thoom wa Kammoon
Palestine and Jordan
Serves 8 to 10

It is believed that cumin was first utilized as a flavoring in the Nile Valley; its use spread to the neighboring countries and as far away as the Indian subcontinent and the Far East. In the eighth century, the Arabs brought it to the Iberian Peninsula, and from there its use spread to all of Europe. This spice, which derives its name in all the European languages from the Arabic kammoon, *became a popular flavoring agent in the cooking of medieval Europe.*

4 tablespoons olive oil
1 head garlic, peeled and crushed
1 small hot pepper, finely chopped
4 tablespoons finely chopped fresh cilantro
4 medium tomatoes, finely chopped
1 medium potato, cut into small cubes
¾ cup lentils, rinsed
2 teaspoons ground cumin
salt and pepper to taste
6½ cups water

Heat oil in a saucepan and sauté garlic, hot pepper, and cilantro over medium heat for 5 minutes. Add tomatoes and sauté another 5 minutes; then stir in remaining ingredients and bring to boil, adding more water if necessary. Cover and cook over medium heat for 45 minutes. Serve hot.

LENTIL AND NOODLE SOUP

Shawrbat 'Adas ma' Sha'reeya
Syria and Lebanon
Serves 8 to 10

In the Arab world legumes—chief among them, lentils—play a starring role in soups. The legumes are all moderately priced and universally available, and are an excellent source of basic nutrition.

8 cups of water
salt and pepper to taste
1 cup brown lentils, rinsed and drained
¼ cup olive oil
2 medium onions, chopped
4 cloves garlic, crushed
½ cup finely chopped fresh cilantro
½ cup fine noodles, broken into small pieces

Place water, salt, pepper, and lentils in a saucepan and bring to boil. Cook for about 30 minutes over medium heat or until lentils are tender but still intact and slightly firm.

In the meantime, place oil, onions, and garlic in a frying pan and sauté over medium heat until the onions begin to turn slightly brown. Add the cilantro and stir-fry for a few more minutes.

Add frying pan contents to lentils; then stir in noodles and bring to boil. Lower heat and simmer for about 20 minutes or until the noodles are done, adding more water if necessary.

Note: Noodles and vermicelli can be used interchangeably.

Lentil Soup with Spinach

Shawrbat 'Adas ma' Sabanakh
Syria and Lebanon
Serves 8 to 10

Cooked lentils can be served as a vegetable with other foods or in salads, but they are most often used as the main ingredient in soups and stews.

Dry lentils do not require soaking and are usually only washed before cooking. But they can be soaked, then requiring only half the time for cooking.

1 cup brown lentils, rinsed
8 cups water
salt to taste
¼ cup finely chopped fresh cilantro
2 large onions, finely chopped
4 cloves garlic, crushed
¼ cup olive oil
½ 10-oz package spinach, washed and chopped
1 cup finely chopped parsley
½ cup lemon juice

Place lentils, water and salt in a saucepan and cook over medium heat until lentils are tender but still intact and slightly firm.

In the meantime, in a frying pan sauté cilantro, onions, and garlic in the oil until they begin to turn brown. Add frying pan contents to lentils, then stir in spinach, parsley, and lemon juice. Simmer until the spinach is cooked; serve hot.

Note: Swiss chard may be substituted for spinach.

LENTIL AND TOMATO SOUP

Shawrabat 'Adas ma' Banadoora
Bahrain
Serves 8

The lentil was introduced into the New World by the Spaniards. Nevertheless, for hundreds of years, it was only in Central and South America that it took root.

1 cup brown lentils, rinsed and drained
7 cups water
4 tablespoons butter
2 medium onions, chopped
4 cloves garlic, crushed
3 medium tomatoes, finely chopped
1 teaspoon cumin
1 teaspoon ground coriander
⅛ teaspoon cayenne
salt and pepper to taste
¼ cup vermicelli, broken into small pieces
3 tablespoons lemon juice

Place lentils and water in a saucepan and bring to boil. Cover and cook over medium heat for 20 minutes.

In the meantime, melt butter in a frying pan and sauté onions and garlic until they begin to turn brown. Stir in tomatoes and sauté for a few minutes more; then add frying pan contents to lentils.

Stir in remaining ingredients, except lemon juice, and simmer over low heat until lentils and vermicelli are well cooked, adding more water if necessary; then stir in lemon juice and serve hot.

MARRAKESH RICE AND LENTIL SOUP

Hareera Marrakashee
Morocco
Serves 8

The ancients in the Middle East and North Africa believed that the herbs and spices in the broth, besides enriching the soup, stimulated the appetite, helped in the circulation of the blood, alleviated rheumatic disorders, and eased diabetic problems. Even if these claims were only myths, these hearty and nourishing concoctions make an appetizing and gratifying meal.

¾ cup lentils, washed and soaked overnight in 7 cups of water
2 tablespoons olive oil
½ cup finely chopped fresh cilantro
1 teaspoon paprika
½ cup rice, rinsed
salt and pepper to taste
1 teaspoon cumin
¼ teaspoon chili powder
2 tablespoons flour, dissolved in ½ cup of water
¼ cup lemon juice
4 tablespoons butter

Place lentils with their water, olive oil, cilantro, and paprika in a saucepan and bring to boil. Cover and cook over medium heat for 25 minutes; then add remaining ingredients except flour, lemon juice and butter. Cook for another 20 minutes or until rice grains are tender but still whole.

Remove from heat; slowly stir in the flour paste, lemon juice, and butter. Return to heat and bring to a boil; then serve immediately.

Moroccan Eggplant & Summer Squash Soup

L'Hamraak
Morocco
Serves 8 to 10

On a trip through the Anti-Atlas Mountains of Morocco, I stopped at a village restaurant where I was served this soup. The day was cold and after consuming a large bowl, I felt sated and content. In my ensuing conversation I asked the proprietor about the ingredients and thereafter prepared the same soup to my own taste.

salt
1 medium eggplant, peeled and cut into ½ inch cubes
½ cup olive oil
1 large summer squash or zucchini (about 7 to 8 inches long), cut into ½-inch cubes
1 small onion, finely chopped
3 cloves garlic, crushed
3 tablespoons finely chopped fresh cilantro
2 large tomatoes, finely chopped
1 teaspoon cumin
½ teaspoon pepper
5½ cups water

Sprinkle salt on eggplant cubes and place in a strainer. Top with a weight and allow to drain for 45 minutes.

Heat oil in a large saucepan; add squash and sauté over medium heat for 3 minutes. Stir in eggplant, onion, garlic, and cilantro; sauté, stirring constantly for 5 minutes, adding more oil if necessary.

Stir in remaining ingredients and bring to boil. Lower heat, cover, and simmer for 30 minutes, adding more water if necessary. Taste and add salt if needed. Serve hot.

Moroccan Vegetable Soup

Hareera
Morocco
Serves 10 to 12

Hareera, *one of Morocco's oldest and most popular soups, plays an important role during* Ramadan, *Islam's annual fast, which lasts 30 days. The end of each day's abstention of food and drink is announced by the firing of a cannon. At that instant, the first taste of food is always a mouthful of* hareera, *often made solely with vegetables.*

The widely prepared hareera *is the ultimate Moroccan soup, adapting to a range of situations. Wealthy city-dwellers add all types of meats to create their delicious* hareeras. *Peasants omit the meat and compensate by richly spicing it with herbs, lemon, or fruit. Spicy, sour, or sweet, the meatless* hareeras *are a match for any soups made with the choicest meat.*

4 tablespoons olive oil
2 medium onions, chopped
3 cloves garlic, crushed
½ cup finely chopped fresh cilantro
1 small hot pepper, finely chopped
2 cups cooked chickpeas
½ cup lentils, soaked overnight
¼ cup rice
4 medium tomatoes, chopped
2 teaspoons ginger
1 teaspoon paprika
1 teaspoon cumin
½ teaspoon turmeric
salt and pepper to taste
9 cups water
4 tablespoons lemon juice

Heat oil in a saucepan and sauté onions over medium heat for 5 minutes. Add garlic, cilantro, and hot pepper and stir-fry for another 5 minutes. Stir in remaining ingredients, except lemon juice, and bring to boil; cook over medium heat for 35 minutes or until rice and lentils are well done. Stir in lemon juice and serve.

OKRA AND CHICKPEA SOUP

Mlokhia L' Hamraak
Morocco
Serves 10 to 12

The okra plant is cultivated mainly for its immature pods, which are dark green in color and can reach a length of 12 inches. The plants are prodigious yielders and must be picked every few days. The pods should be gathered before they mature on the plant and become overly tough and fibrous. They are at their best when tender, fresh, and crisp—usually less than 3 inches long. If the pods turn yellowish with brown spots, they are too mature and not fit for the pot.

4 tablespoons butter
4 medium onions, chopped
4 cloves garlic, crushed
1 small hot pepper, finely chopped
1 19-oz can chickpeas, with liquid
2 cups stewed tomatoes
1 11-oz package frozen okra, thawed and cut into small pieces
6 cups water
1 teaspoon paprika
1 teaspoon cumin
salt and pepper to taste
2 tablespoons finely chopped fresh cilantro
2 tablespoons finely chopped chives

Melt butter in a saucepan and sauté onions, garlic, and hot pepper for 10 minutes. Add remaining ingredients, except cilantro and chives; bring to boil. Cover and cook over medium heat for 30 minutes, adding more water if necessary. Stir in cilantro and chives. Serve hot.

PALESTINIAN LENTIL SOUP

Shawrbat 'Adas Filasteeniya
Palestine and Jordan
Serves 6 to 8

The ancient Egyptians and Greeks believed that lentils would enlighten the mind, open the heart, and render people cheerful. Thus it was a favorite food among both rich and poor. The Romans, on the other hand, believed that lentils made men reserved, indolent, and lazy. A story is told that in one of the many Roman–Parthian wars, a Roman general was convinced that the Romans were going to lose the war because the supply of grain was exhausted and his men had been obliged to eat lentils.

Some writers suggest that these ancient beliefs are the reason lentils flourished in Asia, Africa, Greece, and Spain, which was once under the control of the Arabs, but not in many other European countries.

¼ cup olive oil
2 large onions, chopped
1 cup split lentils
salt and pepper to taste
1 teaspoon cumin
pinch saffron
7 cups boiling water
2 tablespoons rice
4 to 6 teaspoons lemon juice

Heat oil in a saucepan and sauté onions until they turn golden brown. Add lentils, salt, pepper, cumin, saffron, and water. Simmer over low heat until lentils are almost cooked; then add rice and cook 15 minutes more.

Serve in individual bowls, adding lemon juice to taste.

Note: The soup can be puréed if a smoother texture is desired. A Syrian/Lebanese version of this soup uses paprika and fresh cilantro instead of cumin and saffron, demonstrating how a basic recipe can be varied by the use of spices.

POMEGRANATE AND MUSHROOM SOUP

Shawrbat Rumman
Iraq
Serves 10 to 12

The ancient civilizations of the Middle East regarded the pomegranate as a symbol of fertility. The Romans believed its seeds to be an aphrodisiac—a belief that in later centuries spread to all parts of Europe. Many know it as the "love fruit." In Arabic folklore and poetry, the pomegranate is also a symbol for the female breast.

1 cup finely chopped mushrooms
1 medium onion, finely chopped
½ cup fine breadcrumbs
salt and pepper to taste
½ teaspoon cumin
pinch cayenne
¼ cup olive oil
½ cup finely chopped fresh cilantro
4 cloves garlic, crushed
½ cup finely chopped green onions
¼ cup finely chopped fresh mint
½ cup lentils, washed and soaked overnight
1 teaspoon tarragon
¼ teaspoon chili powder
3 tablespoons *dibs rumman* (Pomegranate Concentrate, see p. 4)
8 cups water

Thoroughly combine mushrooms, onion, breadcrumbs, salt, pepper, cumin and cayenne. Add a little water, and form into small balls. Set aside. (If balls fall apart, add a little flour.)

In a saucepan, heat the oil and sauté the mushroom balls over medium heat, gently turning them over until they begin to brown. Stir in cilantro and garlic and sauté for a few more minutes. Stir in remaining ingredients and bring to boil. Cover and cook over medium heat for about 30 minutes. Serve immediately.

Red Lentil Soup with Rice

Shawrbat 'Adas Ahmar ma' Rizz
Syria and Lebanon
Serves 8

Spanish missionaries introduced the lentil to the Americas, but it took many years before people began to appreciate its value. Slowly its cultivation spread, until today it is grown in parts of South America, in the northwestern United States, and in parts of western Canada. Some of the countries in the West now appreciate its food value, but in its native habitat, the Arab world, it has been used as a food since man took up farming.

¾ cup red lentils, rinsed and drained
salt to taste
1 teaspoon pepper
1 teaspoon paprika
8 cups water
4 tablespoons butter
1½ cups chopped onions
4 cloves garlic, crushed
½ cup finely chopped fresh cilantro
¼ cup rice, rinsed

Place lentils, salt, pepper, paprika, and water in a saucepan and cook over medium heat for about 30 minutes or until lentils are tender, but still intact and slightly firm.

In the meantime, melt butter in a frying pan; then add onions and garlic. Sauté until onions begin to turn brown. Stir in cilantro and sauté another 3 minutes; then add the contents of the frying pan and the rice to lentils and stir. Bring to boil, then reduce the heat to low. Simmer until rice is tender but still intact and slightly firm. Serve piping hot.

SEMOLINA SOUP

Sdirr
Tunisia
Serves 6 to 8

For me, sdirr *is always associated with Kairouan, the Islamic capital of Tunisia. On a cold spring day, a friend there had invited me for dinner. The meal began with this soup, and I remember vividly how its hot spicy taste warmed my body.*

As we ate, we discussed Kairouan and its history. In the seventh century AD, *the daring Arab general Uqba ibn Nafi' moved westward, with only a few men, until he occupied the whole of the North African coast. During his advance toward the Atlantic, he halted the march of his small army to lay the foundation of Kairouan, the first Arab city established west of Egypt.*

From its beginning, Kairouan was known as the western citadel of Islam. Only outranked by Mecca, Medina, and Jerusalem, it is a destination for pilgrims, venerated as the fourth holy city in Islam. Some Muslims believe that seven pilgrimages to Kairouan are equal to a pilgrimage to Mecca.

4 tablespoons olive oil
½ head garlic, peeled and crushed
6 cups water
2 tablespoons tomato paste
4 tablespoons chopped parsley
1 teaspoon *hreesa* (see recipe, p. 17)
1 tablespoon dried mint
1 teaspoon ground caraway seeds
1 teaspoon paprika
1 tablespoon pickled capers
1 preserved lemon, chopped (see recipe, p. 17)
salt and pepper to taste
½ cup semolina

Heat oil in a saucepan and sauté garlic for a few minutes until it begins to brown. Stir in remaining ingredients, except semolina, and bring to boil. Cover and cook over medium heat for 15 minutes. Stir in the semolina a little at a time. Then, stirring constantly, bring to boil. Cook for 10 minutes or until semolina is well done; serve piping hot.

Spinach and Yogurt Soup

Hasa Sabanakh ma' Laban
Iraq
Serves 8

An annual potherb of the goosefoot family, spinach is a dark green plant with broad, fleshy and crinkly leaves. Forty-five days after it is planted, spinach is ready for harvesting. If allowed to mature, it will go to seed and become useless as a vegetable.

2 tablespoons olive oil
2 medium onions, chopped
½ hot pepper, finely chopped
1 10-oz package spinach, thoroughly washed and chopped
¼ cup *burghul*
salt and pepper to taste
5 cups water
2 tablespoons finely chopped fresh cilantro
2 cloves garlic, crushed
3 cups yogurt

Heat oil in a saucepan and sauté onions and hot pepper over medium heat for 10 minutes. Stir in spinach, cover, and cook for 5 more minutes, stirring a few times.

Add *burghul,* salt, pepper, and water and bring to boil. Cook over medium heat for 20 minutes, adding more water if necessary. Remove from heat and stir in remaining ingredients; then reheat briefly, stirring constantly. Serve hot.

Tahini and Yogurt Soup

Shawrbat Taheena wa Laban
Palestine and Jordan
Serves 6

The possibilities of yogurt in the kitchen are numerous. It can be made into a cheese, eaten plain or flavored with fruit and other sweets; it appears in appetizers, salads, and soups. Equally appetizing hot or cold, yogurt is always a healthy treat.

4 cups yogurt
4 tablespoons tahini
4 cloves garlic, crushed
2 tablespoons finely chopped fresh cilantro

1 cup water
4 tablespoons lemon juice
½ teaspoon dried crushed thyme
⅛ teaspoon cayenne
salt and pepper to taste

Place all ingredients in a serving bowl and combine thoroughly. Chill and serve.

Tamarind Lentil Soup
Shawrbat 'Adas bit Tamar Hindi
Arabian Gulf
Serves 10

Besides being on the daily menu in India and southeast Asia, tamarind is often used in the Arabian Gulf countries. The Indian workers in the Arabian Gulf lands have acquainted the inhabitants with delicious tamarind candies, chutneys, curries, desserts, preserves, relishes, sauces, stews, and soups.

4 tablespoons olive oil
2 medium onions, chopped
4 cloves garlic, crushed
1 small hot pepper, finely chopped
1 tablespoon grated fresh ginger
1 cup stewed tomatoes
2 tablespoons tamarind paste, dissolved in 8½ cups hot water
1 cup lentils
1 teaspoon cumin
salt and pepper to taste
4 tablespoons chopped fresh mint

Heat oil in a saucepan and sauté onions, garlic, hot pepper, and fresh ginger over medium heat for 10 minutes. Stir in remaining ingredients, except mint; then bring to boil. Cover and cook over medium heat for 40 minutes or until lentils are well cooked, adding more water if necessary. Stir in mint and serve.

TOMATO AND BURGHUL SOUP

Shawrbat al-Jereesh ma' at-Tamata
Arabian Gulf
Serves 8

A quarter century ago, the Arabian Gulf countries were pretty much barren desert lands; since the discovery of oil, they have been totally transformed into ultramodern nations. Spending their wealth wisely, they converted their arid lands into lush fields of greenery. The oil-dollars have seeped down to even the lowest strata of society, giving the people some of the highest living standards in the world. Reflecting this, their cuisine has expanded by leaps and bounds.

4 tablespoons butter
2 medium onions, finely chopped
4 cloves garlic, crushed
½ cup coarse *burghul*
1 5.5-oz can tomato paste, dissolved in 5 cups water
2 tablespoons flour, dissolved in 2 cups milk
½ teaspoon cinnamon
¼ teaspoon nutmeg
salt and pepper to taste
toasted pita bread, broken into small pieces
2 tablespoons finely chopped fresh cilantro

Melt butter in a saucepan and sauté onions over medium heat for 8 minutes. Add garlic and *burghul* and stir-fry for 3 minutes. Add tomato paste–water mixture and bring to boil; then cover and cook over medium heat for 40 minutes, adding more water if necessary. Stir in flour–milk mixture, cinnamon, nutmeg, salt, and pepper; then, stirring constantly, bring to boil and cook for a few minutes.

Place bread and coriander on separate plates. Serve soup hot, allowing each diner to add bread and cilantro to taste.

Tomato and Chickpea Soup

Hasa Tamata ma' Hummus
Iraq
Serves 8 to 10

Chickpeas make a nice change from pastas, potatoes, and rice. They are more nutritious and add an exotic touch to a meal.

2 tablespoons butter
2 medium onions, chopped
4 cloves garlic, crushed
¼ cup finely chopped fresh cilantro
2 cups cooked chickpeas
3 cups tomato juice
4 cups water
½ cup rice, rinsed
salt and pepper to taste
1 teaspoon cumin
½ teaspoon allspice

Melt butter in a saucepan and sauté onions and garlic until they begin to brown. Add cilantro and stir-fry a few minutes more. Stir in remaining ingredients and bring to boil. Cook over medium heat for about 20 minutes or until the rice is cooked.

TUNISIAN NOODLE SOUP

Hlalem
Tunisia
Serves 8

The first time I enjoyed this soup was in Hammamet, Tunisia's most elegant beach resort. In a little restaurant, hidden in a narrow street, I sat with workers all around me, supping on this soup—a meal unto itself.

¼ cup chickpeas, soaked overnight and drained
¼ cup small fava beans, soaked overnight and drained
10 cups water
4 tablespoons olive oil
2 medium onions, finely chopped
4 tablespoons finely chopped fresh cilantro
4 cloves garlic, crushed
4 tablespoons tomato paste
1½ teaspoons *hreesa* (see recipe, p. 17)
1 teaspoon paprika
salt and pepper to taste
4 tablespoons finely chopped celery
1 cup frozen or fresh peas
1 cup noodles broken into small pieces

Place chickpeas, fava beans, and water in a saucepan and bring to boil; then cover and cook over medium heat for 2 hours or until chickpeas are cooked.

In the meantime, heat oil in a frying pan and sauté onions over medium heat for 10 minutes. Stir in cilantro and garlic and stir-fry for a few minutes more. Transfer frying pan contents and remaining ingredients to saucepan; then cook over medium heat for a further 20 minutes, adding more water if necessary. Serve hot.

VEGETABLE SOUP

Hasa al-Khadr
Iraq
Serves 8

Many of the easy-to-make vegetarian Arab soups are served as one-dish meals.

4 tablespoons olive oil
2 medium carrots, peeled and finely diced
2 medium potatoes, peeled and finely chopped

1 medium onion, chopped
4 cloves garlic, crushed
1 cup finely chopped fresh cilantro
5 cups water
2 cups stewed tomatoes
½ teaspoon allspice
½ teaspoon cumin
salt and pepper to taste

Heat oil in a saucepan and sauté carrots, potatoes, onion, garlic, and cilantro over medium heat for 8 minutes, stirring constantly. Stir in remaining ingredients and bring to boil. Lower heat, cover, and simmer until vegetables are tender, adding more water if necessary.

VERMICELLI AND MILK SOUP

Sha'reeya L'Hamraak
Morocco
Serves 8

This is a somewhat sweet soup, unlike the vast majority of soups in the Arab world.

4 cups milk
4 cups water
1 teaspoon salt
1 teaspoon cinnamon
4 tablespoons butter
1½ cups crushed vermicelli
4 tablespoons sugar
½ teaspoon nutmeg

Place milk, water, salt, cinnamon, butter, and vermicelli in a saucepan and, stirring constantly, bring to boil. Cook over low heat for 15 minutes or until vermicelli is cooked, stirring a few times and adding more water if necessary. Stir in sugar; then transfer to serving bowl. Sprinkle with nutmeg and serve hot.

Vermicelli and Paprika Soup

Dweda Zaara
Tunisia
Serves 6

To most Middle Eastern Arabs, Tunisian food is mysterious and exotic, and its history is full of fascinating and romantic tales. According to mythology, Tunisia's Island of Djerba—the country's "Paradise Isle"—was the home of the lotus eaters. In Homer's Odyssey, *some of Ulysses' men almost succumbed when the beautiful maidens of this island fed them the lotus flower. Nina Nelson, in her book* Tunisia, *writes:*

Ulysses sent messengers ahead to see if they would be well received. The island people were indeed lotus eaters, living on a plant named lotus which so dazed their senses that they cared for nothing but dreamy idleness in the languid air of the island, where everything was beautiful and did not change. Even the fruit could be had by stretching out the hand and plucking it from the trees. Once strangers had tasted the flowery food, offered by the gentle islanders, they did not have the desire to leave but wished to remain forever....

When Ulysses saw what a spell the lotus had worked on his messengers he had them dragged back by force, tied to benches on the ships, while the remainder of his men hurried on board before they could eat the flower and fall under the spell of inglorious ease. Toiling at their oars, they left the magic island.

This Tunisian soup is not made with lotus, but is nevertheless seductive.

4 tablespoons olive oil
1 large onion, finely chopped
4 cloves garlic, crushed
5 cups water
4 tablespoons finely chopped celery
2 tablespoons tomato paste
1 tablespoon paprika
1 teaspoon *hreesa* (see recipe, p. 17)
½ teaspoon turmeric
4 bay leaves
salt and pepper to taste
1½ cups crushed vermicelli
2 tablespoons finely chopped fresh cilantro

Heat oil in a saucepan and sauté onion over medium heat for 10 minutes. Add garlic and sauté for a few minutes. Stir in remaining ingredients, except vermicelli and cilantro; bring to boil. Cook over medium heat for 5 minutes; then stir in vermicelli. Cover and cook for another 15 minutes; then stir in cilantro and serve immediately.

Yemeni Vegetable Soup

Shoubra
Yemen
Serves 10 to 12

For many centuries Yemen's imam rulers kept the country in a medieval state. Most Yemenis were poor; only the upper classes could afford meat, eggs, and milk. Among the peasants, this soup was a favored dish.

4 tablespoons olive oil
2 medium onions, chopped
4 cloves garlic, crushed
2 tomatoes, chopped
1 pound zucchini, cut into 1-inch cubes
1 pound scraped carrots, cut into ½-inch cubes
1 pound peeled potatoes, cut into 1-inch cubes
8 cups water
salt to taste
4 tablespoons chopped cilantro
2 tablespoons *hulbah* (Fenugreek Paste, see recipe, p. 12)
4 tablespoons *zhug* (Spicy Relish, see recipe, p. 18)
toasted pita bread or *khobz* (Yemeni Bread, see recipe, p. 10)

Heat oil in a saucepan and sauté onions and garlic for 10 minutes. Add tomatoes, zucchini, carrots, potatoes, water, and salt and bring to boil. Cover and cook over medium heat for 40 minutes or until vegetables are well cooked. Stir in cilantro, *hulbah*, and *zhug*. Serve immediately with toasted pita bread or *khobz*, each diner adding bread to taste.

SALADS

Salads were perhaps the first vegetable dishes people experimented with as they moved to diversify their all-meat diet. In the warm lands where primitive man evolved, wild plants grew in profusion. It would have been natural, even before the invention of fire, to mix some wild vegetables together in an appetizing form and, for the sake of taste, add a few leaves from an aromatic plant. Regardless of how or when vegetarian salads were first invented, they have become a must on the daily menu of most people in the world

In the countries of the Middle East and North Africa, where civilization goes back to the dawn of history, the types of salads that have been enjoyed by both rich and poor are numerous. From the days of Sumer and the Pharaohs to our times, simple, tasty vegetarian salads have graced the tables of humankind. We know this because the inheritors of these civilizations documented a number of their dishes. Some of their recipes, first recorded by the Arabs as early as the ninth century, can still be enjoyed today.

Century after century, from the Atlantic Ocean to the borders of Iran, in what is now known as the Arab world, new salads were developed and added to the tried and true. During the past hundred years, immigrants returning from the Americas have contributed another dimension to Arab salads.

Today, these delicious salads fit easily into the North American's daily menu. Once tried, they are seldom rejected—a tribute to their lasting appeal. Our growing awareness of the health benefits of raw vegetables only adds to their appeal.

Europeans and North Americans typically flavor their salads with many types of dressings—Caesar, French, Italian, Thousand Island. In the lands of the Middle East and North Africa, however, salads are dressed as of old, simply with lemon juice and olive oil. Perhaps the fact that the sons and daughters of the Arab immigrants in the West continue to use this time-honored method is a good indicator of its appeal. Even after three or four generations, they continue to prefer lemon juice and olive oil to the other popular dressings available here.

In fact, in most restaurants and in many homes in North America, you will find a version of this dressing—vegetable oil and vinegar—alongside the popular Western dressings. Nowadays, a few Arab cooks may substitute vinegar for lemon juice, but never vegetable for olive oil. The peoples of the Mediterranean countries love the taste of the oil produced from the fruit of the olive tree, which some believe was first grown in the Garden of Eden.

In response to the European occupation of the Middle East and North Africa, a number of the indigenous salads underwent modification to suit the tastes of the newcomers; the *Avocado Salad* is a good example of this. A good number of ancient salad recipes, however, were not affected; they are still basically the same as those enjoyed by the forefathers of the present inhabitants—a few salads have been around for over five thousand years. All of them—the new, European-influenced and the ancient and unchanging—are wholesome and simple to prepare.

Salads can be served as appetizers at the start of a meal, as entrées, or as accompaniments to the main course. Arab salads are not limited to lettuce and tomatoes; they often combine many vegetables and spices. The variations are endless; feel free to substitute fresh vegetables or spices of your choice. If you prefer it, use vinegar instead of lemon juice, or try combining both. You can substitute vegetable oil or combine oils if you wish, but once you have tried a good-quality olive oil, you may prefer it.

ALGERIAN SALAD

Salata Jaza'iriya
Algeria
Serves 4 to 6

Olives are said to be an acquired taste—if so, one well worth acquiring. In the Mediterranean basin, however, people seem to be born with a taste for them. The oil- or salt-cured olives used in Arabic cooking are far more flavorful than the bland found on North American grocery shelves. For the uninitiated, canned olives are a mild introduction, but I encourage you to try the genuine article, readily available in Mediterranean or Middle Eastern specialty stores.

2 sweet peppers, seeded and finely chopped
4 medium tomatoes
½ cup sliced cucumber
2 small onions, thinly sliced
½ cup black olives, pitted and halved
salt and pepper to taste
2 hard-boiled eggs, quartered
1 teaspoon chopped fresh basil or 1 tablespoon chopped fresh cilantro
3 tablespoons olive oil
1 tablespoon vinegar

Place all ingredients in a salad bowl and toss gently. Serve with pita bread.

ARTICHOKE SALAD

Salatat Khurshoof
Syria and Lebanon
Serves 6

The artichoke is a native of the Mediterranean basin, where it still can be found growing wild. In Europe, for many centuries, it was unknown, although they were once cultivated by the Greeks and the Romans.

The Arabs were responsible for reintroducing artichokes into Europe via the Iberian Peninsula and Sicily. Almost all the European languages derive their name for artichoke from the Arabic al-khurshoof.

1 can artichoke hearts, drained and cut into quarters
½ head lettuce, chopped

1 large tomato, cut into large pieces
1 small onion, finely chopped
1½ cups finely chopped celery
2 cloves garlic, crushed
¼ cup lemon juice
4 tablespoons olive oil
salt and pepper to taste

Combine artichoke, lettuce, tomato, onion, celery, and garlic in a salad bowl. Combine the lemon juice, olive oil, salt and pepper; then pour over the vegetables. Toss and serve.

Note: Frozen artichoke hearts may be used after being cooked according to directions on the package.

AVOCADO SALAD

Salatat Abakadoo
Palestine and Jordan
Serves 4

The Aztec Indians of Mexico believed that the avocado had aphrodisiac qualities. They named it ahacatl, *meaning testicle because it not only resembled a testicle but aroused sexual passion as well. The Spaniards censored the name and phonetically translated the word as* abogado *(meaning "lawyer"), from which we get avocado.*

The Spaniards then brought the avocado back with them to Europe, but it was not until this century that they were introduced to the Middle East and North Africa on an appreciable scale.

1 large avocado, cut into small cubes
1 large tomato, diced
1 medium onion, finely chopped
1 small hot pepper, very finely chopped
2 tablespoons finely chopped fresh cilantro
3 tablespoons olive oil
2 tablespoons lemon juice
salt and pepper to taste

Toss all ingredients together in a salad bowl and serve.

BASIL-FLAVORED TOMATO SALAD
Salatat Tamatim bi Habaq
Palestine and Jordan
Serves 6

On the Indian subcontinent, where it is believed basil was first cultivated, a type of this herb, ocimum sanctum, *is revered as a holy plant. It has been employed by the Hindus in their religious ceremonies for countless centuries. They often plant basil near their homes and temples as an offering to the gods Vishnu and Krishna and as a protection from evil.*

The Hindus believe that basil will guide a human being to Paradise, and they place a leaf of basil on the dead person's chest. Despite, or perhaps because of its revered status, basil is not much used in the cuisine of the Indian subcontinent. Only as a tea is it popular to some extent.

5 medium ripe but firm tomatoes, chopped into small pieces
1 small onion, very finely chopped
4 tablespoons finely chopped fresh basil
2 cloves garlic, crushed
4 tablespoons finely chopped parsley
4 tablespoons olive oil
2 tablespoons vinegar
1/8 teaspoon cayenne
salt and pepper to taste

Thoroughly combine all ingredients in a salad bowl; then serve.

BEET SALAD WITH CHIVES
Salatat Shamandar
Syria and Lebanon
Serves 4 to 6

Essentially a modern vegetable, the beet (or beetroot) was rarely mentioned in ancient literature. Since it grows best in cool, moist climates, Europe became its home. Only in the past few centuries has it become a popular food in Arab lands.

5 large beets
2 cloves garlic, crushed
2 tablespoons finely chopped fresh cilantro

4 tablespoons finely chopped fresh chives
4 tablespoons olive oil
4 tablespoons vinegar
salt and pepper to taste
4 tablespoons parsley, chopped

Boil the beets until tender; when cool enough to handle, peel, dice, and place in a salad bowl. Stir in garlic, cilantro, chives, olive oil, vinegar, salt and pepper, then chill for about an hour. Stir, sprinkle with parsley, and serve.

Beet and Tahini Salad

Salatat Shamandar bi Taheena
Syria and Lebanon
Serves 4 to 6

The Greater Syria area of the Middle East, at the crossroads of world civilizations, has developed a somewhat unique type of cuisine, typified by this salad. It is a specialty of Damascus, which has been an important urban center since the beginning of civilization.

2 medium beets, cooked, peeled, and finely chopped
4 tablespoons tahini
⅓ cup yogurt
½ teaspoon nutmeg
salt and pepper to taste
3 hard boiled eggs, quartered

Place beets in a bowl and set aside.
Thoroughly combine tahini, yogurt, nutmeg, salt and pepper; then pour over beets and mix. Spread on a platter; arrange eggs on top, and serve.

Beet-Green Salad

'Assoorat Shamandar
Syria and Lebanon
Serves 4 to 6

There are many varieties of beets. Most are deep red in color, but there are other hues such as white and yellow. The round, red variety is popular as a table vegetable, while the conical, white type is utilized in the manufacture of alcohol and animal feed. From the latter type, half of the world's sugar supply is derived. Several beet species are cultivated exclusively for their leaves—the most important being Swiss chard, a variety of white beet.

4 tablespoons olive oil
1 small bunch green onions, finely chopped
2 tablespoons finely chopped fresh cilantro
2 cloves garlic, crushed
1 pound beet greens, thoroughly washed and chopped
2 tablespoons water
salt and pepper to taste
2 tablespoons vinegar

Heat oil in a saucepan and sauté onions, cilantro, and garlic over medium heat for 6 minutes. Stir in remaining ingredients, except vinegar; then cover and cook over medium low heat for 20 minutes. Stir in vinegar and serve hot or cold.

Note: You may substitute Swiss chard for the beet greens.

Black Olive and Orange Salad

Salatat Zaytoon
Morocco
Serves 4

Olives come in dozens of shapes and colors. They vary in size from half an inch to two inches. A little over a third are picked green before they ripen; the remainder are harvested when ripe, their hues ranging from purple-blue to black.

Whatever the color, olives are bitter when picked and must be processed before they become palatable. In the Mediterranean countries, all types are usually slit or bruised and soaked in a lye solution to remove their bitterness. They are then washed and preserved in brine or oil. The pits of green olives are sometimes removed and the cavities stuffed with almonds or pimientos. More often, they are marinated in coriander, ginger, hot pepper, lemon juice, thyme, and other herbs or spices.

Olives are usually retailed in bulk, both in their lands of origin and in specialty markets in the West. The enticing pungent odors emanating from the barrels of ripe preserved olives are a recognizable feature of Mediterranean markets.

The following recipe makes an unusual and vividly colored salad that can also be served as a wonderful appetizer.

½ cup black olives, pitted and halved
4 large oranges, peeled, sectioned, and cut into small pieces
½ teaspoon cumin
pinch cayenne

Combine olives and oranges in a salad bowl. Cover and refrigerate for at least 1 hour.

Mix cumin and cayenne in a separate dish and set aside.

Just before serving, sprinkle cumin–cayenne combination over olive–orange mixture and toss.

BREAD SALAD

Fattoosh
Syria and Lebanon
Serves 8

One of the highly favored foods in the eastern Arab world, this salad can serve as a main course—perfect for a summer lunch.

1 loaf pita bread or 4 thin slices white bread, toasted brown, then broken into small pieces
juice of 1 large lemon
1 large English seedless cucumber, chopped, or ½ head of lettuce, chopped
1 small sweet red pepper, chopped
4 firm ripe tomatoes, chopped
1 small bunch green onions, chopped
2 tablespoons finely chopped parsley
2 tablespoons finely chopped fresh mint, or 1 teaspoon of dried crushed mint
2 cloves garlic, crushed
5 tablespoons olive oil
1 teaspoon sumac (see p. 4)
3 tablespoons finely chopped fresh cilantro
salt and pepper to taste

Toss all ingredients together. Taste and add more seasoning if desired; then serve immediately, before the bread becomes soft.

Burghul and Cabbage Salad

Salatat Malfoof wa Burghul
Syria and Lebanon
Serves 8

In the West, burghul *can be purchased, in bulk or packaged, in Middle Eastern markets, health food stores, and a good number of supermarkets. It comes in three sizes: coarse, medium, and fine. The coarse is used in stews; the medium in salads; and the fine as the main component in vegetarian and other patties, as a breakfast cereal, or as a principal element in some desserts.*

½ cup medium *burghul*
3 cups shredded cabbage
2 medium tomatoes, cut into ½-inch cubes
½ cup finely chopped green onions
2 tablespoons finely chopped fresh cilantro
2 tablespoons finely chopped fresh mint
Lemon and Oil Salad Dressing (see recipe, p. 14)

Soak *burghul* in warm water for 10 minutes; then drain by pressing through a strainer. Place in a salad bowl with remaining ingredients, except the dressing and mix thoroughly. Pour salad dressing over top and toss; serve immediately.

Burghul and Chickpea Salad

Salatat Hummus wa Burghul
Syria and Lebanon
Serves 8

One of the most preferred foods in the Middle East, burghul *is now regarded as a health food throughout the Western world.*

½ cup medium *burghul*
1 19-oz can chickpeas, drained
1 cup finely chopped parsley
1 small cucumber (about 5 inches long), peeled and finely chopped
1 large tomato, cut into ½-inch cubes
½ cup finely chopped green onions
4 tablespoons finely chopped fresh mint
Lemon and Oil Salad Dressing (see recipe, p. 14)

Soak *burghul* in warm water for 10 minutes; then drain by pressing the water out through a strainer. Place in a salad bowl with remaining ingredients, except salad dressing, and mix thoroughly. Pour salad dressing over top and toss; serve immediately.

Cabbage Salad with Cumin

Schlada Krump
Morocco
Serves 4

A Moroccan friend told me that this salad was brought back to Morocco by soldiers who had fought with the French army in Indochina. This could well be the case since cabbage does not commonly appear in Moroccan cooking.

4 cups shredded cabbage
1 teaspoon cumin seed
3 tablespoons olive oil
salt and pepper to taste

Place cabbage and cumin in a saucepan, cover with water, and bring to boil. Cover and cook over medium heat for 10 minutes; then drain. Place in a salad bowl; toss with remaining ingredients just before serving.

CABBAGE AND PEPPER SALAD

Salatat Malfoof wa Flayfle
Syria and Lebanon
Serves 8

Originating in Mexico, peppers have been, for hundreds of years, the primary flavoring—the essence of the native cuisine. Hot peppers were more essential than salt and so prized that they were offered as food to the gods.

4 cups shredded cabbage
2 large sweet red peppers, chopped into small pieces
½ cup chopped green onions
2 cloves garlic, crushed
4 tablespoons olive oil
4 tablespoons lemon juice
1 tablespoon finely chopped fresh mint
½ teaspoon ground mustard
⅛ teaspoon cayenne
salt and pepper to taste

Place cabbage, peppers, and green onions in a salad bowl and mix thoroughly. Combine remaining ingredients in a small bowl; just before serving, pour over vegetables and toss.

CARDAMOM-FLAVORED FRUIT SALAD

Salatat al-Fawaakih
Arabian Gulf
Serves 8

For centuries, until the discovery of the Americas, the Indian subcontinent was virtually the only part of the world where cardamom was cultivated. Even today it is still chiefly grown in that part of the world, but its cultivation has spread to Central America and Jamaica. Its use in food, on the other hand, is almost worldwide, especially in the Middle East and surprisingly in the Scandinavian countries.

1 medium cantaloupe (2 pounds) peeled and cut into ½-inch cubes
2 medium oranges, peeled and sectioned; sections cut in half
2 medium apples, peeled, cored, and cut into ½-inch cubes
½ cup seedless raisins

½ cup honey
2 tablespoons water
½ teaspoon ground cardamom seeds
4 tablespoons lemon juice

Place cantaloupe, oranges, apples, and raisins in a salad bowl and set aside.

Place honey, water, and cardamom in a saucepan and bring to boil, stirring a few times and adding a little water if necessary. Stir in lemon juice; then allow to cool.

Add syrup to fruit; then toss and serve immediately.

Note: This salad can also be served as a dessert.

CARROT SALAD

Khissoo
Morocco
Serves 4 to 6

If your children like raw carrots, they will love this salad.

6 large carrots, grated
¼ cup sugar
4 tablespoons lemon juice
4 tablespoons olive oil
1 teaspoon orange-flower water
½ teaspoon cinnamon

Combine all ingredients in a salad bowl. Chill; then stir and serve.

CARROT AND EGG SALAD

Omok-Houria
Tunisia
Serves 8

Whether eaten as daily fare or cooked for an honored guest, a Tunisian meal is a journey into a world of gourmet pleasure. Even if the dishes at first seem strange to a foreigner, they are always inviting, nutritious, yet simple to prepare. Somewhat different from the cuisine of its neighbors, Tunisia's foods have a fascinating hold on the uninitiated. A traveler who was enamored with the Tunisian kitchen once wrote, "Tunisian dishes delight the senses and make a diner relaxed and content."

5 medium carrots, scraped, washed, and sliced into ¼-inch rounds
2 cloves garlic, crushed
4 tablespoons finely chopped fresh cilantro
4 tablespoons lemon juice
4 tablespoons olive oil
⅛ teaspoon cayenne
salt and pepper to taste
2 hard-boiled eggs, sliced
12 pitted black olives, sliced in half
1 small tomato, thinly sliced

Place carrots in a saucepan, cover with water, and bring to boil. Cook for 5 minutes over medium heat; then drain and allow to cool.

Place carrots in a food processor and process briefly until the carrots are coarsely chopped. Transfer to a mixing bowl; then stir in garlic, cilantro, lemon juice, oil, cayenne, salt, and pepper. Place on a flat serving platter; just before serving, arrange the eggs, olives and tomato over the carrots.

CARROT AND OLIVE SALAD

Salatat Jazar wa Zaytoon
Sudan
Serves 6

Carrots have traditionally been a part of the diet of the peoples across North Africa— much less so in the eastern Arab lands. Only in this century have carrots made an appearance on the daily menu of people in the Middle Eastern Arab countries.

2 medium carrots, peeled and sliced into thin rounds
½ medium-sized head of lettuce, coarsely chopped
1 tablespoon finely chopped fresh cilantro
½ cup pitted black olives, halved
2 tablespoons lemon juice
2 tablespoons olive oil
salt and pepper to taste

Place all ingredients in a salad bowl; toss gently just before serving.

CHEESE SALAD

Salatat Jibna
Sudan
Serves 6

Unlike the Greeks, the Arabs rarely use cheese in their salads. Perhaps it was the Greek immigrant population in the Sudan, at one time considerable, who introduced this dish to that country.

1½ cups onion, finely sliced
1½ cups cabbage, finely sliced
1 cup carrots, grated
1½ cups tomatoes, cubed
4 tablespoons olive oil
4 tablespoons lemon juice
1 clove garlic, crushed
salt and pepper to taste
½ cup crumbled feta cheese

Combine onion, cabbage, carrots, and tomatoes in a salad bowl and set aside
Combine olive oil, lemon juice, garlic, salt, and pepper; then pour over vegetables and toss. Sprinkle with cheese and serve.

COOKED SPINACH SALAD

'Assoora
Syria and Lebanon
Serves 4 to 6

The Arabs, who became familiar with spinach in Persia, introduced it to Europe by way of Spain. Its name in almost all European languages comes from the Arabic isbanakh.

¼ cup olive or vegetable oil
2 large onions, sliced
2 pounds fresh spinach, thoroughly washed and chopped
salt and pepper to taste
2 tablespoons lemon juice

   Heat oil in a saucepan and sauté onions over medium heat until they turn golden brown. Add spinach, cover, and continue cooking for 20 minutes. Remove cover, but leave on heat until water has evaporated and spinach becomes tender. Stir in salt, pepper, and lemon juice; then allow to cool before serving.

Note: Never add water to the spinach; its own moisture is sufficient for cooking.

CUCUMBER SALAD

Salatat Khiyar
Kuwait
Serves 6

The cuisine of the petroleum-rich lands of the Arabian Gulf has been influenced in recent years by the thousands of workers flooding in from the Indian subcontinent. This Kuwaiti salad has a touch of India and Pakistan.

¼ cup olive oil
1 large onion, finely chopped
1 medium sweet pepper, finely chopped
1 teaspoon ginger
salt to taste
2 cups yogurt
2 medium cucumbers, peeled and chopped

Heat oil in a frying pan and sauté onion and pepper until onion turns limp, but not brown. Transfer frying pan contents to a serving bowl; allow to cool. Stir in remaining ingredients; then refrigerate for at least one hour. Serve well chilled.

CUCUMBER SWEET SALAD

Schlada Feggous
Morocco
Serves 4

Morocco is a fine example of the saying: To know a country and its people is to know its food. The country's cuisine vividly reflects the vast differences in its landscape and ethnic mixture.

1 large English cucumber (1 pound), grated
2 tablespoons sugar
2 tablespoons vinegar
1 teaspoon dried thyme
salt and pepper to taste

Thoroughly combine all ingredients, place on a serving platter, and serve.

CUCUMBER AND YOGURT SALAD

Khiyar bi Laban
Syria and Lebanon
Serves 6

Long ago, the Arabs discovered that cucumber and yogurt go well together, as this dish demonstrates.

3 cloves garlic, crushed
salt to taste
1 quart plain yogurt
2 medium cucumbers, peeled and diced
2 tablespoons dried mint

Place garlic, salt, and yogurt in a serving bowl and mix thoroughly. Stir in cucumbers and mint and mix; chill before serving.

Dandelion Greens Salad

Salatat Hindba
Syria and Lebanon
Serves 6

Dandelion greens are used in the salads of the Mediterranean lands, but in North America are usually considered just a weed. Although cultivated dandelion greens can be purchased, wild greens are much tastier, especially when the plants are at their tenderest before flowering. Their refreshing bitterness may take some getting used to for those accustomed to blander greens.

1 bunch dandelion greens, thoroughly washed and chopped into medium pieces
1 large tomato, cut into medium pieces
1 medium Spanish onion, finely chopped
Lemon and Oil Salad Dressing (see recipe, p. 14)

Place dandelion greens, tomato, and onion in a salad bowl and toss. Pour dressing over the salad; then toss again just before serving.

Note: Spinach may be substituted for the dandelion greens.

Eggplant and Cucumber Salad

Salatat Bathinjan wa Khiyar
Syria and Lebanon
Serves 8

The nutritional value of eggplants is above average, and they are ideal for those who watch their weight as they are not high in calories.

1 large eggplant, peeled and cut into ½-inch cubes
½ cup plus 2 tablespoons olive oil
2 large tomatoes, diced
1 medium cucumber, peeled and diced
1 clove garlic, crushed
1 bunch green onions, finely chopped
½ cup finely chopped parsley
2 tablespoons lemon juice
1 teaspoon sumac (see p. 4)
¼ cup olives, pitted and quartered
salt and pepper to taste

Sprinkle eggplant with salt and place in a strainer. Top with a weight and allow to drain for 45 minutes.

Heat the ½ cup of olive oil in a frying pan and sauté eggplant over moderately high heat until it turns light brown, adding more oil if necessary. Remove from oil with a slotted spoon and place in a strainer; set aside to drain and cool.

Combine remaining ingredients, including the 2 tablespoons of oil, in a salad bowl; add eggplant cubes and toss gently. Serve immediately.

EGGPLANT AND PEPPER SALAD

Schlada Bathinjan wa Fulful
Morocco
Serves about 6

In almost all the Mediterranean countries eggplants, known as "the peasant's meat," appear on the daily menu. It is said that if all the eggplant recipes of these countries were gathered, there would be well over a thousand.

1 large eggplant
2 cloves garlic, crushed
2 tablespoons finely chopped parsley
2 tablespoons finely chopped fresh cilantro
½ teaspoon cumin
½ teaspoon paprika
2 tablespoons olive oil
1 medium onion, finely chopped
1 large sweet red pepper, finely chopped
2 tablespoons lemon juice
salt to taste

Bake eggplant in a 425°F oven for about 1 hour, turning frequently. It will become quite charred. Cool; then peel and mash pulp until smooth. Add garlic, parsley, cilantro, cumin, and paprika; mix thoroughly and set aside.

Heat oil in a frying pan and sauté onion until it turns golden brown. Add pepper and sauté a few minutes longer. Stir frying pan contents, lemon juice, and salt into the eggplant mixture; then place on a platter and chill at least one hour before serving.

Fava Bean Salad

Salatat Fool
Syria and Lebanon
Serves 4

It is not just the inhabitants of the Arab world who rely on fava beans as a dietary staple. The peoples of the Indian subcontinent have enjoyed fava beans for thousands of years. Today, it is a rare garden in India or Pakistan that does not have at least one patch of this ancient vegetable.

2 cups green fava beans
½ cup chopped parsley
¼ cup finely chopped green onions
2 tablespoons chopped cilantro
2 cloves garlic, crushed
2 tablespoons lemon juice
4 tablespoons olive oil
salt and pepper to taste

Place fava beans in saucepan, cover with water, bring to boil, and cook over medium heat for 15 minutes. Drain and allow to cool.

Thoroughly combine with remaining ingredients, place in a salad bowl, and serve.

Note: To make this salad more substantial, add three chopped hard-boiled eggs; then sprinkle with paprika.

Fava Beans with Yogurt

Fool ma' Laban
Syria and Lebanon
Serves 6 to 8

Fava beans are delicious when picked green and still tender. Harvested at this stage, the whole pod is tasty and enjoyable, and the beans themselves can be eaten raw. In the Arab East, where the fava bean is known as fool, *rare is the evening banquet or gourmet meal where* fool *is not served as an hors d'oeuvre.*

2 pounds fresh fava beans
1 teaspoon brown sugar
1 teaspoon lemon juice
1 teaspoon mustard powder

pinch nutmeg
1 clove garlic, crushed
1 teaspoon finely chopped fresh mint
½ teaspoon freshly ground pepper
1 cup yogurt
salt to taste
1 egg, beaten

Shell beans; then cook in boiling water until tender, about 15 minutes. Drain; then return to the pot. Set aside.

Combine all remaining ingredients, except egg. Pour this mixture over beans and heat gently; then stir in egg. Allow mixture to thicken over low heat; then serve at once.

FRIED CARROT SALAD

Schlada Dsjada
Morocco
Serves 4 to 6

A root vegetable, carrots are noted for their high vitamin A content. In addition, they contain 87% water, 9.4% carbohydrate, 1% protein, .2% fat and .9% minerals— mainly potassium, sodium and phosphorus.

1 pound carrots, scraped and sliced into thin rounds
3 cloves garlic, crushed
½ teaspoon salt
2 tablespoons olive oil
3 tablespoons lemon juice
1 tablespoon finely chopped fresh cilantro
1 teaspoon paprika
¼ teaspoon cumin
⅛ teaspoon cayenne

Place carrots, garlic, and ¼ teaspoon of the salt in a saucepan; cover with water and bring to a boil. Cover and cook over medium heat for 20 minutes; then drain.

Heat oil in a frying pan and stir-fry carrots over medium heat for 10 minutes or until they are cooked, adding more oil if necessary.

Combine remaining ingredients, including remaining ¼ teaspoon of salt, in a salad bowl. Stir in carrots; serve hot or cold.

FRIED PEPPER SALAD

Schlada Fulful
Morocco
Serves 4 to 6

The salads of Morocco are, for the most part, different from those in the eastern Arab world in that the vegetables are cooked rather than raw.

½ cup olive oil
4 large sweet peppers
3 medium tomatoes, diced
1 teaspoon paprika
salt and pepper to taste
½ teaspoon cumin
2 cloves garlic, crushed
1 teaspoon lemon juice
¼ cup finely chopped parsley

Heat oil in a frying pan and fry whole peppers over medium high heat, turning them until they become soft. Remove and set aside to cool.

In the same frying pan, sauté tomatoes with paprika, salt, pepper, cumin, and garlic until tomatoes are cooked but still a little firm.

Peel peppers and remove the seeds; then dice. Combine peppers, lemon juice, and tomatoes; then place in serving bowl. Garnish with the parsley; serve warm.

GRILLED VEGETABLES

Salata Fikteeb
Morocco
Serves 6

Simple to prepare, this salad is often eaten by the inhabitants of the hilly, coastal Riff region in Morocco.

4 medium tomatoes, quartered
4 medium onions, quartered
4 medium peppers, quartered
salt and pepper to taste
lemon juice

Place vegetables in a bowl and sprinkle with salt and pepper; toss. Place on skewers and grill or roast in oven until cooked but still firm. Place on serving plates; sprinkle with lemon juice just before serving.

GRILLED VEGETABLE SALAD
Mechouia
Tunisia
Serves 6 to 8

Ever since I first tasted mechouia *in an eating stall in the Medina (the old section of Tunis), I have been a devotee of this tasty salad.*

2 large red sweet peppers
4 firm medium tomatoes
3 medium onions, peeled
1 small hot pepper
3 tablespoons lemon juice
3 tablespoons olive oil
1 teaspoon oregano
1 teaspoon salt
½ teaspoon pepper
2 hard boiled eggs, chopped
¼ cup crumbled feta cheese

Grill red peppers, tomatoes, onions, and hot pepper in the oven, turning them over once or twice until they are soft. (The onions will take longer than the other vegetables.) Allow to cool.

Remove the skin and seeds from peppers; then chop all vegetables into small pieces and place in a mixing bowl. Stir in lemon juice, oil, oregano, salt, and pepper; then place on a serving platter. Spread egg and cheese evenly over top and serve.

KISHK SALAD

Salatat Kishk
Syria and Lebanon
Serves 6 to 8

Considered a peasant food, kishk *is rejected by almost all modern urban Arabs. As they trip over one another trying to fashion their menus after Western models, they have abandoned this wholesome staff of life which kept their ancestors healthy. Only the farmers and the villagers of Syria and Lebanon, and the sons and daughters of Arab peasant immigrants in the Americas, appreciate the taste and food value of* kishk.

1 bunch of dandelion greens, or a 10-oz package of spinach, coarsely chopped
1 bunch green onions, finely chopped
1 large tomato, finely chopped
½ cup *kishk* (Powdered Cheese, see recipe, p. 16)
salt and pepper to taste
4 tablespoons olive oil
2 tablespoons lemon juice

In a salad bowl, mix thoroughly dandelion greens or spinach, onions, tomato, *kishk,* salt, and pepper. Add olive oil and lemon juice and toss. Serve immediately.

LEMON SALAD

Salatat Laymoon
Syria and Lebanon
Serves 4 to 6

Before becoming known in the West, lemons were cultivated on the Indian subcontinent, where for hundreds of years they flourished. Around 1100 AD, the Arabs introduced them into the Iberian Peninsula, from whence their cultivation spread to the remainder of Europe. The name for lemons in Italian, Portuguese, Spanish, and other languages is derived from laymoon, *an Arabized Persian word.*

3 medium lemons
1 medium onion, very finely chopped
1 large bunch parsley, thoroughly washed, stemmed, and finely chopped
4 tablespoons crushed walnuts
4 tablespoons olive oil
1 teaspoon dried mint

salt and pepper to taste
12 pitted black olives, sliced in half

Remove rind of the lemons (reserve for other recipes), leaving the white skin underneath intact. Finely chop lemons, discarding seeds, and place in a salad bowl. Add remaining ingredients, except olives; then toss. Decorate with olives and serve.

LENTIL SALAD
Salatat 'Adas
Syria and Lebanon
Serves 8 to 10

In some parts of Spain, Don Quixote's Friday meal of lentils is still the mainstay of many peasants and urban poor. This recipe could well have been Quixote's repast.

1 cup lentils, washed
6 cups water
6 tablespoons olive oil
½ cup lemon juice
1 bunch green onions, finely chopped
3 large tomatoes, diced
1 cup of cooked chickpeas, (canned chickpeas can be used)
½ cup finely chopped parsley
1 large sweet red pepper, finely chopped
salt and pepper to taste

Cook lentils in water until tender, but still intact and slightly firm; allow to cool. Drain lentils, and mix thoroughly with remaining ingredients just before serving.

LENTIL AND YOGURT SALAD

Salatat `Adas wa Laban
Syria and Lebanon
Serves 8

Lentils have very little fat; there are only 116 calories in a half cup of cooked lentils. This relatively cheap and nutritious food is also full of minerals: folic acid, iron, magnesium, phosphorus, potassium, and thiamin. A boon to diabetics, lentils assist the body in controlling blood sugar and insulin levels.

1 cup lentils, rinsed
6 cups water
6 cups plain yogurt, chilled
2 tablespoons finely chopped fresh cilantro
2 cloves garlic, crushed
½ teaspoon thyme
pinch of cayenne
salt and pepper to taste

Place lentils and water in a saucepan and bring to boil; then cover and cook over medium heat for 30 minutes or until lentils are tender but not mushy. Drain; then allow to cool.

Place in a serving bowl with the remaining ingredients; mix thoroughly and serve immediately.

Note: Besides being served as a salad, this dish can be served as an appetizer or for snacks.

MOROCCAN EGGPLANT SALAD

Schlada Bathinjan
Serves 4 to 6

According to tradition, an Arab bride learns quickly to master the art of making tempting eggplant meals. An Arab proverb says: "A woman, after marriage, controls her husband with her beauty; then in his middle age by feeding him delicious eggplant stews; and in his old age by beating him with her bathroom clogs."

1 large unpeeled eggplant, cut into 1-inch cubes
3 cloves garlic, finely chopped

5 cups water
salt to taste
1 teaspoon cumin
1 teaspoon paprika
¼ cup lemon juice
¼ cup olive oil

Place eggplant, garlic, water, and salt in a saucepan and bring to boil. Cover and cook over medium heat for ten minutes, or until eggplant cubes are cooked but still firm. Drain eggplant in a strainer, allowing to cool; then transfer to a salad bowl. Sprinkle with salt, cumin, and paprika and toss gently. Just before serving, add lemon juice and olive oil; gently toss again just before serving.

ONION AND SUMAC SALAD

Salatat Basal wa Summaaq
Syria and Lebanon
Serves 4 to 6

According to R. Landry, in his book The Gentle Art of Flavoring, *some historians believe that the dish of lentils that Jacob gave Esau was seasoned with berries of Rhus coriaria, or sumac. Sumac (from the Arabic* summaaq) *may be the last of the great condiments still to be introduced into the West.*

This tangy seasoning has been employed for thousands of years by Middle Eastern cooks, often as a replacement for lemon juice or vinegar.

3 large Spanish onions, thinly sliced
1 cup water
½ cup vinegar
salt to taste
2 tablespoons sumac (see p. 4)

Place onions, water, vinegar, and salt in a salad bowl; then let stand for 2 hours, gently tossing two or three times.

Drain well, then sprinkle in sumac and gently toss just before serving.

ORANGE SALAD

Schlada Latsheen
Morocco
Serves 4

This simple dish can be served as a salad or dessert.

5 large oranges
2 teaspoons orange-flower water (*mazahar*)
½ teaspoon ground cinnamon

Slice oranges thinly; then arrange slices on a serving plate. Sprinkle *mazahar* evenly over the slices; chill for at least one hour.

Just before serving, sprinkle cinnamon evenly over the orange slices.

ORANGE AND OLIVE SALAD

Salatat Burtagal wa Zaytoon
Saudi Arabia
Serves 4

Saudi Arabia today has one of the highest living standards in the world, yet a little over a quarter century ago, in this Holy Land of Islam, poverty reigned supreme. In the last few decades, however, the country has evolved into a land where ultramodern highways have obliterated the camel trails, towering skyscrapers have taken the place of mud huts, spots of desert land are now green oases, up-to-date factories have overwhelmed the artisan stalls, and schools are now plentiful. No other country has advanced from the middle ages into the twentieth century in such a short period of time.

4 large oranges, peeled, sectioned, and cut into small pieces
½ cup olives, pitted and halved
2 small onions, thinly sliced
salt and pepper to taste
2 tablespoons lemon juice
1 tablespoon olive oil
lettuce leaves

Place oranges, olives and onions in a mixing bowl; set aside.

Combine salt, pepper, lemon juice, and olive oil; then gently stir into mixing bowl contents.

Place lettuce leaves on a serving plate, top with salad, and serve.

Oregano Salad

Salatat Za'tar Tilyaanee
Syria and Lebanon
Serves 6 to 8

Oregano, which is also called wild marjoram or origan and is often confused with marjoram, is a perennial plant of the mint family, native to the Mediterranean region. In classical Arabic, oregano is called anrar, *but in the eastern colloquial Arabic, the various types of oregano and thymes are lumped together under the name* za'tar.

In bygone ages, oregano was employed to improve eyesight, to cure indigestion, and to soothe insect bites.

There are many types of oregano, but for this salad a very mild fresh oregano should be used.

4 cups (lightly packed) fresh mild Italian oregano leaves
4 medium onions, chopped
1 cup crumbled feta cheese
2 cloves garlic, crushed
4 teaspoons olive oil
3 tablespoons lemon juice
2 tablespoons sumac
salt and pepper to taste

Combine oregano, onions, and cheese in a salad bowl; set aside.

Thoroughly combine remaining ingredients; then stir into salad bowl mixture and serve immediately.

Parsley and Burghul Salad (Tabbouli)

Tabboola
Syria and Lebanon
Serves 6 to 8

Popular in the West now as a health food, tabboola *is regarded by Middle Easterners as the epitome of salads. It is different from the salads familiar to the Western palate, different also in its preparation: the main ingredients must be very finely chopped. It can be served as an appetizer or as a side dish with an entrée.*

¼ cup medium *burghul*
2 medium ripe but firm tomatoes, finely chopped
1 cup finely chopped fresh green onions
2 large bunches of parsley, stems removed and leaves finely chopped
1 clove garlic, crushed
2 tablespoons finely chopped fresh mint leaves
4 tablespoons olive oil
4 tablespoons lemon juice
salt and pepper to taste
about a dozen romaine lettuce leaves, washed

Place *burghul* in a bowl and cover with water; let stand for 15 minutes. Drain in a strainer, pressing out as much water as possible; then place in a mixing bowl.

Add remaining ingredients except lettuce leaves and mix thoroughly. Line a salad bowl with lettuce leaves, place *tabboola* on top, and serve.

Note: This salad keeps very well; any left over may be used the next day, as it does not become soggy or lose its flavor.

Parsley and Pepper Salad

Schlada Madnousse
Morocco
Serves 8

The Arabs are one of the few peoples in the world who have discovered the culinary delights of parsley. In the West, unfortunately, it is used mainly to decorate other food. There are numerous Arab salads, like this dish, in which parsley is the main ingredient.

1 large bunch wide leaf parsley, washed, stemmed, and chopped
2 medium tomatoes, finely chopped
1 medium sweet red pepper, finely chopped

1 large Spanish onion, finely chopped
1 clove garlic, crushed
2 tablespoons finely chopped fresh mint
4 tablespoons lemon juice
4 tablespoons olive oil
salt and pepper to taste
¼ cup black olives, pitted and halved

Place all ingredients, except olives, in a salad bowl and mix thoroughly. Garnish with olives and serve immediately.

Peanut Salad

Salatat Fool
Sudan
Serves 8

An unusual way to use what most Westerners think of as a snack food.

2 cups unsalted peanuts
¼ cup water
2 large tomatoes, finely chopped
1 medium onion, finely chopped
4 tablespoons olive oil
pinch of cayenne
juice of 1 lemon
salt to taste
4 tablespoons chopped parsley

Grind or pulverize peanuts until they are as fine as cornmeal; then add water and stir.

Add tomatoes, onion, olive oil, cayenne, lemon juice, and salt, and mix thoroughly. Place on a serving platter and garnish with the parsley. Chill and serve.

Pepper and Tomato Salad

Schlada L'Fulful
Morocco
Serves 6

Moroccan cuisine has a unique history. Many Moroccan dishes were first prepared in the kitchens of Baghdad; from there they were brought to Al-Andalus, the paradise the Arabs had created in the Iberian Peninsula. When the Arabs were expelled from their Eden in Europe, they took their food with them to North Africa. Here, the food traditions of Baghdad and Al-Andalus were enriched by those of the Berbers. This is why in Morocco—and, to a lesser degree, the remainder of North Africa—the cuisine is different from that of the Arab East.

4 medium ripe, but firm, tomatoes
4 medium green peppers
8 cloves garlic, crushed
1 teaspoon cumin
salt to taste
⅛ teaspoon cayenne
4 tablespoons vinegar
4 tablespoons olive oil

Place tomatoes and peppers in boiling water. After 3 minutes, remove tomatoes with a slotted spoon; after 8 minutes, remove peppers. Immediately plunge vegetables into cold water. Peel tomatoes and cut into thin slices. Peel peppers, remove seeds, and core; then cut into ½-inch thick strips. Place tomatoes and peppers in a salad bowl.

Combine remaining ingredients; then pour over tomatoes and peppers. Chill; then stir and serve.

Potato Salad

Batata Mutabbala
Syria and Lebanon
Serves 6

Although the potato is not native to the Arab countries, it was adopted by these lands soon after the potato was discovered in America. This Arabic version of potato salad makes a refreshing change from the kind made with mayonnaise and is perfect for picnics and barbecues.

5 large potatoes, cooked, peeled, and cut into ½-inch cubes
2 eggs, hard-boiled and chopped
¼ cup finely chopped green onions
¼ cup finely chopped parsley
2 tablespoons finely chopped fresh mint
¼ cup olive oil
2 cloves garlic
salt and pepper to taste
¼ cup lemon juice

Place all ingredients, except garlic, salt, pepper, and lemon juice in a salad bowl.

Mash garlic with salt; then stir in pepper and lemon juice. Add this to ingredients in salad bowl; toss gently, taking care not to break up potatoes and eggs. Serve well chilled.

POTATO SALAD WITH CARAWAY

Salatat Batata
Tunisia
Serves 4 to 6

Potato salads are now common throughout the Arab world. Unlike most Western versions, they are rather spicy, and olive oil is always used as part of the dressing.

¼ cup olive oil
3 tablespoons lemon juice
1 teaspoon ground caraway
¼ teaspoon cayenne
salt to taste
5 large potatoes, cooked, peeled, and cubed
2 tablespoons finely chopped fresh mint
2 tablespoons finely chopped cilantro
¼ cup finely chopped parsley

Heat olive oil in a frying pan over medium heat; add lemon juice, caraway, cayenne, and salt, stirring constantly. Cook for 3 to 5 minutes, until some of the liquid in the frying pan evaporates.

Remove from heat; add potatoes and turn gently with a fork until they are coated with the seasoned oil. Place in a salad bowl; then add mint, cilantro, and parsley and toss. Chill; then toss again and serve.

POTATO AND CHEESE SALAD

Salatat Batata wa Jiban
Tunisia
Serves 8

The red-hot embers barely kept us warm as we huddled around a Tunisian earthenware kanoun (a small stove) on a cold January day. Nevertheless we were not thinking of the cold. The aroma coming from the kitchen was arousing our hunger as we waited for our lunch. Soon we were relishing a tasty vegetarian meal, which we had requested from our host the previous evening.

Among the half dozen dishes was this salad, common to many Mediterranean countries.

8 medium potatoes, boiled and peeled
1½ cups crumbled feta cheese
4 hard-boiled eggs, chopped
4 tablespoons finely chopped fresh cilantro
2 cloves garlic, crushed
4 tablespoons lemon juice
5 tablespoons olive oil
salt and pepper to taste
¼ cup pitted green olives, sliced in half

Cut potatoes into ¾-inch cubes and place in a salad bowl. Add remaining ingredients, except olives and toss gently. Garnish with olives, and serve immediately.

POTATO AND YOGURT SALAD

Salatat Batata wa Laban
Palestine and Jordan
Serves 6

For those wishing to cut down on the amount of fat, cholesterol, and calories they consume, yogurt made from skim milk is a good substitute for mayonnaise, sour cream, or similar products. The combination of yogurt and potatoes is delicious and nourishing.

2 tablespoons olive oil
1 large onion, chopped

4 cloves garlic, crushed
2 tablespoons finely chopped fresh cilantro
½ small hot pepper, finely chopped
salt and pepper to taste
4 large potatoes (about 1 pound), peeled and diced into ½ inch cubes
¾ cup water
1 cup plain yogurt

Heat oil in a saucepan and sauté onion over medium heat for 8 minutes. Add garlic, cilantro, and hot pepper and stir-fry for a few more minutes. Add remaining ingredients, except yogurt. Bring to boil; then cover and cook over medium heat for 20 minutes or until potatoes are done. Place in a serving bowl; then stir in yogurt and serve.

RADISH SALAD
Salatat Fijil
Tunisia
Serves 4 to 6

Radishes originated in China, but are now cultivated in all parts of the world. According to W. Root's Food: An Authoritative and Visual History and Dictionary of the Foods of the World, *Herodotus, the ancient Greek historian who has been called the father of history, saw an inscription in Egypt honoring radishes, along with onions and leeks, as the food of the workers who built the pyramids. And radishes mixed with honey were considered a "love food" by the Egyptians as early as 500 BC.*

Radishes come in many varieties, but the most widely eaten are the familiar red or red and white types. All species are dieters' delights since they are low in carbohydrates and contain vitamin B, iron, and sulphur.

2 bunches of radishes, tops cut off, thinly sliced
4 tablespoons finely chopped celery
4 tablespoons finely chopped parsley
2 tablespoons olive oil
2 tablespoons lemon juice
salt and pepper to taste
2 hard-boiled eggs, chopped
6 olives, pitted and sliced in half

Combine radishes, celery, parsley, oil, lemon juice, salt, and pepper; place on a serving platter. Decorate with eggs and olives and serve immediately.

Radish and Orange Salad

Salatat Fijl wa Latsheen
Morocco
Serves 4 to 6

The first time that I enjoyed this salad was in a friend's home in Casablanca, during my first trip to Morocco in 1961. It left a lasting impression on me since it was not a salad found on my parents' table.

6 seedless oranges, peeled
½ cup lemon juice
a few drops orange-flower water (*mazahar*)
salt to taste
3 tablespoons sugar
1 bunch red radishes, tops removed
¼ tablespoon cinnamon

Section oranges; then place in a salad bowl and set aside.

In another bowl, combine lemon juice, orange-flower water, salt, and sugar; stir until sugar and salt are dissolved.

Grate radishes coarsely; then add with lemon mixture to oranges and toss gently. Sprinkle with cinnamon and serve.

Note: This salad must be served immediately. If allowed to stand for too long, the taste will not be as fresh and sharp.

Red Pepper Salad

Mahamara
Syria and Lebanon
Serves 8 to 10

Popular in the cities of Syria, especially its birthplace Aleppo, this tasty dish adds color to any meal. It can also be served as an appetizer, a fine addition to any maza *table.*

¼ cup fine *burghul*
4 large sweet red peppers
½ cup pine nuts
1 tablespoon tamarind paste
2 tablespoons lemon juice

½ teaspoon cumin
⅛ teaspoon cayenne
salt to taste
2 tablespoons olive oil

Soak *burghul* in warm water for 10 minutes; then drain in a strainer, pressing out as much water as possible. Set aside.

Place the peppers in an oven and broil, turning them a number of times, until they blister on all sides. Remove from oven and allow to cool, then remove seeds and skin. Chop finely, then thoroughly combine with *burghul* and remaining ingredients, except the olive oil.

Place on a platter and chill. Just before serving sprinkle with olive oil. Serve with crackers or pita bread.

Note: If you do not want to serve it immediately, place in a covered container. When needed, place on a platter and sprinkle with a little olive oil just before serving. The flavor is enhanced if refrigerated for about a week.

SEASONED BEANS
Loobiya Mutabbal
Syria and Lebanon
Serves 4 to 6

Along with avocados, potatoes, tomatoes, and dozens of other food plants, green beans were contributed to the world by the Indians of Central America. In the Arab lands, green beans have become a vital ingredient in the daily menu. It is safe to say that very few people in these countries know that they are a Mexican gift to the culinary art of the Middle East and North Africa.

1 pound frozen green beans
3 cloves garlic, crushed
3 tablespoons lemon juice
3 tablespoons olive oil
salt and pepper to taste

Place beans in a saucepan, cover with water, and bring to boil. Turn heat to medium and cook for 8 minutes. Drain and allow to cool; then place in a serving bowl. Stir in remaining ingredients just before serving

Spinach Salad

Schlada Baqoola
Morocco
Serves 6 to 8

Baqoola in the Moroccan dialect is a type of mallow not available elsewhere. Spinach is a good substitute.

2 10-oz packages spinach, thoroughly washed and chopped
½ hot pepper, finely chopped
1 teaspoon oregano
4 tablespoons olive oil
1 cup finely chopped parsley
2 cloves garlic, crushed
¼ teaspoon cumin
salt and pepper to taste
4 tablespoons lemon juice

Place spinach, hot pepper and oregano in a pot, cover with water, and bring to boil. Cook over medium heat for 3 minutes; then remove from heat and drain.

Heat oil in a saucepan and add spinach and remaining ingredients, except lemon juice, and stir-fry for 5 minutes. Remove from heat; then stir in lemon juice. Place on a serving platter and serve hot or cold.

Spinach and Coriander Salad

Salatat Sabanakh wa Kuzbara
Syria and Lebanon
Serves 4 to 6

"Come on, eat your spinach. Don't you want to grow up and be as strong as Popeye?" How many times have parents used such words to urge their long-suffering children to consume the vegetable made famous by that comic-strip hero.

More often than not, children have to be forced to eat this healthy green—which, all too often is prepared in an unappetizing way. If mothers only knew that, besides being a body-building food, spinach can be cooked into a mouth-watering dish, children's traditional dislike might vanish.

¼ cup lemon juice
2 tablespoons olive oil

salt and pepper to taste
1 10-oz package spinach, thoroughly washed and chopped
3 medium tomatoes, cut into ½-inch cubes
½ cup finely chopped fresh cilantro
2 tablespoons finely chopped fresh mint

Make a dressing by mixing lemon juice, oil, salt, and pepper; set aside. Combine all remaining ingredients in a salad bowl. Add dressing just before serving and toss.

Note: Young, tender dandelion leaves may be substituted for the spinach.

SPINACH AND YOGURT SALAD
Salatat Sabanakh wa Laban
Palestine and Jordan
Serves 6

An excellent blood builder, spinach is without question as wholesome and health-giving a food as can be imagined. It contains over 90 percent water, is low in calories, has no cholesterol, and is a rich source of minerals and vitamins.

3 tablespoons olive oil
2 medium onions, chopped
½ hot pepper, finely chopped
1 10-oz package spinach, thoroughly washed and chopped
salt and pepper to taste
2 cloves garlic, crushed
1 teaspoon crumbled dried mint leaves
2½ cups yogurt

Heat oil in a frying pan and sauté onions and hot pepper over medium heat for 12 minutes. Add spinach, salt, and pepper, cover, and cook for 5 minutes, stirring a few times.

Transfer to a salad bowl and allow to cool. Stir in garlic, mint, and yogurt and serve.

Tangy Beet Salad

Schlada Barba
Morocco
Serves 4 to 6

*Beets were employed for medical purposes long before they became a common food.
Both the roots and leaves (greens) have nutritional value: they are rich in aspartic acid,
calcium, phosphorous, potassium, and contain some carbohydrates, iron, magnesium,
protein, sodium, traces of fat, and small amounts of vitamins A, B, and C. Beet greens,
too often thrown away, are richer in iron than spinach, and the skin of the roots
contains a good amount of minerals.*

*Beets have no cholesterol. Half a cup contains about 40 calories, and they provide
excellent food for red blood corpuscles. In the middle ages, herbalists recommended
them for dysentery, headaches, menstrual problems, toothaches, and ailments of the
bladder, kidney, and liver.*

1 pound cooked beets, sliced
6 tablespoons vinegar
1 teaspoon powdered mustard
½ teaspoon salt
½ teaspoon nutmeg
2 tablespoons water

Place beets in a salad bowl and set aside.

Place remaining ingredients in a small saucepan and bring to boil; then cover
and cook over medium heat for 5 minutes. Pour over beets and allow to cool.
Chill; then stir and serve.

TOMATO SALAD

Salatat Banadoora
Syria and Lebanon
Serves 8

Tomatoes provide North Americans with a greater percentage of their nutrition than any other vegetable. This is not to say that they contain more nourishment than any other garden produce, but that they are widely consumed.

The tomato is a dieter's delight—a medium tomato has about 30 calories, contains no cholesterol, and is low in carbohydrates. When sun ripened, tomatoes are rich in vitamins A and C and minerals, especially potassium. In addition, they contain some calcium, chlorine, iron, magnesium, phosphorus, and traces of fat, protein, sodium, and vitamins B, E, and G.

6 large firm tomatoes
1 medium Spanish onion
½ cup finely chopped green onions
3 cloves garlic, crushed
¼ teaspoon thyme
1 teaspoon dried mint
¼ cup lemon juice
¼ cup olive oil
salt and pepper to taste

Cut tomatoes into thin slices and place in a salad bowl. Slice onion very thin and add to tomatoes. Add remaining ingredients and mix gently. Chill; toss lightly just before serving.

Tomato and Coriander Salad

Salatat Tamatim wa Kuzbara
Yemen
Serves 4 to 6

Coriander has long been known to almost every Asian, African, and European civilization. In ancient China, it was believed that coriander bestowed immortality on those who faithfully used it in their cooking. In the Egypt of the Pharaohs, this herb was considered a food fit for the gods. Coriander seeds have been found in ancient Egyptian tombs, apparently as a food offering to the next world. The Bible *(Exodus 16:31) compares coriander to the manna that fell from Paradise.*

The Romans, who employed it extensively, did not agree on its qualities. Pliny labeled coriander "a very stinking herb." In later centuries, Charlemagne, who loved its taste, ordered that it be grown in all his imperial gardens. In the same era, the Arabs used this herb on a massive scale, not only enjoying its exotic tang but also believing it stimulated sexual desire. The well-known Arabian classic, A Thousand and One Nights, *mentions it as an aphrodisiac.*

This simple salad demonstrates coriander's ability to enhance other ingredients while maintaining its own definite taste.

5 medium tomatoes, diced
¾ cup fresh coriander leaves (cilantro), chopped
⅛ teaspoon cayenne
3 tablespoons lemon juice
2 tablespoons olive oil
salt and pepper to taste

Combine tomatoes and cilantro in a salad bowl.

In a separate bowl, thoroughly mix remaining ingredients; then pour over tomatoes and toss just before serving.

Tomato and Vegetable Salad

Salatat Tamatim
Palestine and Jordan
Serves 8

Known for hundreds of years as love apples, tomatoes became the favorite of sweethearts and a symbol of passion. This sobriquet came about by mistake.

The Spaniards, who were known to many Europeans as Moors, first introduced tomatoes to neighboring countries in the sixteenth century. According to one story, the Italians called tomatoes pomi dei Moro *(apples of the Moors). Another version speculates that the first tomato seen in Italy was probably yellow—the original color of tomatoes in the Americas—and hence was called* pomo d'oro *(apple of gold). To the French, both names sounded like* pomo d'amore *(apple of love), leading to their reputation as an aphrodisiac.*

The name for tomatoes in Syria and Lebanon, banadoora, *is probably derived from* pomo d'oro *since it is believed that Italian merchants first introduced them into the Middle East.*

3 medium tomatoes, diced
1 large sweet pepper, diced
1 medium cucumber, diced
½ bunch parsley, finely chopped
2 tablespoons finely chopped fresh mint
½ bunch green onions, finely chopped
1 clove garlic, crushed
4 tablespoons olive oil
juice of two lemons
6 red radishes, chopped
10 pitted olives, chopped
salt and pepper to taste
¼ cup feta cheese, crumbled

Combine all ingredients, except the cheese, in a salad bowl and allow to marinate for 10 minutes. Sprinkle evenly with cheese and serve.

Tossed Salad

Salata
Syria and Lebanon
Serves 8

Eastern Arab dressings for salads combine olive oil and lemon juice (or vinegar); crushed garlic is usually added along with salt and pepper. These dressings are tangier than vinaigrettes in the West because more lemon juice is used in proportion to the oil. The Middle Eastern cook may use as much lemon as oil, or more. You can, of course, adjust these dressings to taste. Salads are never served without having been tossed in their dressing.

1 small head lettuce, chopped into large pieces
3 medium-to-large tomatoes, chopped into large pieces
½ bunch green onions, finely chopped
¼ cup of fresh finely chopped mint leaves, or 1 teaspoon dried mint
¼ cup of fresh chopped parsley leaves
2 cloves garlic, crushed
½ teaspoon oregano
salt and pepper to taste
⅓ cup olive oil
¼ cup lemon juice

Place all ingredients in a salad bowl; then toss lightly and serve immediately.

Vegetable Salad

Salatat Khudr
Egypt
Serves 4 to 6

Due to their long experience of European colonialism, Egyptians have incorporated many aspects of Western cooking into their kitchens. This recipe is an example of an Arab dish with a Western influence.

1 cup fresh green peas, cooked
1 cup fresh green beans, cooked
3 tomatoes, diced
½ cup pickled white onions, halved
3 tablespoons lemon juice
3 tablespoons olive oil
¼ cup sour cream
salt and pepper to taste
1 large beet, cooked, peeled, and sliced thin
3 tablespoons chopped parsley

Combine peas, beans, tomatoes, onions, lemon juice, olive oil, and sour cream in a salad bowl. Sprinkle with salt and pepper; then toss. Garnish with beets and parsley; serve chilled.

Yogurt and Dandelion Greens Salad

Salatat Laban ma' Hindba
Iraq
Serves 6 to 8

Three times as easy to digest as milk, yogurt is rich in vitamin B and calcium, and high in protein. Plain yogurt contains few calories, a boon in low-calorie diets.

In the Middle East and the Balkans, millions rely on yogurt as a remedy for numerous ailments, especially digestive problems.

1 small bunch of dandelion greens, washed and finely chopped
½ cup finely chopped fresh cilantro
1 clove garlic, crushed
2 tablespoons lemon juice
2 tablespoons olive oil
salt and pepper to taste
2½ cups yogurt

In a serving bowl, thoroughly mix all ingredients, except yogurt. Gradually stir in yogurt. Serve chilled.

Yogurt and Vegetable Salad

Salatat Laban
Sudan
Serves 6 to 8

Yogurt has long been associated with magical power. Cleopatra, the famous Egyptian queen, attributed her great beauty to yogurt baths. The ancient Greek physicians prescribed yogurt to clear the digestive tract of body poisons, and Genghis Khan, the notorious Mongolian conqueror, believed the extraordinary bravery of his warriors was due to their regular consumption of yogurt.

1 cup plain yogurt
2 tablespoons vinegar
4 tablespoons olive oil
1 teaspoon chili powder
salt to taste
1 clove garlic, crushed
1 head lettuce, chopped
2 medium tomatoes, diced
½ bunch green onions, finely chopped

Combine yogurt, vinegar, oil, chili power, salt, and garlic in a salad bowl; then add remaining ingredients. Thoroughly mix; then serve.

EGG DISHES

*A*s do most Westerners, Arabs today get their eggs from modern chicken factories. Gone are the days when they gathered eggs from the chickens scratching for food in the fields or in the barnyard. But as in the past, eggs are still very popular throughout the Arab world.

I can personally testify to the superior taste of eggs produced by barnyard chickens. During the Depression years when our family did not have the money to buy feed, our chickens survived on the meager food they found while scratching in the barn and the surrounding fields. When I think of those eggs, my mouth still waters. Of course, it may well have been our spartan diet that made those eggs so appetizing. In any case, I still remember with fondness the eggs produced by our scraggly chickens.

The Arab omelet is made with numerous vegetables, and sometimes meats, and is very tasty. It is believed that the Spanish *tortilla* was introduced, like many other foods, into the Iberian Peninsula by the Arabs. Arab omelets are flat, like the *tortilla* or the Italian *frittata*, as opposed to the folded or souffléed types more commonly known in the West.

Besides omelets, there are dozens of other ways Arabs prepare their eggs, all with their special appeal.

An Arab poet once wrote:

> My wife always brings me
> For breakfast a covered tray
> Containing the best of treats,
> But for only one I pray.
>
> When I find eggs offered,
> Like a penetrating sun ray,
> They revive my spirits,
> And nourish me for
> the day.

Asparagus and Egg Soup

Shawrbat Halyoon wa Bayd
Syria and Lebanon
Serves 8

After it is harvested, asparagus should be cooked as soon as possible. It does not keep well and quickly loses its delicate flavor and much of its vitamin C. Newly picked or frozen fresh, it is excellent in a wide range of dishes, from appetizers to main courses.

I first came to taste this soup in a village in Lebanon, at the home of a family who had emigrated to the United States and then returned. I'm not really sure whether the dish originated in Syria or Lebanon or among the Arab immigrants in North America.

1 pound asparagus
4 tablespoons olive oil
2 medium onions, chopped
4 cloves garlic, crushed
1 small hot pepper, finely chopped
6 cups water
4 tablespoons finely chopped fresh cilantro
salt and pepper to taste
2 eggs, beaten
½ cup crumbled feta cheese

Wash asparagus; cut off and discard tough ends. Chop spears into small pieces and set aside.

Heat oil in a saucepan and sauté onions, garlic and hot pepper over medium heat for 12 minutes. Add asparagus and stir-fry for 3 minutes more. Add water, cilantro, salt, and pepper and bring to boil. Cover and cook over medium heat for 25 minutes; then stir in eggs and cook for a few moments.

Place in serving bowls, garnish with cheese, and serve.

Asparagus Omelet

'Ujjat Halyoon
Syria and Lebanon
Serves 6

Appealing to the eye, asparagus is a healthy and delectable member of the lily-of-the-valley family of plants. Its smooth velvety flavor melts in the mouth and leaves a lasting delicate aftertaste—an ideal vegetable for gourmet meals.

A. J. Arberry, in his book Aspects of Islamic Civilization, *quotes the scribe Mahmood ibn al-Husayn ibn al-Sindi Kushaajim describing asparagus:*

Lances we have, the tips whereof are curled,
Their bodies like a hawser turned and twirled,
Yet fair to view, with ne'er a knot to boot.
Their heads bolt upright from the shoulders shoot,
And, by the grace of Him who made us all,
Firm in the soil they stand, like pillars tall.

1 pound asparagus
4 tablespoons butter
1 medium onion, finely chopped
½ cup water
4 eggs, beaten
1 tablespoon finely chopped fresh cilantro
⅛ teaspoon cayenne
salt and pepper to taste

Wash asparagus; cut off and discard tough ends. Chop spears into small pieces and set aside.

Melt butter in a frying pan and sauté onion over medium heat for 10 minutes. Add asparagus and water; cover and cook for 10 minutes.

Thoroughly combine remaining ingredients; then add to asparagus and stir-fry briefly. Serve hot.

Basil-Flavored Eggs

Bayd ma' Habaq
Palestine and Jordan

In France, Greece, Italy, Portugal, Spain and the Arab countries basil is a popular herb that turns up in a vast number of dishes. Its delightful odor and pungent flavor appeal

alike to the ordinary housewife and the gourmet cook. Chefs combine basil with garlic to make a condiment that is used in numerous dishes, especially soups and stews. Sometimes, the herb is used alone to flavor appetizers, salads, or just sprinkled on a simple food, as in this recipe.

eggs
salt, pepper and dry basil to taste

Fry eggs sunnyside up; then sprinkle lightly with salt, pepper, and basil just before serving

Cabbage and Egg Salad

Salatat Hanim
Syria and Lebanon
Serves 8 to 10

It has been established that people suffering from ulcer experience relief by consuming cabbage. Researchers have found that this vegetable has ulcer-healing properties. Raw cabbage juice is well-documented as having remarkable success in treating peptic ulcers. Nutritionists have found that a compound in cabbage appears to strengthen the stomach lining's resistance to acid attacks and also to rejuvenate cells—actually helping to heal ulcers.

This dish, a favorite of the Syrian Damascenes, makes the consumption of cabbage not only a healthful, but an enjoyable event.

4 cups shredded cabbage
1 cup finely chopped green onions
2 cloves garlic, crushed
4 tablespoons olive oil
3 tablespoons vinegar
salt and pepper to taste
⅛ teaspoon cayenne
3 hard boiled eggs, chopped
12 pitted black olives, sliced in half

Place cabbage and green onions in a mixing bowl and set aside.
Combine garlic, olive oil, vinegar, salt, pepper, and cayenne; then pour over cabbage and green-onion mixture. Thoroughly mix; then place on a serving platter. Spread eggs evenly over top; then decorate with olives and serve.

CASSEROLE OF EGGS AND PEAS

Shakshooka des Pois
Tunisia
Serves 4

The first time I tasted this dish was in a simple restaurant edging the main street of the Kasbah (old city) of Tunis. It was early morning and, today, what I remember most was the mouth-watering aroma emanating from the kitchen that made dining on this dish a memorable event. Like a good number of dishes in North Africa, versions of this Tunisian dish are also found in the Iberian Peninsula.

3 tablespoons olive oil
2 medium onions, finely chopped
2 cloves garlic, crushed
5 tablespoons finely chopped fresh cilantro
2 cups fresh or frozen peas
¾ cup water
salt and pepper to taste
¼ teaspoon cumin
4 eggs
1 teaspoon paprika

Heat oil in a frying pan; add onions, garlic, and cilantro, and sauté over medium heat until the onions begin to brown. Transfer to a casserole. Add peas, water, salt, pepper, and cumin; then cover and bake in an oven preheated to 350°F, for 20 minutes or until peas are done.

Break eggs, side by side, over peas; cover casserole and bake for another 10 minutes or until the eggs are set but still soft. Garnish with paprika and serve from casserole.

EGG AND DILL OMELET

'Ujjat Bayd bish-Shummar
Syria and Lebanon
Serves 4

Dill, called shabath *in classical Arabic, is confused in eastern Arab colloquial speech with* shummar, *the name for fennel.*

The dill plant has been prized for its leaves and seeds ever since it was first grown in Babylonia and Assyria for its magical and medicinal powers. To the Romans, dill was a symbol of vitality; to the Greeks it was a remedy for hiccups.

For millennia, herbs such as dill have been used medicinally, and from the time of recorded history, the ancient peoples of the Arab lands played their part in the discovery and use of herbs to cure diseases. Papyrus writings and paintings found on the walls of ancient temples, tell of Egyptians who traveled widely to collect and classify herbs. These writings speak of the contribution to herbal science made by the pre-Islamic Arabs.

In later centuries, books such as al-Adwiyah al-Mufradah (Simple Drugs) *by the twelfth century's Abu Jafar al-Ghafiqi and* al-Jami' li Mufradat al-Adwiyah wal-Aghthiyah (A Summary of Drugs and Food) *by the thirteenth century's Ibn Baitar are examples of famous writings by Arab scientists in this field.*

4 large eggs, beaten
½ cup finely chopped dill
¼ teaspoon cumin
salt and pepper to taste
pinch of cayenne
2 tablespoons butter

Thoroughly combine all ingredients, except butter.

Melt butter in a frying pan; pour in egg mixture. Cook over medium low heat until eggs set; then turn over. Cook a few moments more; then serve hot.

Eggs and Fried Bread

Fattoot
Yemen
Serves 4

Often served for breakfast, this dish is tasty—but not to be indulged in by those who are on low-fat diets.

4 tablespoons butter
1 8-inch loaf pita bread, cut into small pieces
1 tablespoon finely chopped fresh cilantro
5 eggs
salt and pepper to taste

Melt butter in a frying pan and add bread pieces and cilantro. Stir-fry over medium heat until bread pieces turn light brown; then stir in eggs, salt, and pepper. Continue to stir-fry until eggs are cooked; then serve hot.

Eggs in Mint Yogurt Sauce

Bayd bil-Laban
Syria and Lebanon
Serves 6

I always recall with fondness the cold winter days on the prairies when my mother cooked this dish for us children.

2 cloves garlic
2 tablespoons dried mint, or 3 or 4 sprigs fresh mint
salt to taste
2 tablespoons butter
1 tablespoon cornstarch, dissolved in 2 cups water
1 quart plain yogurt
6 eggs

Mash garlic, mint, and salt together; then sauté in butter for 3 minutes and set aside.

Mix dissolved cornstarch with yogurt in a heavy saucepan; then bring to boil over medium heat, stirring constantly in one direction to prevent curdling.

Break eggs, dropping quickly into boiling yogurt and allow to cook over medium heat for a few minutes. Stir in sautéed garlic mixture and continue to cook for 10 minutes, stirring a number of times. Serve hot with plain rice.

Eggs and Mushroom Stew

Tajin Tufaya
Morocco
Serves 4 to 6

People who come to know Moroccan cooking usually find it among the most sensual in the world—as this dish will no doubt bear witness.

3 tablespoons butter
2 medium onions, finely chopped
salt and pepper to taste
½ teaspoon paprika
pinch cayenne
pinch saffron
1 pound fresh mushrooms, washed and sliced

½ cup water
¼ cup finely chopped fresh cilantro
4 tablespoons olive oil
½ cup slivered almonds
3 large eggs

Melt butter in a saucepan and stir-fry onions, salt, pepper, paprika, cayenne, saffron, and mushrooms over medium heat for 5 minutes. Add water and cilantro, then cover and cook for an additional 10 minutes. Remove from heat and set aside.

Heat oil in a frying pan and sauté almonds until they turn golden brown. Remove from oil with a slotted spoon and set aside.

Hard-boil eggs; then shell and divide into quarters.

Place mushrooms with their sauce on a serving platter; then garnish with almonds and arrange the egg quarters in a pattern on top just before serving.

EGGS AND PEAS

Bayd ma' Bizayla
Palestine and Jordan
Serves 4

Broad beans are often substituted for the peas in this dish. Made with either, it is wholesome and tasty.

2 tablespoons olive oil
1 tablespoon finely chopped cilantro
2 cloves garlic, crushed
⅓ cup water
1 cup fresh or thawed frozen peas
salt and pepper to taste
4 eggs

Heat oil in a frying pan and sauté cilantro and garlic over medium heat for 3 minutes. Stir in remaining ingredients, except eggs and bring to boil. Cover and cook over medium low heat for 15 minutes.

Break eggs over top; then stir. Cook for a few minutes until eggs are done; then serve immediately.

Egg and Potato Omelet

Bayd ma' Batata
Morocco
Serves 4 to 6

Somewhat like a Spanish tortilla, this Moroccan dish may have some link with the cuisine of the Iberian Peninsula. According to some food historians, this simple dish was prepared (with other vegetables before potatoes were brought back from the New World) from Baghdad to Cordoba during the time when the Arab/Islamic world stretched from France to China. The Arabs could very well have introduced it into Spain.

½ cup cooking oil
5 medium potatoes, peeled and diced into very small pieces
1 cup water
salt and pepper to taste
½ teaspoon paprika
5 eggs, beaten

Heat oil in a frying pan and add potatoes, water, salt, pepper, and paprika. Cook over medium heat until water has been absorbed by potatoes, which should be tender but still intact.

Pour eggs over the potatoes; then reduce heat to very low. Cook without stirring for about 5 minutes, or until eggs are done.

Egg and Tomato Casserole

Shakshooka
Tunisia
Serves 6

Tunisia is an Arab country that has entered the modern age, but has not discarded many of the fine traditions from its past. Its enchanting modern resort structures incorporate a good number of beautiful architectural gems from the middle ages. Tunisia's inhabitants enjoy an open society that fits into the twentieth-century lifestyle, yet they jealously preserve the best elements from their history. As to food, its cuisine is a world of delectable delights, perfected through the centuries.

4 tablespoons olive oil
1 small green pepper, finely chopped
1 medium onion, finely chopped
5 medium tomatoes, chopped

2 cloves garlic, crushed
salt and pepper to taste
¼ teaspoon cumin
pinch allspice
pinch chili powder
6 eggs

Heat oil in a frying pan and sauté green pepper and onion over medium heat for 3 to 5 minutes. Stir in tomatoes and garlic; continue to sauté until tomatoes are tender. Turn heat to low; then mash tomatoes with fork. Stir in salt, pepper, cumin, allspice, and chili powder; cook for 5 more minutes. Break in eggs; then cover and cook until eggs are done.

EGGS WITH TOMATOES

Bayd ma' Banadoora
Syria and Lebanon
Serves 4

The attractive coriander plant, an annual of the parsley family, can be grown by simply planting the seeds sold as a spice. It grows from one to two feet high with slender, hollow stems, feathery leaves, and tiny pinkish-white flowers. The plant will grow easily in all types of gardens, but to thrive it needs a dry, sunny climate and a well-drained light soil. The fresh leaves (cilantro) are a frequent addition to many Middle Eastern dishes. When mature, it produces a small oval fruit containing a pungent oil. The smell of this oil repels insects from the plant itself and from neighboring plants. When dried, the fruit is pleasantly aromatic and makes a tasty spice.

2 tablespoons butter
1 medium potato, cut into 1-inch cubes
2 tablespoons finely chopped fresh cilantro
2 tomatoes, finely chopped
5 eggs, beaten
salt and pepper to taste
¼ teaspoon cumin

Melt butter in a frying pan; add potato cubes and sauté over medium heat until they begin to brown. Stir in cilantro and sauté for a few minutes longer; then add tomatoes and stir-fry for another 3 to 5 minutes.

In the meantime, combine remaining ingredients; then add to frying pan contents and mix well. Cover and turn the heat to low; cook until eggs are done. Serve hot.

EGG AND TOMATO PIES

Fatayar Bayd wa Banadoora
Syria and Lebanon
Makes 18 pies

Fatayars, *known as* empanadas *or* empanaditas *in the Spanish-speaking countries, pasties in the British Isles,* pirozhki *in Russia,* patties *in Jamaica,* samosas *in India,* tiropittakia *in Greece, and dumplings in Chinese teahouses where they form a part of the* dim sum *meal, are delightful for snacks or as an accompaniment to meals.*

In Turkey, the pies are known as borek, *in Tunisia as* brik, *and in the eastern Arab lands, besides* fatayar, lahma bi-'ajeen *and* samboosa.

4 tablespoons olive oil
2 large onions, chopped
2 cloves garlic, crushed
2 tablespoons finely chopped fresh cilantro
2 pounds tomatoes, chopped
5 eggs, beaten
4 tablespoons chopped green olives
1 teaspoon dried basil
⅛ teaspoon cayenne
salt and pepper to taste
1 basic dough (see recipe, p. 11)
extra olive oil

Prepare (or defrost) dough and set it to rise.

Make filling: heat oil in a frying pan and sauté onions, garlic, and cilantro over medium heat for 5 minutes. Stir in tomatoes and continue to sauté for another 8 minutes; then stir in remaining ingredients, except dough and extra olive oil. Stir-fry until eggs begin to set; then remove from heat and allow to cool. Divide into 18 parts and set aside.

When dough has doubled in bulk, form into 18 balls and place on a floured tray. Cover with a damp cloth and set in warm place for 30 minutes.

Roll balls into 5- to 6-inch rounds; then place a portion of filling in the middle of each round. Fold dough to enclose filling in one of two ways: fold in half to create a half-moon shape or lift sides to meet in the middle, dividing the round into thirds and creating a triangle. In either case, pinch edges of dough firmly. Continue until all balls are folded.

Place on greased baking trays; then bake in an oven preheated to 400°F for 20 minutes or until pies turn golden brown. Remove from oven; then brush with olive oil and serve warm.

Eggs with Truffles

Kama ma' Bayd
Syria and Lebanon
Serve 4

There are two kinds of truffles: European and Arabian. There are at least thirty species of truffles, which grow wild in the root systems of hazel, juniper, poplar, willow, and especially oak trees. They range in color from black or brown to cream, pink, and white. The most famous European truffles are the French Perigord, *black in color, and the Italian* Piedmont, *a white variety.*

All the European species give out a strong aroma and have a slight garlic-peppery taste. They are usually consumed raw in salads or as a condiment.

The Arab truffle, known in North Africa as terfez *and in the eastern Arab world as* kama, kamaieh, *or* faqa'a, *are larger in size and much blander than the European species. They are white in color, shaped like a pear, and have a meaty mushroom taste. In classical times, they were the only type of truffles known and, then as now, the best variety comes from the area around Palmyra in Syria. In the desert around this oasis town, they are still found in abundance and are quite cheap, especially when compared to the expensive European types.*

3 tablespoons butter
½ cup canned Moroccan or Syrian truffles, thoroughly washed and chopped
2 cloves garlic, crushed
6 eggs
salt and pepper to taste

Melt butter in a frying pan and sauté truffles and garlic over medium heat for 4 to 5 minutes.

In the meantime, beat eggs with salt and pepper; then stir into truffles. Stir-fry over medium heat for few moments until eggs are cooked; then serve immediately.

Note: Moroccan and Syrian canned truffles can be purchased in Middle Eastern markets and some specialty food shops.

EGGPLANT OMELET

Bathinjan ma' Bayd
Syria and Lebanon
Serves 4 to 6

The eggplant is a very versatile vegetable and goes well with other foods, as this recipe will testify.

1 medium eggplant, peeled and cut into small cubes
salt to taste
6 tablespoons olive oil
1 medium onion, finely chopped
2 cloves garlic, crushed
½ teaspoon pepper
5 eggs, beaten

Sprinkle eggplant pieces with salt and place in a strainer. Top with a weight and allow to drain for 45 minutes.

Heat oil in a frying pan and add eggplant pieces, onions, and garlic. Sprinkle with a little salt and pepper, if needed; then gently stir-fry over medium heat until eggplant pieces are cooked, adding more oil if necessary.

Stir in eggs; then lower heat and continue to stir gently for a few minutes until eggs are cooked.

FAVA BEANS AND EGGS

Fool biz-Zayt
Yemen
Serves 6 to 8

Although green fava beans (fresh, frozen, or canned) are employed to some extent in cooking, most favas are allowed to dry on the plant before being harvested. The dry fava is brown in color and can be purchased packaged or in bulk.

2 cups dried small fava beans, soaked overnight
¼ cup olive oil
2 tablespoons tahini
6 tablespoons lemon juice
salt and pepper to taste
5 eggs, hard-boiled and chopped
¼ cup finely chopped fresh cilantro

Place fava beans in a saucepan and cover with water to an inch over beans. Cook over medium heat for 1 hour or until they are tender but not soft enough to break up, adding more water if necessary. Drain; then place in a mixing bowl and allow to cool.

In the meantime, thoroughly mix olive oil, tahini, lemon juice, salt, and pepper; then add to beans and mix well. Add half the chopped eggs and toss gently. Place on a platter and garnish with remaining chopped eggs and cilantro just before serving.

GARLIC OMELET

Bayd ma' Thoom
Syria and Lebanon
Serves 4

In the Arab East, bayd ma' thoom, *a tasty garlic omelet, is served to a mother who has just given birth. It is believed that the garlic purifies the blood and speeds the recovery of the new mother. No one has proved that this omelet purifies the blood, but it makes a delicious breakfast dish.*

1 large head of garlic
4 tablespoons olive or vegetable oil
6 eggs, beaten
salt and pepper to taste

Peel garlic cloves, mince, and set aside.

Heat oil in a frying pan and stir-fry garlic until golden brown. Remove garlic with a slotted spoon. Reserve oil in frying pan.

Combine eggs with salt, pepper, and fried garlic. Pour into frying pan and cook over very low heat until eggs are set.

Note: For a slightly different omelet, after the eggs are beaten, stir in 1 tablespoon of pomegranate concentrate (*dibs rumman*).

HARD-BOILED EGGS WITH CUMIN

Bayd Maslooq ma' Kammoon
Morocco

In Morocco, vendors in the streets sell eggs sprinkled with seasoning. The following simple preparation is similar.

1 teaspoon salt
2 teaspoons cumin
12 hard-boiled eggs

Mix salt and cumin in a small bowl. Serve eggs whole, accompanied by the bowl of salt and cumin, with each person dipping eggs into the seasoning.

KISHK WITH EGGS

Kishk ma' Bayd
Syria and Lebanon
Serves 4

This dish can be served for breakfast, lunch, dinner, or as a snack. Hearty and tasty, it is also an exotic treat.

2 tablespoons butter
2 cloves garlic, crushed
1 small onion, finely chopped
3 cups water
¼ cup *kishk* (Powdered Cheese, see recipe, p. 16), dissolved in ½ cup milk
salt and pepper to taste
4 eggs

Melt butter in a saucepan and sauté garlic and onion until they begin to brown. Stir in remaining ingredients except eggs and bring to boil. Turn heat to low and cook for 10 minutes, stirring once in a while.

Break eggs into *kishk* mixture; then cook for another 5 minutes. Serve 1 whole egg in a bowl of *kishk* to each person.

POTATOES WITH EGGS

Batata ma' Bayd
Iraq
Serves 4

Some food writers believe the Iraqis acquired this dish from British troops after the First World War. However, a similar dish, called zunood al-banaat, *has been prepared in Damascus for hundreds of years, using ground meat instead of the potatoes.*

2 cups mashed potatoes
1 tablespoon flour
salt and pepper to taste
4 hard-boiled eggs
1 raw egg, beaten
4 tablespoons breadcrumbs
oil for frying

Thoroughly combine potatoes, flour, salt, and pepper; divide into 4 portions. Flatten 1 portion and place 1 hard-boiled egg on it. Fold the potato over eggs and pat into an oval shape; repeat until all hard-boiled eggs are used.

Place beaten raw egg in a small bowl and place breadcrumbs on a dish. Dip each oval in egg; then roll in breadcrumbs until well coated.

Heat oil, about 2 inches deep, in a saucepan; then fry ovals until they turn golden brown. Serve whole, or cut each oval into 4 parts.

SCRAMBLED EGGS WITH MUSHROOMS & PEPPERS

Shakshooka de Champignons
Tunisia
Serves 4

Tunisian cuisine is neither Western nor Oriental but a mixture of both. It has borrowed much from the neighboring Mediterranean countries and from civilizations that thrived in that land at various times in history. Phoenicians, Romans, Arabs, Andalusian Muslims, Turks, French, and the native Berbers have all contributed to the modern Tunisian kitchen.

¼ cup olive oil
½ pound large mushrooms, cut into ½-inch pieces
2 cloves garlic, crushed
¼ teaspoon caraway
2 large tomatoes, cut into eighths
¼ cup water
salt and pepper to taste
2 sweet peppers (green, yellow, or red) with seeds removed,
    cut into ½-inch strips
3 eggs, beaten

Heat oil in a frying pan over high heat until sizzling; add mushrooms, garlic and caraway. Stir-fry for about 3 minutes; then add tomatoes, water, salt, and pepper. Lower heat to medium and cook until most of liquid in frying pan has evaporated.

Add sweet peppers and cook, partially covered, for about 10 minutes. Stir eggs into frying pan contents; then cook over low heat until eggs are done.

SCRAMBLED EGGS WITH YOGURT

'Ujja ma' Laban
Palestine and Jordan
Serves 4

Simple to prepare, this dish makes an excellent morning treat.

5 eggs, beaten
salt and pepper to taste
5 tablespoons *labana* (Yogurt Cheese, see recipe, p. 22)
2 tablespoons butter

Thoroughly mix eggs, salt, pepper, and *labana*. Melt butter in a frying pan and pour in the egg–yogurt mixture. Stir for a few minutes over low heat until eggs are cooked; then serve hot.

TURMERIC-FLAVORED EGGS

'Ujjat Bayd ma' Kurkum
Arabian Gulf
Serves 4

This dish, from the greater Syria area, has been modified by influences from the Indian subcontinent. The addition of turmeric gives the eggs a somewhat subtle taste.

In India, yellow is a sacred or noble color. The golden yellow turmeric is much in demand at birth, marriage, and death ceremonies, and as a magical symbol to protect against evil. A turmeric-soaked thread is to this day the binding symbol of Hindu marriages.

4 tablespoons olive oil
1 medium onion, finely chopped
2 cloves garlic, crushed
1 large tomato, finely chopped
4 eggs
2 tablespoons finely chopped fresh cilantro
½ teaspoon turmeric
salt and pepper to taste

Heat oil in a frying pan and sauté onions for 10 minutes. Stir in garlic and tomatoes; then cover and simmer over low heat for 15 minutes, stirring a few times.

In the meantime, beat eggs with remaining ingredients. Stir into frying pan contents and cook, stirring, until eggs are done; serve hot.

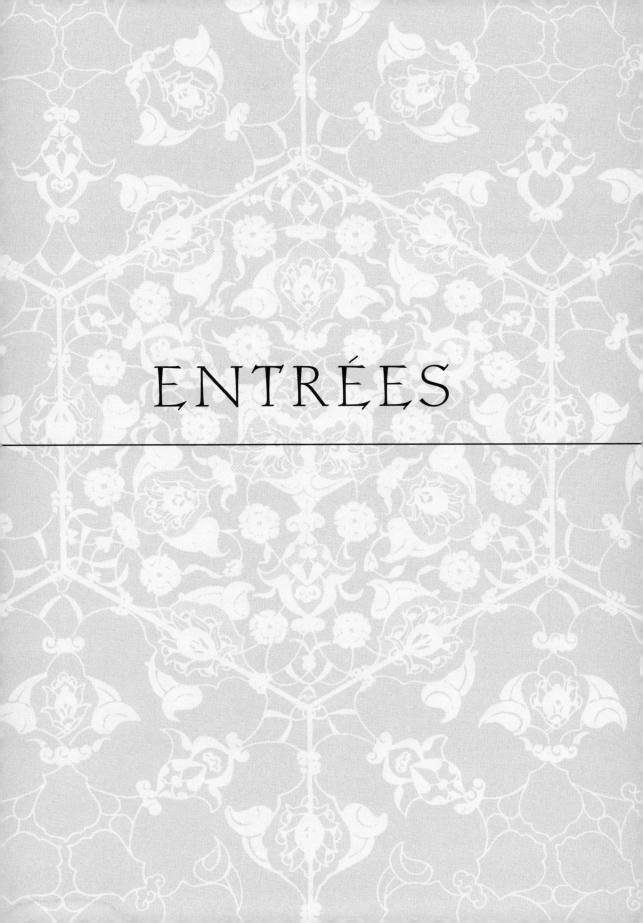

ENTRÉES

Mad cow disease! High cholesterol! Unexpected heart attacks! Obesity! Depression! These words bombard us daily in the media. We worry and we try to watch our diet, but nothing seems to work. Too many of us just give up and gorge ourselves with meats and fats, enjoying the taste, but living in fear of heart attacks. We live from day to day, in a fantasy land, waiting to be crippled or killed.

This has happened to many of us: we look forward to a banquet, but then after feasting, we regret our indulgence. After eating meat and other rich foods, it usually takes us a number of days to get back to normal. In the meantime, we suffer the discomfort of overeating and, at the same time, gain a few unnecessary pounds.

Never again! This is the last time! These are the phrases we often express, only to forget them when the next banquet rolls around. Our resolve seems to melt away in the presence of the rich foods on display.

Yet, one can cut down on anxiety, revel in a delicious feast, remain healthy until old age, and not rue the decision to overeat. In fact, a repast can be a wholesome and healthy meal if we leave the world of meat and enter the vegetarian kitchen—a more healthy and tasty abode. In this simple culinary world, cereals and legumes make great replacements. Prepared with the right amount of condiments, these fiber-rich edibles make a healthy and satisfying substitute.

The Arabs who occupied the Iberian Peninsula in the eighth century not only introduced into Europe the art of courtly love, magnificent architecture, mathematics, haunting music, advanced sciences, and irrigation; they also enriched the European table with a good number of new fruits, spices and vegetables.

These foods, augmented by new foods from the Americas, drastically changed the meat-based European diet. But Westerners stubbornly clung to the idea that a meatless diet engendered weakness and poor health. In *Walden*, author and philosopher Henry David Thoreau, a vegetarian, relates his encounter with a farmer at his work who insisted that no one could live on vegetables alone, and that meat was necessary for the strengthening of bones. As Thoreau accompanied the farmer behind his sturdy oxen, he observed how the vegetable-made bones of the animals jerked the farmer and his heavy plow through every obstacle in the way. The myth of vegetarianism as a cause of physical debility has been disproved by generations of peasants the world around, a fact that Westerners have come to recognize only in the last half century.

ALGERIAN VEGETARIAN STEW

Ijwaz
Algeria
Serves 8 to 10

Algeria is a land of green coastal plains, towering mountains, and vast deserts. Parts of it have been colonized by Romans, Vandals, Greeks, Spaniards and, most recently, the French. All have left their traces in the country's cuisine. Today a mixture of Arabs and Berbers inhabit Algeria, and their cuisine dominates the land. However, the French who ruled the country for over 130 years, have had a hand in creating the exciting and delicious cuisine of Algeria.

4 tablespoons olive oil
2 medium zucchinis, cut into ¾-inch cubes
1 large eggplant, peeled and cut into ¾-inch cubes
2 large green peppers, chopped into small pieces
1 medium carrot, peeled and chopped into small pieces
3 medium onions, chopped
1 head garlic, peeled and crushed
salt and pepper to taste
2 cups water
2 cups stewed tomatoes
1 tablespoon dried basil

Heat oil in a saucepan; add all ingredients, except tomatoes and basil. Cover and cook over medium heat for 45 minutes; then stir in tomatoes and cook for another 15 minutes. Stir in basil; then place in a serving bowl and serve with cooked rice or mashed potatoes.

ARABIAN PIZZA

Safeehat Hadeetha
Syria and Lebanon
Serves 4

Pizzas have now traveled to the Arab world—where they have been transformed. This simple pizza is popular among the Arabs who have lived many years in North America. It is simple to make and very tasty.

1 large (about 12 inches in diameter) loaf of pita bread, opened
4 medium tomatoes, cut into ¼-inch slices
1 medium onion, thinly sliced
1 tablespoon oregano
salt to taste
½ teaspoon garlic powder
¼ teaspoon pepper
1 cup, crumbled feta cheese
2 tablespoons olive oil

Place opened bread on a greased baking pan; cover evenly with tomato and onion slices. Sprinkle with oregano, salt, garlic powder, and pepper; then spread cheese evenly over top, and, lastly, sprinkle with olive oil.

Bake in an oven preheated to 350°F for 10 to 15 minutes, until the edges of loaves turn dark brown; then broil for 3 minutes. Serve hot.

ARTICHOKE TAJIN

Tajin Khurshuf M'qualli
Morocco
Serves 6

The Spaniards brought the artichoke plant to the Americas. They thrived in California where, today, almost the entire United States commercial crop of about 70 million pounds is grown. Castroville, CA claims to be the artichoke capital of the world.

1 pound fresh or frozen fava beans
4 cloves garlic, peeled and crushed
2 cups cooked chickpeas
4 tablespoons olive oil
1 tablespoon finely chopped fresh ginger

salt and pepper to taste
pinch of saffron
1 14-oz can artichokes, drained and quartered
½ cup pitted green olives

Place beans, garlic, chickpeas, oil, ginger, salt, pepper, and saffron in a saucepan; barely cover with water and bring to boil. Cook over medium heat for 30 minutes; then add the remaining ingredients. Cook for another 20 minutes; then serve hot.

BAKED TOMATOES
Ad-Duqous
Arabian Gulf
Serves 4 to 6

In the last few decades, the wealth generated by the petroleum industry has been instrumental in adding new foods to the once mostly meat diet of the people. Today, there are a wide variety of vegetarian dishes served in the abodes of both the rich and poor.

4 large tomatoes (about 2 pounds), sliced about ¼-inch thick
6 cloves garlic, crushed
4 tablespoons finely chopped fresh cilantro
4 tablespoon olive oil
1 teaspoon paprika
⅛ teaspoon cayenne
salt and pepper to taste

Place tomato slices in a shallow baking dish.
Combine remaining ingredients and spread evenly over tomatoes. Bake in an oven preheated to 350°F, for 25 minutes. Serve hot from casserole.

BASIL-FLAVORED RICE PILAF

Aeesh Alhabaq
Arabian Gulf
Serves 4 to 6

In some parts of the world, basil is a symbol of love. The ancient Greeks employed the herb extensively as a love charm and as an aphrodisiac.

In Italy, country maidens give their beaus basil sprigs to win their love, or they place a pot of basil in the window as a signal to their lovers. If an Italian gentleman comes courting wearing a sprig of basil, he signals his serious intentions.

In the Middle East, it is believed the fragrant odor that a few pots of basil give a room creates an atmosphere conducive to romance.

4 tablespoons butter
2 medium onions, finely chopped
1 cup rice, rinsed
2 cups boiling water
salt and pepper to taste
4 tablespoons pine nuts or slivered almonds, toasted
⅛ teaspoon cayenne
1 teaspoon dried basil

Melt butter in a frying pan and sauté onions until they begin to brown. Add rice and stir-fry for 3 minutes; then add remaining ingredients, except basil, and bring to boil. Cover and cook over medium low heat for 25 minutes. Turn off heat; then allow the pilaf to cook in its own steam for 30 minutes. Stir in basil and serve immediately.

BASIL-FLAVORED TOMATOES

Banadoora bi Habaq
Syria and Lebanon
Serves 4

Unlike the Greeks who ascribed a mystical lure to basil, the Romans did not much appreciate this herb. For some unknown reason, they believed that basil produced scorpions in the human body. This belief put a damper on its use as a condiment. In later centuries, however, the Italians became enamored with this herb of folklore, becoming its largest consumer.

2 tablespoons butter
5 medium tomatoes, chopped
salt and pepper to taste
pinch of cayenne
4 tablespoons finely chopped fresh basil or 2 teaspoons dried basil

Melt butter in a frying pan and add tomatoes, salt, pepper, and cayenne. Cover and simmer over medium low heat for 15 minutes, stirring a few times. Stir in basil; then serve.

BEAN AND CHICKPEA STEW

Tbikhat Fool Masri
Tunisia
Serves 8

A large percentage of Tunisian cooking is connected to the Arabs from Spain. From the time of the fall of Cordoba and Seville in the middle of the thirteenth century until 1609, the expelled Spanish–Arab Muslims came to North Africa in waves. During this period, as many as 150,000 refugees made Tunisia their home.

The immigrants, though Arabic speaking, did not melt into Tunisian society. They established themselves in separate quarters in the cities and built their own villages. Today these quarters and villages, even though not exclusively inhabited by the descendants of the Arab–Andalusian refugees, are still known as Andalusian quarters and Andalusian towns.

The Spanish Arabs sparked a renaissance in Tunisia in all areas of life, including the country's cuisine. Many Tunisian dishes in our time still bear the aura of the Iberian Peninsula.

1 cup dried navy beans, soaked overnight and drained
1 cup dried chickpeas, soaked overnight and drained
6 cups water
6 tablespoons olive oil
3 medium onions, chopped
4 cloves garlic, crushed
2 tablespoons finely chopped fresh cilantro
4 medium tomatoes, chopped
2 cups raw pumpkin, peeled and cut into ½-inch cubes
2 teaspoons *hreesa* (see recipe, p. 17)
1 teaspoon paprika
salt and pepper to taste

Place beans, chickpeas, and water in a saucepan and bring to boil; then cover and cook over medium heat for 2 hours or until beans and chickpeas are tender, adding more water if necessary.

In the meantime, heat oil in a frying pan and sauté onions over medium heat for 10 minutes. Stir in garlic, cilantro, and tomatoes and sauté for another 10 minutes. Transfer frying pan contents to saucepan; then stir in remaining ingredients and bring to boil. Cover and cook over medium heat for 30 minutes or until pumpkin is well cooked, adding more water if necessary. Serve hot with cooked rice.

BEANS AND MUSHROOMS

Fasoolya ma' Futr
Syria and Lebanon
Serves 8

This dish was apparently brought back to the Middle East by immigrants returning from North America. In the past mushrooms were not eaten to a great extent in the countries of the Fertile Crescent.

2 cups dried beans, white or navy, soaked overnight and drained
8 cups water
4 tablespoons olive oil
1 large onion, chopped
6 cloves garlic, finely chopped
1 pound mushrooms, thoroughly washed and sliced
2 cups stewed tomatoes
4 tablespoons molasses
1 teaspoon cumin
1 teaspoon ground coriander seeds
¼ teaspoon cayenne
salt and pepper to taste

Place beans with 8 cups water in a saucepan and bring to boil. Cover and cook over medium heat for 2½ hours.

In the meantime, heat oil in a frying pan and sauté onion and garlic over medium heat for 10 minutes. Add mushrooms and stir-fry for another 10 minutes.

Add frying pan contents and remaining ingredients to beans and bring to boil. Cover and cook over medium heat for 1 hour or until beans are well cooked, adding more water if necessary.

BEANS AND RICE

Fasoolya ma' Rizz
Syria and Lebanon
Serves 6 to 8

In the West, the bean dish most people are familiar with is pork and beans. In contrast, the Arabs prepare innumerable bean dishes using almost all the known types of beans—and many of these dishes are vegetarian.

½ cup dried kidney beans, soaked overnight and drained
6 tablespoons butter
1 cup rice, rinsed
salt to taste
2 cups boiling water
2 medium onions, chopped
2 cloves garlic, crushed
½ teaspoon cumin
½ teaspoon pepper
pinch cayenne

Place beans in a saucepan and cover with water; bring to a boil, then reduce heat and cook for about an hour until beans are tender but still firm. Drain and set aside.

While beans are cooking, melt 4 tablespoons of butter in a frying pan. Add rice and, stirring continually, sauté over high heat for 2 minutes. Add water and salt and bring to boil; then turn the heat to low and cover. Cook for 25 minutes; then turn off heat and allow to finish cooking in its own steam for another 30 minutes.

In another frying pan, melt remaining butter; add onions and garlic and sauté until they turn golden brown. In a serving bowl place fried onions and garlic, beans, rice, and remaining ingredients; mix thoroughly and serve hot with a salad.

BEAN STEW

Loobiya
Morocco
Serves 8

Moroccans are noted for their pride, dignity, and a certain delicacy in their manners. They treat a guest as one of the family. Courtesy and custom govern their daily lives among themselves and in interaction with strangers. While visiting a friend in Fez, Morocco's preserved medieval city, I was made welcome and comfortable by my host, setting the background for enjoying this tasty dish.

2 cups dried navy beans, soaked for 24 hours and drained
4 tablespoons olive oil
2 medium onions, chopped
½ head garlic, peeled and crushed
½ cup finely chopped fresh cilantro
1 small hot pepper, finely chopped
2 cups stewed tomatoes
1 teaspoon paprika
½ teaspoon allspice
salt and pepper to taste
pinch of saffron
4 tablespoons lemon juice

Place beans in a pot and cover with water 2 inches above beans; bring to boil. Cook over medium heat for 2½ hours or until beans are cooked, adding more water if necessary.

In the meantime, heat oil in a frying pan and sauté onions over medium heat for 10 minutes. Add garlic, cilantro, and hot pepper and stir-fry for another 5 minutes.

Add frying pan contents and remaining ingredients, except lemon juice, to beans and bring to boil. Cook for 30 minutes over medium heat, adding more water if necessary. Stir in lemon juice. Serve hot or cold.

Bread and Potato Delight

L'Khobz bi Batata
Morocco
Serves 4

Europeans once thought that potatoes—botanically related to the tomato but not to the sweet potato—had the power to cure impotence. This is perhaps one of the reasons that ever since the Spaniards brought them back to the Old World under the name batata, *their consumption has increased until today they are the world's fourth largest crop after wheat, rice, and corn.*

In our modern age, they are enjoyed in most countries. In North Africa this dish is often prepared by the farmers and laborers of Morocco. It can be served as an appetizer or a snack, as well as a main dish.

2 cups mashed potatoes, still warm
1 cup well-toasted bread, broken into very small pieces
3 tablespoons butter
4 tablespoons finely chopped fresh cilantro
salt and pepper to taste
¼ teaspoon cumin
½ teaspoon paprika
8 black olives, pitted and quartered

Thoroughly combine all ingredients, except paprika and olives; place on a platter. Sprinkle with paprika, then spread olives evenly over top and serve immediately.

BURGHUL CABBAGE ROLLS

Mihshee Malfoof bi Burghul
Syria and Lebanon
Serves 8

Burghul *is prepared by cooking, drying, and breaking up wheat kernels. In the past, the wheat was dried. Today this first-rate wheat product, called by some "the noblest food achieved by man," is produced by machines and electrically controlled ovens.*

1 medium cabbage
2½ cups cooked chickpeas
1 cup coarse *burghul*
2 medium onions, finely chopped
4 tablespoons tomato paste
2 tablespoons finely chopped fresh cilantro
2 tablespoons butter
2 tablespoons finely chopped mint
½ teaspoon allspice
½ teaspoon cumin
⅛ teaspoon cayenne
salt and pepper to taste
8 cloves garlic
2 cups tomato juice

Place cabbage in a pot of boiling water and cook for a few minutes to soften leaves. Remove from water and, with a knife, loosen leaves from the base. If the leaves are still not soft, boil again for a few minutes. When all leaves are cut free, trim the thick ribs, cut large outer leaves in half, and set aside, saving trimmings.

To make filling, place all remaining ingredients, except garlic and tomato juice, in a bowl and thoroughly mix.

Place some filling on the wide end of a cabbage leaf and roll, tucking in the ends in the process. Continue until all leaves are finished.

Cover bottom of saucepan with saved cabbage ribs and any extra leaves. Arrange rolls side by side in layers. Sprinkle a little extra salt and place some of the garlic cloves over each layer. Place an inverted plate on top of the last layer. Add tomato juice and enough water to cover plate. Bring to boil; then cover and cook over medium heat for 50 minutes or until *burghul* is well done. Serve hot or cold.

BURGHUL PILAF

Burghul Mufalfal
Syria and Lebanon
Serves 4

Simple to prepare and versatile, burghul *is inexpensive, natural, wholesome, and flavorful. It is often used instead of rice and cooked in the same fashion. It can be employed in every course and in every meal of the day.*

4 tablespoons butter
1 cup coarse *burghul*
2¼ cups water
salt and pepper to taste

    Melt butter in a frying pan and stir-fry *burghul* over medium heat for 3 minutes. Stir in remaining ingredients and bring to boil. Cover and cook over medium low heat for 25 minutes; then shut off heat and allow to steam for 30 minutes.

Note: Can be served as a side or main dish.

BURGHUL AND POTATO PIE

Kibbet Batata
Syria and Lebanon
Serves 8

In my youth, I always looked forward to my mother preparing this dish—which was quite often. Even though many years have passed, its succulent taste still wins me.

1 cup *burghul*
3 cups mashed potatoes
3 tablespoons flour
½ teaspoon dried basil
½ teaspoon cinnamon
½ teaspoon cumin
⅛ teaspoon cayenne
3 cups finely chopped onions
salt and pepper to taste
6 tablespoons olive oil
4 cloves garlic, crushed
2 tablespoons finely chopped fresh cilantro
½ cup pine nuts or slivered almonds

Soak *burghul* for 10 minutes in warm water; then drain in a strainer, pressing out as much water as possible.

Thoroughly combine *burghul*, potatoes, flour, basil, cinnamon, cumin, cayenne, 1 cup of the onions, salt, and pepper. Divide into two even portions and set aside.

Heat 4 tablespoons of the olive oil in a frying pan and sauté remaining onions, garlic, cilantro, and pine nuts or almonds over medium heat for 10 minutes. If needed, stir in more salt and pepper; then set aside.

Spread a portion of *burghul*–potato mixture evenly in an 7 x 11 inch well-greased pan. Spread frying pan contents evenly over top. Spread second portion of burghul–potato mixture evenly over top. Cut into 2-inch squares; then sprinkle with remaining oil.

Bake in an oven preheated to 400°F for 30 minutes or until the edges turn golden brown. Serve hot or cold.

BURGHUL WITH TOMATOES

Burghul bi Banadoora
Syria and Lebanon
Serves 4 to 6

More versatile than any other vegetable, tomatoes can be canned, dried, frozen, pickled, puréed, or made into a paste. They can be eaten raw, baked, broiled, fried, or stewed; they are the main component in ketchups, relishes, sauces, soups, and a garnish for all types of dishes.

½ cup butter, melted
2 onions, finely chopped
¼ cup pine nuts
4 medium tomatoes, chopped
2 cups water
salt and pepper to taste
¼ teaspoon cinnamon
¼ teaspoon allspice
¼ teaspoon ground coriander
1 cup coarse burghul, rinsed

Melt 3 tablespoons of butter in a frying pan and sauté onions and pine nuts until they turn light brown. Add tomatoes and cook over medium heat for 5 minutes. Stir in water, salt, pepper, cinnamon, allspice, and coriander; then bring to rolling boil. Stir in burghul; then cover and cook over low heat for 25 minutes. Turn off heat and allow to steam for 30 minutes. Spoon remaining butter over the top, then stir lightly and serve immediately.

CABBAGE ROLLS IN OIL

Mihshee Malfoof bi Zayt
Syria and Lebanon
Serves 8

Stuffed vegetable leaves, such as cabbage, kohlrabi, Swiss chard, and wild grape leaves, make an excellent main course for any meal, even a banquet. The herbs and spices soak into the rice and blend with the lemon juice and vegetables, enhancing their flavor. For lovers of vegetarian foods, these stuffed leaves are among the most tasty of meatless dishes.

1 medium head cabbage
1 cup rice, rinsed
½ 19-oz can chickpeas, drained
1 medium onion, finely chopped
1 small bunch green onions, finely chopped
½ cup finely chopped parsley
½ cup finely chopped fresh cilantro
½ cup finely chopped fresh mint
1 cup olive oil
salt and pepper to taste
2 large tomatoes, finely chopped
6 cloves garlic, coarsely chopped
⅔ cup lemon juice

Core cabbage; then place in a large pot. Cover with water, bring to boil, and cook until leaves soften. Separate leaves and trim thick ribs. (Return to pot and boil again for a few minutes if inner leaves are still hard.) Cut large outer leaves in half; then cover bottom of a pot with rib trimmings.

To make the filling, mix remaining ingredients except the garlic and lemon juice. Place a heaping tablespoon of filling on the bottom (stem end) of a leaf; then roll, tucking in the ends. Repeat. Squeeze the rolls gently; then place compactly in pot on top of trimmings, sprinkling garlic pieces between the layers.

When leaves are all rolled and placed in pot, add lemon juice. Place an inverted dish on top of rolls and add water to cover rolls. Bring to boil; then cover and cook over medium heat for 30 minutes. Turn heat to low and simmer for 15 minutes. Serve either hot or cold as a main dish or for snacks.

Note: Swiss chard and other vegetable leaves or grape leaves may be substituted for the cabbage.

CARROTS WITH YOGURT

Jazar ma' Laban
Egypt
Serves 4 to 6

The Spanish word for carrots, zanahoria, *is taken from the Arabic* isfannariya, *which is Arabic for parsnips. In modern Arabic this word does not connote carrots.*

2 pounds carrots, scraped, then cut lengthwise into quarters
salt and pepper to taste
boiling water
¼ cup butter
4 cloves garlic, crushed
1½ cups yogurt
¼ cup finely chopped fresh cilantro
1 teaspoon chili powder

Place carrots, salt, and pepper in a saucepan; add enough boiling water to cover carrots. Cover and cook for 20 minutes; then remove and drain. Set aside.

Melt butter in a frying pan; then add garlic and carrots and sauté over medium heat for 10 minutes, turning carrots over once or twice.

Arrange carrots on a flat serving dish; then pour yogurt evenly over carrots. Garnish with cilantro; then sprinkle with chili powder and serve hot.

CASHEW NUT KIBBEH

Kibbet Kashew
Syria and Lebanon
Serves 6 to 8

This dish is a relatively new invention—a testimony to the ever-evolving Arab cuisine. A gourmet delight, it makes a rich addition to the vegetarian kitchen.

1 cup fine *burghul*
1 cup raw cashew nuts
3 cups chopped onions
2 tablespoons flour
1½ teaspoons salt
¾ teaspoon pepper
¼ teaspoon allspice
¼ teaspoon cumin
¼ teaspoon cinnamon
⅛ teaspoon cayenne
8 tablespoons olive oil
3 cloves garlic, crushed

Soak *burghul* in warm water for 10 minutes; place in strainer and press out water. Set aside.

Place in the bowl of a food processor cashews, 1 cup of the onions, flour, 1 teaspoon of the salt, ½ teaspoon of the pepper, allspice, cumin, cinnamon, cayenne, 2 tablespoons of the oil, and *burghul*; then process into a coarse paste and set aside.

Heat 4 tablespoons of the olive oil in a frying pan and stir-fry remaining onions and garlic over medium heat until they begin to brown. Stir in remaining salt and pepper; then set aside.

Divide food processor mixture into two equal portions. Spread one portion evenly in 7 x 11-inch greased pan. Spread frying pan contents over top, then spread second portion of mixture evenly over top of onions. Cut into 2-inch squares; then sprinkle with remaining olive oil.

Bake in an oven preheated to 350°F for 40 minutes. Serve hot or cold.

CHEESE PIZZA
Safeehat Jiban
Syria and Lebanon
Makes 12 individual pies

The Arabs of Syria and Lebanon have their own kind of pizzas, which they call safeeha. *Like the well-known pizzas of North America, the Arab versions come with a variety of toppings. This traditional cheese pizza is wholesome and tasty, especially fresh out of the oven—great for breakfast.*

1 basic dough (see recipe, p. 11)
2 large onions, finely chopped
1 cup black olives, pitted and quartered
1 teaspoon marjoram
⅛ teaspoon cayenne
salt and pepper to taste
3 tablespoons olive oil
1½ cups grated mozzarella cheese

Form dough into 12 balls; then cover with a damp cloth and allow to rest for 30 minutes.

In the meantime, combine remaining ingredients, except cheese, to make a topping; set aside.

Roll dough balls into 6-inch rounds; then pinch edges to make a raised rim. Place rounds on greased baking pans. Spread topping inside rims; then sprinkle with cheese.

Bake in an oven preheated to 350°F, for 20 minutes or until rims of pizzas turn golden brown. Serve hot.

Note: An alternate topping can be made from 2 cups tomato sauce, 1 teaspoon dried basil, 1 teaspoon garlic powder, and salt and pepper to taste; sprinkle with 2 cups of grated mozzarella cheese.

Chickpea and Burghul Patties

Kibbet Hummus
Syria and Lebanon
Makes about 60 small patties

Vegetarians in the West are always searching for new dishes to add variety to their meals. One day they will discover kibbeh with chickpeas, and when they do, it will surely become a favorite.

1 cup dry *burghul*
1 19-oz can chickpeas, drained
2 medium onions, chopped
4 cloves garlic, crushed
¼ cup finely chopped fresh cilantro
1 teaspoon baking powder
1 teaspoon baking soda
½ teaspoon cumin
½ teaspoon allspice
pinch cayenne
salt and pepper to taste
1 cup flour
oil for frying

Soak *burghul* in boiling water for 5 minutes; then drain in a strainer, pressing out as much water as possible.

Place all ingredients, except flour and oil, in a food processor and process until a soft paste is formed. Place in a mixing bowl; then add flour and mix thoroughly. Form into balls the size of walnuts. (If batter is too sticky, add more flour; if too stiff, add a little water.) Flatten into patties, about ¼-inch thick.

Heat oil about ½ inch deep in a saucepan and fry patties a few at a time over medium high heat until they turn golden brown, turning them over once (about 10 minutes on each side). Remove and place on paper towels to drain.

Serve either hot or cold. (They reheat well on foil plates in the oven.)

Note: To make *kibbet 'adas* (lentil *kibbeh*), 1 19-oz can of lentils may be substituted for the chickpeas.

CHICKPEAS WITH GREEN BEANS

Hummus ma' Loobya
Syria and Lebanon
Serves 4 to 6

This dish is often on the Middle Eastern daily menu. It is tasty, simple to prepare, and very nourishing.

4 tablespoons olive oil
4 medium onions, chopped
1 cup chickpeas, soaked for 24 hours and split (see p. 3 for directions)
1 pound green beans, washed, trimmed, and halved
salt and pepper to taste
½ teaspoon allspice
4 large tomatoes, chopped into small pieces

Heat oil in a saucepan and sauté onions over medium heat until they begin to brown. Add chickpeas and green beans and stir-fry for 10 minutes. Add remaining ingredients and cover with water; then cover saucepan and cook over medium heat for about an hour or until chickpeas are tender. Serve hot or cold.

Chickpea Kababs

Kabab An-Nikhi
Arabian Gulf
Makes about 36 patties

Like numerous other dishes now common in the Arabian Gulf countries, this dish probably came from the Indian subcontinent. Wholesome and tasty, these fried patties can be served as an entrée, as a side dish, and for snacks.

1 19-oz can chickpeas, drained
1 medium onion, chopped
1 medium tomato, chopped
½ cup fresh or frozen green peas
½ small sweet green pepper, chopped
1 teaspoon baking powder
½ cup flour
1 teaspoon cumin
1 teaspoon ground coriander seeds
salt and pepper to taste
2 tablespoons finely chopped fresh cilantro
2 eggs
oil for frying

Place all ingredients, except oil, in a food processor and process into soft dough, adding as much water or flour as necessary. Make sure that chickpeas are well ground.

Place oil in a saucepan, about 1½ inches deep; then heat. Spoon dough, by heaping spoonfuls a few at a time, into the oil. Fry until golden brown, turning kababs over once. If kababs tend to break up in the oil, add more egg or flour to the dough. Continue until all the dough is used. Drain kababs on paper towels; then serve warm.

CHICKPEA AND LENTIL STEW

Markit Ommalah
Tunisia
Serves 8

After savoring a delicious traditional soup at the home of a friend in Tunisia one winter day, a servant came in with a steaming dish of markit ommalah, *a chickpea stew accompanied by* tajin, *a Tunisian shepherd pie filled with eggs and cheese. To add flavor to our meal, she set before each person a small dish of* hreesa, *a fiery sauce of red-hot peppers, garlic, and salt.*

After the meal was finished, when we praised our host for the tasty food, he smiled: "Wait until my wife returns from her vacation, then you will never forget the delights of the Tunisian cuisine."

4 tablespoons olive oil
2 medium onions, chopped
4 cloves garlic, finely chopped
½ cup finely chopped fresh cilantro
1 cup lentils, soaked overnight and drained
3 cups cooked chickpeas
4 medium tomatoes, chopped
1 teaspoon cumin
½ teaspoon thyme
⅛ teaspoon cayenne
salt and pepper to taste
3 cups water
¼ cup chopped green olives
2 tablespoons lemon juice

Heat oil in a saucepan and sauté onions, garlic, and cilantro for 5 minutes. Stir in remaining ingredients, except olives and lemon juice, and bring to boil. Cover and cook over medium heat for 40 minutes or until lentils are well cooked, adding more water if necessary. Stir in olives and lemon juice; then simmer for 5 minutes and serve.

CHICKPEAS WITH MACARONI

Macaronis Lablabee
Tunisia
Serves 6

In availability, price, food value, versatility, and flavor, chickpeas are without match when compared to other legumes. There is no better way to convince the uninitiated than by sampling a few dishes that make use of this tasty and nourishing legume.

2 tablespoons olive oil
2 medium onions, chopped
3 cloves garlic, crushed
¼ cup finely chopped fresh cilantro
1 small hot pepper, very finely chopped
1 19-oz can stewed tomatoes
1 19-oz can chickpeas, with its liquid
1½ cups elbow macaroni
1 cup water
salt and pepper to taste
¼ teaspoon allspice
¼ teaspoon cumin

Heat oil in a frying pan and sauté onions and garlic over medium heat until they begin to turn brown. Stir in cilantro and hot pepper and sauté for another few moments. Transfer frying pan contents to a casserole. Add remaining ingredients and stir; then bake in an oven preheated to 350°F, for about 40 minutes or until the macaroni is cooked.

CHICKPEA OPEN-FACED PIE

Safeehat Hummus
Syria and Lebanon
Makes 20 pies

To the eastern Christians in the Arab world, Lent, the great feast beginning seven weeks before Easter, is the most important time of the religious year. As it approaches, households prepare for the feast. For the wealthy especially, the daily menu undergoes a drastic change from rich dishes to vegetarian ones. Excluded from the diet are all types of meats, as well as cheese, eggs, and milk.

These tasty pies are one of the dishes prepared for the feast.

¾ cup dried chickpeas
1 teaspoon baking soda
1 basic dough (see recipe, p. 11)
6 tablespoons olive oil
2 tablespoons sumac
½ teaspoon oregano
½ teaspoon salt
½ teaspoon pepper
½ teaspoon nutmeg

Soak chickpeas overnight in water and baking soda. Drain.

Form dough into 20 balls; then cover and allow to rest for 30 minutes.

In the meantime, combine remaining ingredients, except chickpeas, and set aside.

Roll balls into rounds 4 to 5 inches in diameter; then place on well-greased baking trays. Brush tops with spice mixture; then press the chickpeas into the dough.

Bake in an oven preheated to 350°F, for 20 minutes or until edges of pies turn golden brown. Serve hot.

CHICKPEAS WITH SPICES

An-Nikhi
Arabian Gulf
Serves 6 to 8

Simple to prepare, delicious and nutritious, this dish has been on the daily menu in Arabian Gulf households for centuries. When broad beans are substituted for the chickpeas, the dish is called bajelah; *when black-eyed peas are substituted for the chickpeas, the dish is called* luba. *For centuries the toiling masses have depended on these dishes for sustenance. For many they are more important than fish—the mainstay of the people of the Arabian Gulf.*

2 cups dried chickpeas
1 teaspoon baking soda
1 hot pepper, finely chopped
4 tablespoons olive oil
1 teaspoon ground coriander seeds
1 teaspoon cumin
salt and pepper to taste
3 tablespoons lemon juice

The day before, place chickpeas in a bowl and cover with 6 cups water; then stir in baking soda. Allow to stand overnight.

Drain chickpeas and place in a saucepan. Cover with water to about 2 inches over chickpeas; stir in remaining ingredients, except lemon juice, and bring to boil. Cover and cook over medium heat until chickpeas are tender, adding more water if necessary. Stir in lemon juice; serve in deep dishes with cooking liquid.

CHICKPEAS WITH TOMATOES & SWEET PEPPERS

Yahnee
Libya
Serves 6 to 8

Chickpeas can be found in Arab, Armenian, Greek, Indian, Italian, and Spanish food stores as well as in many supermarkets. They can be purchased in bulk, in packages, or precooked in cans.

2 cups chickpeas, soaked for 24 hours, drained, and split
    (see p. 3 for instructions)
½ cup olive oil
2 medium sweet red peppers, chopped into small pieces
1 small hot pepper, finely chopped
1 large onion, chopped into small pieces
2 cloves garlic, crushed
1 pound fresh tomatoes, chopped into small pieces
2 tablespoons parsley, finely chopped
salt to taste
½ teaspoon black pepper
½ teaspoon basil
½ teaspoon tarragon

Place chickpeas in a pot and add water to about an inch over chickpeas. Bring to boil; then cover and cook over medium heat for about an hour or until chickpeas are tender, adding more water if necessary.

In the meantime, heat oil in a saucepan; stir-fry sweet and hot peppers, onion, and garlic over medium heat until vegetables turn limp. Stir in remaining ingredients; then cover. Turn heat to low and simmer for 30 minutes. Stir in chickpeas; then simmer for another ten minutes and serve immediately.

Note: If a thicker stew is desired, the chickpeas can be drained after being cooked.

CHICKPEA AND YOGURT PLATTER

Fattat Hummus
Syria and Lebanon
Serves 6

When visiting friends in Damascus, I was often served this tasty dish, usually as part of a hearty breakfast.

2 medium loaves pita bread, toasted and broken into small pieces
1 19-oz can chickpeas, drained
1 cup plain yogurt
1 clove garlic, crushed
salt and pepper to taste
seeds of one pomegranate
2 tablespoons lemon juice
1 tablespoon tahini
2 tablespoons butter
4 tablespoons pine nuts
2 tablespoons chopped parsley

Place bread on a platter; then spread chickpeas evenly over top and set aside.

Thoroughly combine yogurt, garlic, salt, pepper, pomegranate seeds, lemon juice, and tahini; then spread over chickpeas.

Melt butter in a frying pan and sauté pine nuts until they begin to brown. Spread pine nuts and butter over the yogurt mixture; then garnish with parsley and serve.

Dates with Rice

Aeesh Altamar
Arabian Peninsula
Serves 6

Main courses cooked with fruit are common in the Arabian Peninsula and in Morocco, the extreme east and west of the Arab world. Oddly, in the countries in between, you seldom find entrées cooked with fruit.

1 cup rice, rinsed
2¼ cups water
salt to taste
5 tablespoons butter, melted
½ cup blanched slivered almonds
2 tablespoons raisins
¾ cup dates, chopped
½ teaspoon cinnamon
pinch of ground cloves

In a pot, cook rice in 2 cups of the water and salt for 10 minutes. Drain, rinse with warm water, and set aside.

In the meantime, place 2½ tablespoons of the butter in a frying pan and sauté almonds until they begin to brown; then stir in raisins, dates, cinnamon, and cloves. Sauté for 3 minutes over low heat; then add remaining ¼ cup of water and simmer for 20 minutes, stirring often to make sure the contents do not burn, adding a little extra water if necessary.

Place half of rice in a saucepan; then dot with 1 tablespoon of the butter. Top with frying pan contents; then cover with the remainder of the rice. Dot with remaining 1½ tablespoons of butter; then top with inverted plate and cover. Simmer over very low heat for 15 minutes; then turn off heat and allow to steam for another 15 minutes. Serve hot.

EGGPLANT AND CHEESE CASSEROLE

Bathinjan ma' Jiban
Syria and Lebanon
Serves 6 to 8

Appealing to the eye, delicious, and versatile, eggplants are a vegetarian's ideal vegetable. In all shapes, from round or egg-shaped to fingerlike and tiny and in colors from jet-black to light purple, this attractive vegetable is catching the fancy of an increasing number of people.

1 large eggplant, peeled and cut into ½-inch slices
½ cup olive oil
2 cups stewed tomatoes
¼ pound feta or other white cheese, very thinly sliced
½ cup finely chopped parsley
¼ cup finely chopped fresh cilantro
3 large eggs, beaten
1 large onion, finely chopped
salt and pepper to taste
¼ teaspoon allspice
¼ teaspoon oregano
¼ teaspoon sage
pinch of cayenne

Sprinkle eggplant slices with salt; then place in a strainer. Top with a weight and allow to drain for 45 minutes.

Heat oil in a frying pan and sauté eggplant slices over moderately high heat until they begin to turn golden brown, adding more oil if necessary. Remove slices from oil and place in a strainer or on paper towels to drain.

Place eggplant slices in a casserole; then cover evenly with tomatoes, cheese, parsley, and cilantro, in that order.

In a separate bowl, combine eggs with onion, pepper, allspice, oregano, sage, and cayenne; then pour evenly over the top of ingredients in casserole. Cover the casserole and bake in an oven preheated to 300°F, for 30 minutes. Remove cover, and bake for another 10 minutes. Serve hot or cold.

EGGPLANT AND CHICKPEA STEW

Munazalit Bathinjan
Syria and Lebanon
Serves 8

Fried, pureed, made into salads or stuffed, eggplants stimulate the appetite and make diners smack their lips. They are at their finest as ingredients in stews. Browned in olive oil or butter, then simmered in herbs and spices, they enhance the other ingredients.

1 medium eggplant, peeled and cut into 1-inch cubes
salt to taste
6 tablespoons olive oil
1 large onion, finely chopped
3 cloves garlic, crushed
1 19-oz can chickpeas, with their liquid
2 zucchinis (about 5 inches long), cut into 1-inch cubes
1 19-oz can tomatoes
3 tablespoons finely chopped fresh cilantro
¼ teaspoon pepper
¼ teaspoon nutmeg

Sprinkle eggplant cubes with salt; then place in a strainer. Top with a weight and allow to drain for 45 minutes.

Heat oil in a saucepan and sauté eggplant cubes over moderately high heat until they begin to brown, adding more oil if necessary. Add onion and garlic and gently stir-fry for a few minutes more. Stir in chickpeas with their liquid, zucchini cubes, tomatoes, cilantro, pepper, and nutmeg, and bring to boil. Cover and turn heat to low. Simmer for 30 minutes, adding more water if necessary. Serve hot or cold.

EGGPLANT IN OIL

Bathinjan bi Zayt
Palestine and Jordan
Serves 8

Requiring long warm summers to mature, eggplants thrive best in the tropical parts of the world. They grow from one to two feet high and produce fruit weighing from a few ounces to over two pounds. They are attractive plants, at times grown for ornamental purposes. However, they are mainly cultivated for their edible fruit.

salt to taste
2 medium eggplants, peeled and cut into ½-inch thick slices
¾ cup olive oil
4 large onions, cut into ¼-inch slices
3 cloves garlic, crushed
¼ cup finely chopped fresh cilantro
5 medium tomatoes, cut into ½-inch slices
½ teaspoon pepper
¼ teaspoon allspice
¼ teaspoon tarragon
pinch of cayenne
1 cup water

Sprinkle salt on eggplant slices and place in a strainer. Top with a weight and allow to drain for 45 minutes.

Heat oil in a frying pan; add onions, garlic, and cilantro. Sauté until onions begin to brown; then remove with a slotted spoon and place at bottom of a casserole. Sauté eggplant slices in same oil until they turn soft, adding more oil if necessary.

Remove eggplant slices from oil and drain on paper towels or in a strainer. Place eggplant and tomato slices in alternate layers on top of onions. Sprinkle with pepper, allspice, tarragon, cayenne, and salt if needed. Pour water over top; then place in an oven preheated to 350°F, and bake for 30 minutes. Serve hot or cold from casserole; accompany with cooked rice.

FALAFEL, EGYPTIAN-STYLE

Ta'amia
Egypt
Makes about 40 patties

This tasty vegetarian delight is the "hamburger" of the Middle East. The simplest way to make it is to purchase the falafel, or ta'amia, *powder ready-made in stores selling Arabic or Middle Eastern foods.*

Although ready-made falafel is simple to prepare, it is not as tasty as that made from scratch. This recipe, common in Egypt, is how true ta'amia *is made.*

4 cups dried fava beans, soaked overnight and drained
3 large onions, coarsely chopped
1 head of garlic, peeled
1 large bunch of parsley, washed, stems removed
2 hot green peppers, seeds removed
2 teaspoons cumin
salt to taste
1 teaspoon pepper
1 teaspoon ground coriander seeds
1 teaspoon baking powder
1 teaspoon baking soda
oil for frying

Place beans, onions, garlic, parsley, and hot pepper in a food processor; then process until beans are very finely ground. Add cumin, salt, pepper, coriander, baking powder, and baking soda; then process to a dough-like paste. Remove from processor and form into patties. If patties tend to crumble, process further or add a little flour.

Heat oil in a deep fryer or saucepan; fry patties, turning them over once or twice, until they turn golden brown and crisp on the outside.

Serve patties sandwiched in half-rounds of pita bread stuffed with tossed salad ingredients. Patties can also be served as an entrée with tossed salad on the side.

Falafel, Syrian and Lebanese-Style

Falaafil
Syria and Lebanon
Makes 20 patties

In the lands that rim the eastern Mediterranean, falafel are a snack food par excellence. Their mouth-watering aromas waft from the cooking stalls in Aleppo, Damascus, Jerusalem, and other Middle Eastern cities, enticing passers-by as if begging to relieve their hunger pangs.

In the West, these Old World croquettes are now quite popular in large urban centers. The word falafel, derived from the Arabic word fulful *or* filfil *meaning "pepper," has now entered the English vocabulary and can even be found in English-language dictionaries.*

1 cup fava beans, soaked overnight and drained
1 cup chickpeas, soaked overnight and drained
3 medium onions, chopped
1 small bunch parsley, chopped
8 cloves garlic, crushed
1 teaspoon ground coriander
1 teaspoon cumin
2 teaspoons salt
1 teaspoon pepper
¼ teaspoon chili powder
1 teaspoon baking soda
oil for frying

Place fava beans, chickpeas, and onions in a food processor and process until beans and chickpeas are very finely ground. Add remaining ingredients, except oil; process to a dough-like paste. Form into patties—if patties tend to crumble, process further or add a little flour.

Heat oil in a saucepan and fry patties over medium heat, turning until they are golden brown on both sides.

Serve patties warm as main dish with fresh vegetables and Sesame Tahini Sauce (see p. 18) on the side or in sandwiches of half-rounds of pita bread stuffed with salad vegetables and topped with Tahini Mix (see pp. 48-49).

FALAFEL, YEMENI-STYLE

Falaafil Yamanee
Yemen
Makes about 48 small patties

This Yemeni version is like falafel made in the Fertile Crescent countries and Egypt, but consists wholly of chickpeas and includes eggs in the ingredients.

2 cups dried chickpeas, soaked for 24 hours and drained
½ head garlic, peeled and crushed
½ cup finely chopped fresh cilantro
1 cup finely chopped parsley
1 cup finely chopped green onions
1 egg
salt and pepper to taste
1 teaspoon ground coriander seeds
1 teaspoon cumin
1 teaspoon baking soda
¼ teaspoon cayenne

Place chickpeas in food processor and process until they are very finely ground. Add remaining ingredients and process until dough-like paste is formed.

Shape into patties and place on a pan or baking sheet coated with oil. Bake in an oven preheated to 350°F, for 30 minutes or until done.

Note: Patties may be deep fried, a less healthy but more flavorful version.

Fava Beans of Fez

Fool Fass
Morocco
Serves 4

Fava beans (also known as fool, broad, vicia, Windsor, English, dwarf, or horse beans) have been grown in western Asia and North Africa from earliest recorded history. Through the centuries, their cultivation has spread to every corner of the globe.

There are numerous types of fava beans. The most common plant grows from two to four feet high and produces large thick pods with flat angular seeds. The size of the seeds (or beans) varies from that of a pea to over an inch long and half-an-inch wide.

2 cups fresh or frozen fava beans
4 tablespoons olive oil
1 large sweet red pepper, finely chopped
4 cloves garlic, crushed
salt to taste
1 teaspoon cumin
1 tablespoon finely chopped fresh cilantro
¼ teaspoon chili powder

Place all ingredients in a saucepan and cover with water; cook for 10 to 15 minutes until fava beans are tender. Serve hot or cold.

Fava Beans in Oil

Fooliyya
Syria and Lebanon
Serves 4 to 6

The cool climate of Europe is ideal for growing fava beans. From Roman times to the discovery of America, fava beans were the only edible beans known to the inhabitants of that continent. In pre-Columbian Europe, this legume, which some have called "the bean of history," nourished all strata of society. It was only after the discovery of the New World that it was replaced by beans newly introduced from the Americas.

Why fava beans lost favor is still a mystery, as they are among the most delicious of legumes. Perhaps the long period required for growth had something to do with their falling out of favor. Other types of beans grow in a much shorter time from seed to harvest. To produce a good crop, fava beans must be planted very early in spring.

4 tablespoons olive oil
3 cloves garlic, crushed
1 large onion, chopped
salt and pepper to taste
¼ teaspoon allspice
1 tablespoon finely chopped fresh cilantro
3 cups shelled fresh fava beans
3 tablespoons lemon juice

Heat olive oil in a saucepan; add garlic, onion, salt, pepper, allspice, and cilantro. Sauté over medium heat until onions begin to brown; then stir in fava beans. Barely cover with water and cook over medium heat for approximately 30 minutes or until beans are tender. Stir in lemon juice; then cook a few more minutes. Serve hot or cold.

Fava Bean Pottage

Fool Mudammas
Egypt
Serves 4

In Egypt fool mudammas *is the usual breakfast for most of the population. In the early morning hours, the streets of the cities in the Nile Valley are filled with people lined up in front of vendors selling tempting* fool mudammas *from earthenware pots.*

Even though in the West there are no vendors with pots of steaming fava beans, anyone can produce delicious fool mudammas *with hardly any effort by following this recipe.*

1 cup dried fava beans, soaked overnight and drained
4 tablespoons olive oil
salt and pepper to taste
½ teaspoon ground coriander
½ teaspoon cumin
4 tablespoons lemon juice
2 cloves garlic, crushed
4 hard-boiled eggs, shelled
2 tablespoons finely chopped fresh cilantro

Place beans in a saucepan and top with 2 inches of water. Cover and cook over medium heat for 45 minutes to an hour or until beans are very tender, adding more water if necessary. Drain beans and place in a mixing bowl; add 2 tablespoons of the olive oil, salt, pepper, ground coriander, cumin, lemon juice, and garlic. Stir well, allowing some of beans to become slightly crushed.

Transfer to 4 soup bowls and place an egg in the center of each bowl. Sprinkle each with remaining oil; then garnish with cilantro and serve.

Fava Beans and Tomatoes

Fool ma' Tomatim
Palestine and Jordan
Serves 4 to 6

Unlike green vegetables, tomatoes lose few of their vitamins in cooking. Canned tomatoes are the most widely utilized of all canned garden products. Yearly, the average North American consumes about 23 pounds of processed tomatoes out of a total of 58 pounds for all vegetables.

4 tablespoons olive oil
2 medium onions, finely chopped
2 cloves garlic, crushed
2 cups fresh shelled fava beans
2 tablespoons finely chopped fresh cilantro
¼ teaspoon chili powder
¼ teaspoon cumin
salt and pepper to taste
2 cups stewed tomatoes

Heat oil in a saucepan and stir-fry onions and garlic until they begin to brown. Add beans and cilantro and stir-fry a few more minutes. Stir in remaining ingredients and add water to barely cover beans; bring to a boil. Cover; then turn heat to low and simmer for about 1 hour, adding a little water if necessary. Serve hot or cold.

FEZ CARROTS

Jazar Fass
Morocco
Serves 4 to 6

In the Arab world, cooking carrots with sugar is unique to North Africa. For a good number of food connoisseurs, carrots cooked in this way reach their ultimate in taste.

4 tablespoons butter
1 pound carrots, peeled and sliced into ½-inch thick rounds
2 medium onions, thinly sliced
½ teaspoon nutmeg
salt to taste
¼ cup white grape juice
¼ cup seedless raisins, soaked in water for 30 minutes and drained
1 tablespoon sugar

Melt butter in frying pan and sauté carrots for 5 minutes over medium heat. Turn heat to low; then add onions, nutmeg, salt, and grape juice. Cover frying pan and simmer, stirring occasionally, until carrots are tender. Add raisins and sugar and cook uncovered, stirring, for a few minutes. Serve.

FRIED CUCUMBERS

Khiyar Maqlee
Syria and Lebanon
Serves 4

Even though cucumbers prepared in this fashion are perhaps a bit unusual, their flavor is excellent.

1 large cucumber, peeled and cut into ½-inch rounds
salt and pepper to taste
½ cup flour
¼ teaspoon garlic powder
¾ cup olive or vegetable oil
½ cup green onions, finely chopped

Sprinkle both sides of cucumber rounds with salt and allow to stand in a strainer for 30 minutes, draining excess water.

Thoroughly combine flour, pepper, and garlic powder; then roll cucumber rounds in seasoned flour.

Heat oil in a frying pan and fry cucumber rounds until they turn evenly brown, adding more oil if necessary. Place on a serving platter; then sprinkle with chopped onions and serve.

FRIED EGGPLANT

Bathinjan Maqlee
Syria and Lebanon
Serves 4

When eggplants are to be fried or used in salads or stews, after slicing or cubing, they should be sliced or diced according to the recipe, then placed in a strainer and sprinkled with salt. A weight is placed on top and the eggplant pieces are allowed to drain. This removes the bitter juices.

At the start of cooking, fry the eggplant pieces quickly over high heat to cut down on the amount of oil or other fat that is absorbed.

1 large eggplant, unpeeled, cut into ½-inch thick slices
salt to taste
¼ teaspoon pepper
½ teaspoon garlic powder
½ teaspoon ground coriander

½ cup olive oil
2 tablespoons lemon juice

Sprinkle eggplant pieces with salt and place in a strainer. Top with a weight and allow to drain for 45 minutes.

Combine pepper, garlic powder, and coriander and sprinkle this mixture on the drained eggplant slices.

Heat oil in a frying pan and fry eggplant slices over high heat on both sides until they are evenly browned, adding more oil if necessary.

Place on a serving platter and sprinkle with lemon juice. Serve hot or cold as a side dish.

Note: Eggplant cooked this way also makes an excellent sandwich with pita bread.

FRIED EGGPLANT, PALESTINIAN-STYLE
Bathinjan Maqlee Falasteeni
Palestine and Jordan
Serves 4

Centuries of experience have demonstrated that olive oil is the perfect medium for cooking or preserving eggplants.

1 large eggplant, peeled and cut into ½-inch slices
salt to taste
½ cup olive oil
2 cloves garlic, crushed
1 hot green pepper, very finely chopped
3 tablespoons lemon juice
6 tablespoons finely chopped parsley

Sprinkle both sides of eggplant slices with salt; then place in a bowl and cover with water. Allow to soak for 15 minutes; then remove eggplant slices from water and allow to dry on paper towels. [This method of salting is common to some parts of Palestine and Jordan. The fried eggplant that has been salted in this manner tends to be crispier on the outside and moist inside.]

Heat oil in a frying pan and fry eggplant slices over high heat, turning them over until they brown on both sides; adding more oil if necessary. Remove with a slotted spoon, place on a serving platter, and set aside.

Prepare a sauce by mixing remaining ingredients, except parsley. Spread sauce evenly over eggplant slices. Garnish with parsley and serve.

FRIED EGGPLANT WITH YOGURT SAUCE

Bathinjan Maqlee bi Laban
Palestine and Jordan
Serves 4

Arab recipes that combine yogurt and vegetables are as old as time itself. Every town and city has its own version; the variations are endless. The vegetables and seasonings may be interchanged with others, or omitted to suit the diner's taste. The yogurt enhances any combination.

1 large eggplant, peeled, quartered lengthwise, and cut into ½-inch slices
salt to taste
½ cup olive oil
½ cup yogurt
1 clove garlic, crushed
2 tablespoons very finely chopped fresh cilantro
½ teaspoon pepper
pinch of cayenne

Sprinkle eggplant slices with salt and place in a strainer. Top with a weight and allow to drain for 45 minutes.

Heat oil in a frying pan and sauté eggplant slices over high heat, turning until they brown on both sides. Add more oil if necessary. Place eggplant slices on paper towels and drain; then arrange on a serving platter and set aside to cool.

Prepare a sauce by thoroughly mixing yogurt, garlic, cilantro, pepper, cayenne, and salt if desired. Spoon sauce over eggplant slices, or serve separately, allowing diners to add sauce to their taste.

Fried Tomatoes with Garlic

Banadoora Maqliya ma' Thoom
Palestine and Jordan
Serves 4

Botanically a fruit, but in practice a vegetable, tomatoes belong to the nightshade family. Nightshades to include some deadly types—no doubt, the root of the belief, held for centuries, that they are all are poisonous. A rapid-growing short-lived sun-loving annual, they come in hundreds of varieties. It is said that every year a new type of tomato is developed. Very prolific, they are simple to grow—in fields, gardens, patios or in pots on window sills.

4 cloves garlic, crushed
salt and pepper to taste
½ small hot pepper, very finely chopped
4 tablespoons chopped fresh parsley
2 tablespoons olive oil
2 large, firm tomatoes, cut in slices

Thoroughly combine garlic, salt, pepper and hot pepper; then stir in parsley and set aside. Heat oil in a frying pan and fry tomato slices over medium heat for about a minute on one side. Turn slices over and sprinkle with garlic, hot pepper, and parsley mixture. Fry for another minute, shaking the pan occasionally; then turn slices again and fry for another 2 minutes. Slide tomato slices onto a plate and serve immediately.

Note: Do not try to cook more than two servings at a time or the tomatoes will end up overcooked. This tomato dish is great scooped up with pita bread.

GARLIC FRIED POTATOES

Batata Maqliya ma' Thoom
Palestine and Jordan
Serves 4

The English eat their fried potatoes or "chips" with vinegar; North Americans consume them with ketchup or vinegar. The Arabs relish their fried potatoes with garlic and lemon.

5 large potatoes (about 2 pounds)
oil for frying
½ head garlic, peeled and crushed
4 tablespoons finely chopped fresh cilantro
salt and pepper to taste
⅛ teaspoon cayenne
2 tablespoons butter
1 lemon, cut into wedges

Peel and dice potatoes into ½-inch cubes.

Place oil in saucepan 2 inches deep and heat. Fry potato cubes until they barely begin to brown; then drain on paper towels.

Combine remaining ingredients, except butter and lemon wedges, in a bowl; then stir in potato cubes.

Melt butter in a frying pan and add potato mixture. Stir-fry for about 3 minutes. Place on a serving platter; then garnish with lemon wedges. Serve hot. Each diner squeezes lemon juice over potatoes.

GRAPE LEAVES STUFFED WITH LENTILS

Mihshee Waraq 'Inab ma' 'Adas
Syria and Lebanon
Serves 6 to 8

In the eastern Arab world, grape leaves are stuffed with various combinations: rice and meat, rice and burghul, *rice and onions, rice and lentils. The latter three, of which this recipe is one, are excellent vegetarian dishes.*

¾ cup brown or green lentils
½ cup oil
¼ cup lemon juice
¾ cup rice, rinsed
1 cup finely chopped fresh mint, or 3 tablespoons dried mint
1 bunch green onions, finely chopped
½ teaspoon allspice
salt and pepper to taste
1 teaspoon cumin
1 pound canned or bottled grape leaves, thoroughly washed and drained
1½ cups tomato juice
water

Place lentils in a saucepan and cover with water; then cook about 15 minutes until half-cooked and drain. Make stuffing by mixing the lentils, ¼ cup of the oil, half the lemon juice, rice, mint, onions, allspice, salt, pepper, and cumin.

Place about 1 heaping tablespoon of the stuffing on each grape leaf and roll, tucking in the ends. If grape leaf is small, decrease stuffing; if large increase stuffing.

Place a few unstuffed grape leaves in the bottom of the pot. Arrange rolled grape leaves in the pot in layers. Pour tomato juice, remaining oil, and lemon juice over the rolls; invert a plate over the rolls to keep them from floating. Pour in enough water to cover the plate; then bring to boil. Reduce heat and simmer over low heat for 40 minutes or until rice inside the rolls is tender but still intact. Serve hot or cold.

Leek Pies

Fatayar Kurath
Syria and Lebanon
Makes 15 to 20 pies

Green onions may be substituted for the leeks in this dish. Also, if desired, the feta cheese may be omitted.

1 bunch (3 or 4) leeks
6 medium onions, peeled and chopped
3 teaspoons sumac
salt and pepper to taste
½ cup feta cheese
½ cup lemon juice
4 tablespoons olive oil
1 basic dough (see recipe, p. 11)
extra olive oil

After cutting off the roots and any damaged or brown parts of the leeks, separate them and cut crosswise into ½-inch pieces. Wash thoroughly two or three times to remove all sand and grit; then drain and set aside.

Make a filling by thoroughly mixing leeks, onions, sumac, salt, pepper, cheese, lemon juice, and olive oil in a bowl; allow to sit for about 30 minutes.

In the meantime, divide dough into 15 to 20 balls. After allowing to rest for 30 minutes, roll out into 5-inch rounds.

Stir filling well; then place about 2 heaping tablespoons, including some of the juice, on dough rounds. Fold rounds in half, forming half-moons, and pinch edges together.

Place on a greased baking pan and bake in an oven preheated to 400°F, for 20 minutes or until pies turn lightly brown on the bottom and edges. Brush with olive oil and serve warm.

Lemon Dumplings

Kibbet Haamid
Syria and Lebanon
Serves 12

When I prepare this dish, my mind goes back to our farm years in the western prairies. In the cool autumn weather, after working all day threshing, we would return home for the evening meal. Many a time when we opened the door, the appetizing aroma of

kibbet haamid *would greet us. At times the* kibbeh *was stuffed with meat; at other times, with various crushed nuts. Whatever the filling, we were always contented after dining on this dish.*

1½ cups fine *burghul*
1 cup flour
¼ cup milk
salt and pepper to taste
4 tablespoons butter
4 medium onions, chopped
6 cloves garlic, crushed
1 cup pulverized almonds
2 cups cooked chickpeas
1 cup lemon juice
1 teaspoon thyme
1 teaspoon allspice
½ teaspoon nutmeg
¼ teaspoon cayenne
8 cups water
extra salt and pepper

Soak *burghul* in water for 10 minutes; then drain in a strainer, pressing out as much water as possible.

Place *burghul,* flour, milk, salt ,and pepper in a mixing bowl; then mix and knead dough, adding more flour or milk if necessary. Form dough into balls the size of golf balls and set aside.

Heat butter in a saucepan and sauté onions and garlic for about 10 minutes. Move half the onion–garlic mixture to a mixing bowl, leaving the remainder in saucepan.

Add almonds to the onions in the mixing bowl and combine. Divide into portions equal to number of balls and set aside.

Wet hands and place a ball of dough in the palm of one hand. With a finger of the other hand make a ¾-inch-deep hole in the middle; then twirl ball around finger until a hollow shell is formed. Stuff with a portion of onion–almond mixture; then seal and reshape into a sphere. Continue until all balls are used, wetting hands each time.

Place the remaining ingredients, including a little extra salt and pepper, in the saucepan containing the reserved sautéed onions and garlic. Bring to boil. Slip in spheres; then cover saucepan. Cook over medium heat for 40 minutes. Serve dumplings piping hot with sauce from the pot.

Lentil Dumplings

Harrak bi Isba'hu
Syria and Lebanon
Serves 8 to 10

Damascus has been an urban center since the beginning of civilization with a rich cuisine all its own. From among its many unique dishes, this makes a tasty and wholesome addition to any feast.

1 cup lentils, rinsed
7 cups water
½ basic pie dough (see recipe, p. 11)
salt to taste
½ teaspoon pepper
½ teaspoon cumin
⅛ teaspoon cayenne
3 tablespoons lemon juice
4 tablespoons olive oil
cooking oil
1 large onion, chopped
½ cup chopped cilantro
4 cloves garlic, crushed

Place lentils and water in a saucepan and bring to boil. Cook for 30 minutes over medium heat.

In the meantime, roll dough to about ⅛-inch thick, then cut into ½-inch squares. Add half the squares, salt, pepper, cumin, and cayenne to lentils and boil for an additional 15 minutes or until dough is cooked.

Add lemon juice and stir; then set aside, keeping hot.

Heat olive oil in a frying pan and sauté onions until they turn light brown. Stir frying pan contents into lentils.

In the same frying pan, add cooking oil and deep-fry remainder of dough until squares turn light brown. Remove with a slotted spoon and place in serving dish.

Combine cilantro and garlic, then place in a serving bowl and set aside.

Serve lentils in soup bowls. Diners add fried dough squares and coriander–garlic seasoning to taste.

Lentil Loaf

Ragheef 'Adas
Palestine and Jordan
Serves 10

This dish was invented by a Palestinian friend who immigrated to North America. She had become familiar with the meatloafs of the West and was inspired to create this healthy vegetarian dish.

2 cups lentils, rinsed
8 cups water
3 medium onions, chopped
6 cloves garlic, crushed
1 hot pepper, chopped
4 tablespoons finely chopped fresh cilantro
1 cup fine bread crumbs
1 5½-oz can tomato paste
4 tablespoons butter
4 eggs, beaten
1 teaspoon thyme
1 teaspoon cumin
salt and pepper to taste
2 tablespoons olive oil
2 tablespoons honey

Place lentils and water in a saucepan and bring to boil; then cover and cook over medium heat for 30 minutes or until lentils are cooked. Drain, place in a food processor, and process briefly. Add remaining ingredients, except olive oil and honey and process into a paste.

Place in a greased loaf pan; then sprinkle with olive oil. Cover with aluminum foil and bake in an oven preheated to 350°F, for 45 minutes. Remove aluminum foil and brush with honey; then bake for 10 minutes more. Serve hot or cold.

LENTILS AND NOODLES

Rishta
Syria and Lebanon
Serves 4 to 6

Lentils, almost unknown in North America during my youth, are now cultivated in many places throughout this continent. In fact, Canada's western province of Saskatchewan is today the second largest exporter of lentils in the world, exceeded only by Turkey.

1 cup lentils, rinsed
5 cups water
2 tablespoons butter
2 medium onions, chopped
2 tablespoons finely chopped cilantro
2 cloves garlic, crushed
4 ounces fine egg noodles
salt and pepper to taste
pinch of cayenne
2 tablespoons lemon juice

Place lentils with water in a pot, cover, and bring to boil. Cook over medium heat for about 25 minutes or until lentils are tender but not mushy.

In the meantime, melt butter in a frying pan and sauté onions, cilantro, and garlic until onions begin to brown. Add frying pan contents to lentils; then add noodles, salt, pepper, and cayenne. Bring to boil; then lower heat to medium and simmer for about 10 minutes or until noodles are tender, adding more water if necessary. Stir in lemon juice; then serve hot accompanied by a tossed salad.

LENTIL PIES

Fatayar 'Adas
Syria and Lebanon
Makes 18 pies

A tasty vegetarian delight, these pies must have been an invention of a creative cook. As a main dish or snack, they always make a special treat.

1 basic dough (see recipe, p. 11)
1 cup lentils, rinsed
5 cups water
3 medium onions, finely chopped
4 cloves garlic, crushed
1 small hot pepper, finely chopped
1 5½-oz can tomato paste
4 tablespoons butter
4 tablespoons lemon juice
1 teaspoon ground coriander seeds
1 teaspoon cumin
salt and pepper to taste

Form dough into 18 balls; then cover with a damp cloth and allow to rest for 30 minutes.

In the meantime, place lentils and water in a saucepan and bring to boil. Cover and cook over medium heat for 40 minutes or until lentils are well cooked. Drain and mash; then allow to cool.

Make a filling by mixing the lentils with the remaining ingredients.

Roll each dough ball into a 4- to 5-inch circle; then place 2 heaping tablespoons of filling in the center. Fold dough over and pinch edges firmly together. Continue until all balls are finished.

Place on well-greased baking sheets; then bake in an oven preheated to 350°F for 20 minutes. If needed, brown under broiler for a minute or two; then brush with olive oil and serve hot.

LENTIL POTTAGE
Mujaddara
Syria and Lebanon
Serves 4 to 6

In the eastern Arab world, the most common dish made from lentils is mujaddara, *which has been popular since Biblical times. According to tradition,* mujaddara *is the food referred to in the Biblical account of Esau's great hunger: for a dish of this pottage, he sold his birthright as first born to his twin brother Jacob. Perhaps this story gave rise to an ancient saying, "A hungry man would be willing to sell his soul for a dish of* mujaddara.*" The dish in* The Bible *was probably made with red lentils, but other types of lentils can be used as well.*

When Arab immigrants came to North America, they brought with them not only their love for mujaddara *but also their custom of not serving it to guests. Perhaps the few cents it costs to make leads to the belief that it cannot possibly be good enough to serve visitors. In my view, it should be at the top of the list of dishes served to honored guests.*

1 cup lentils, rinsed
5 cups water
6 tablespoons olive or vegetable oil
2 large onions, chopped
¼ cup rice or *burghul*, rinsed
salt and pepper to taste
½ teaspoon cumin
2 tablespoons butter

Place lentils and water in a saucepan and bring to boil. Cover and cook over medium heat for 30 minutes.

In the meantime, heat oil in a frying pan; add onions and sauté until they turn golden brown.

Add contents of frying pan to lentils, along with remaining ingredients, except butter; stir, then cook for 20 minutes more or until rice or *burghul* are tender but still slightly firm, adding more water if necessary. Remove from heat; then stir in butter and serve.

Note: If this recipe is prepared as a main course, it will serve only 4. As a side dish, it will serve 4 to 6.

LENTILS WITH RICE

Aeesh Al dal
Arabian Gulf
Serves 6

The origin of the Arabian Gulf cuisine is said to be the marriage between the bedouin and pearl-diving cultures, with the Indian subcontinent as the mother-in-law. This combination has given birth to many tasty foods. Among these is this dish, relished by all classes of society.

4 tablespoons butter
1 cup rice, rinsed
½ cup lentils, soaked overnight and drained
2¾ cups water
½ teaspoon cumin
½ teaspoon ginger
2 crushed cardamom seeds
⅛ teaspoon cayenne
salt and pepper to taste
4 tablespoons olive oil
2 medium onions, sliced
½ teaspoon cinnamon

Melt butter in a saucepan; add rice and stir-fry for 3 minutes. Add remaining ingredients, except olive oil, onions, and cinnamon, and bring to boil. Cover and cook over medium low heat for 25 minutes; then turn off heat and allow to steam for 30 minutes more.

In the meantime, heat oil in a frying pan and sauté onion slices until they turn light brown.

Place rice–lentil mixture on a serving platter; spread onions evenly over top. Sprinkle with cinnamon and serve.

LENTIL STEW

Yakhnat 'Adas
Syria and Lebanon
Serves 8

In addition to being a nourishing food, lentils have some medicinal benefits. They are recommended for anemia, emaciation, low blood pressure, and ulcers. In a number of cultures, people believe they are also an aphrodisiac. In a few Asiatic countries, cooked lentils with onions, rice, and olive oil are a food favored by lovers.

1 cup lentils, rinsed
5 cups water
4 tablespoons olive oil
2 medium onions, chopped
4 cloves garlic, crushed
¼ cup rice, rinsed
¼ cup broken vermicelli or fine noodles
2 cups stewed tomatoes
1 teaspoon ground ginger
salt and pepper to taste
4 tablespoons finely chopped fresh basil, or 2 teaspoons dried crushed basil

Place lentils and water in a saucepan and bring to boil. Cover and cook over medium heat for 20 minutes.

In the meantime, heat oil in a frying pan and sauté onions over medium heat until they begin to brown. Stir in garlic and rice and stir-fry for another 3 minutes.

Add frying pan contents along with remaining ingredients, except basil, to lentils and bring to boil. Cook another 20 minutes, adding more water if necessary. Remove from heat and stir in basil; serve immediately.

Molokhia Vegetable Stew

Molokhia Khudra
Syria and Lebanon
Serves 8

Molokhia *is said to have been the favorite food of the ancient Egyptians—a taste that has never left that historic land. Today in Egypt, this leafy green vegetable continues to be a food preferred by rich and poor alike. The wealthy cook it with meat and the poor with vegetables. The plant is so much in demand that nearly every farmer grows a little patch for his or her own use or for sale.*

In the Fertile Crescent area, this green is fast catching on. In response, more tasty dishes have been created, of which this recipe is an example.

1 large potato, peeled and cut into large chunks
1 medium carrot, scraped clean and cut into small pieces
1 small yellow turnip, peeled and cut into small pieces
1 medium zucchini, cut into large pieces
3 large tomatoes, cut into large pieces
2 medium onions, chopped into small pieces
½ teaspoon cumin
pinch of allspice
salt and pepper to taste
8 cups water
½ pound fresh *molokhia* leaves, very finely chopped, or 1 cup dried and crushed
4 tablespoons butter
½ head garlic, peeled and crushed
½ cup finely chopped fresh cilantro
⅛ teaspoon cayenne

Place potato, carrot, turnip, zucchini, tomatoes, onions, cumin, allspice, salt, pepper, and water in a saucepan; cover and cook over medium heat until water begins to boil. Lower heat and simmer for about 30 minutes or until vegetables are tender but still intact. Remove vegetables with a slotted spoon, placing on a serving platter. Keep warm.

Add *molokhia* to vegetable stock; cover and simmer over medium heat for 20 minutes, stirring occasionally.

In the meantime, melt butter in a frying pan and sauté garlic, cilantro, and cayenne until the garlic turns golden brown. Add to stock and simmer for a few moments, stirring occasionally.

Adjust seasoning; then serve *molokhia* hot with the vegetables—each diner tops the vegetables with *molokhia* and broth to taste.

OKRA AND CHICKPEA STEW

Bamya wa Hummus
Syria and Lebanon
Serves 6

Okra can be baked, boiled, or fried. It should never be cooked in aluminum, iron or tin, however, as the metal is likely to darken the pods. It is best cooked in enameled or glass pans and pots. When cooking fresh okra, take great care not to break the pods. The mucilaginous juice of okra gives it an undesirable slimy texture if not cooked properly. The frozen okra is a safe bet until you gain experience with fresh.

4 tablespoons olive oil
2 medium onions, chopped
4 cloves garlic, crushed
½ hot pepper, finely chopped
1 10.6-oz package frozen okra, thawed
1 19-oz can chickpeas, drained
4 tablespoons lemon juice
½ teaspoon cumin
½ teaspoon ground coriander seeds
½ teaspoon ground mustard
salt and pepper to taste
½ cup water

Heat oil in a saucepan and sauté onions, garlic, and hot pepper over medium heat for 10 minutes. Add okra and gently stir-fry for another 3 minutes. Stir in remaining ingredients and bring to boil; cover and simmer over medium low heat for 25 minutes, adding more water if necessary. Serve hot or cold with cooked rice.

OKRA AND TOMATO STEW

Mlokhia Tajin
Morocco
Serves 4

Once treasured as a delicacy in Moorish Spain, okra originated in Ethiopia, from where it traveled north to the Mediterranean shores and east to India. The African Arabs called it uekha, *from which the name okra may have been derived. They carried it to West Africa and the Iberian Peninsula. In Spain after the Christian conquest, okra fell out of favor, but in much of Africa and the eastern Mediterranean countries it became a much relished food.*

In the seventeenth century it came to North America from West Africa along with the slaves brought by the French to Louisiana. Since its introduction, it has been extensively cultivated in the Mississippi delta, its original American home.

4 tablespoons olive oil
1 10-oz package frozen okra, thawed
2 medium onions, finely chopped
4 cloves garlic, crushed
½ small hot pepper, finely chopped
2 cups stewed tomatoes
½ cup water
¼ teaspoon allspice
½ teaspoon cumin
salt and pepper to taste
2 tablespoons lemon juice

Heat oil in a saucepan and sauté okra over medium heat for 8 minutes or until pods begin to brown. Remove with a slotted spoon and set aside.

In same oil (adding more if necessary) sauté onions, garlic, and hot pepper over medium heat for 10 minutes or until onions begin to brown. Stir in remaining ingredients, including okra, but not lemon juice. Cover and simmer over medium heat for 25 minutes; then stir in lemon juice and serve.

Oregano Cheese Pies

Fatayar Za'tar ma' Jiban
Syria and Lebanon
Makes 20 pies

If one likes delicate tangy foods, this pie fits the bill. It is tasty, somewhat spicy, but not overly so. Note that oregano comes in many varieties; it is important to use the wide-leaf, mild Italian oregano.

1 basic dough (see recipe, p. 11)
4 cups mild fresh Italian oregano leaves
4 medium onions, finely chopped
1 cup crumbled feta cheese
salt and pepper to taste
4 tablespoons olive oil
3 tablespoons sumac
2 tablespoons finely chopped fresh cilantro
extra olive oil

Form dough into 20 balls; then cover with a damp cloth. Allow to stand for 30 minutes in warm place.

In the meantime, make filling by mixing remaining ingredients, except extra olive oil; set aside.

Roll dough into 3- to 5-inch rounds.

Divide filling into 20 portions. Place 1 portion on each dough round. Fold edges of dough over filling to make a half-moon shape; firmly pinch edges together. Place on well-greased baking sheets and brush heavily with extra olive oil.

Bake in an oven preheated to 400°F, for about 20 minutes or until pies turn light brown. Serve hot.

PEPPER AND RICE

Rizz ma' Flayfle
Syria and Lebanon
Serves 4 to 6

"Pepper yet not a pepper" is the contradictory description of the fruits of the capsicums, which range in taste from sweet to spicy hot. They are of no relation at all to the plant that produces the peppercorns we use ground. In many countries, capsicums have all but replaced that spice, which in medieval Europe was more expensive than gold.

4 tablespoons butter
1 large sweet pepper, finely chopped
1 medium onion, finely chopped
2 cloves garlic, crushed
1 cup rice, rinsed
2 cups water
⅛ teaspoon cayenne
salt and pepper to taste

Melt butter in a frying pan and sauté sweet pepper, onion, and garlic over medium heat for 12 minutes. Add rice and stir-fry for 2 minutes; then stir in remaining ingredients and bring to boil. Cover and cook over medium low heat for 25 minutes, then turn off heat and allow rice to steam for 30 minutes. Serve hot.

POMEGRANATE PIZZA

Manaqeesh Rumman
Palestine and Jordan
Makes four 8- to 10-inch pizzas

The seeds of the pomegranate are used to garnish salads and desserts. Besides giving a bright adornment to these foods, they add a piquant flavor. However, they reach their pinnacle of color and taste when employed in stuffings and in pizzas, such as in this recipe.

1 basic pie dough (see recipe, p. 11)
1 cup feta cheese, crumbled
1 cup pomegranate seeds
2 medium onions, finely chopped
2 cloves garlic, crushed
½ cup finely chopped green onions
1 5½-oz can tomato paste
1 teaspoon paprika
½ teaspoon ground coriander seeds
¼ teaspoon cayenne
salt and pepper to taste
4 tablespoons olive oil

Form dough into 4 balls; cover with damp cloth and allow to stand for 1 hour.

In the meantime, make a topping by combining the remaining ingredients and set aside.

Roll balls into rounds about ⅛-inch thick; then fold and pinch edges to make a rim. Divide topping mixture into 4 parts and spread on the 4 rounds. Place on greased baking sheets; then bake in an oven preheated to 350°F, for 15 minutes or until rims of pizzas turn light brown. Serve hot.

POTATO CROQUETTES

'Ajijat
Algeria
Serves 8

During 130 years of French occupation, elements of French cuisine made their way into the Algerian kitchen. Any dishes borrowed from France, however, were altered with the addition of spices and herbs to make them fit Algerian taste—Algerian food was and still is highly seasoned. These potato croquettes are one example of a dish borrowed from France but flavored with an Algerian touch.

6 medium potatoes
6 eggs
1 large onion, finely chopped
1 bunch parsley, stemmed and finely chopped
6 green onions, finely chopped
1 tablespoon finely chopped mint leaves
1 teaspoon cinnamon
½ teaspoon nutmeg
⅛ teaspoon cayenne
pinch of dried sage
salt and pepper to taste
1 cup flour
oil for frying

Wash and boil potatoes until tender; then peel and mash. Add 2 eggs, onion, parsley, green onions, mint, cinnamon, nutmeg, cayenne, sage, salt, and pepper; then combine thoroughly.

In a shallow bowl, beat 4 remaining eggs; set aside.

Place flour on a flat plate; set aside.

Form potato mixture into spheres the size of golf balls; then dip in beaten egg and roll in the flour. Flatten into patties; then place on floured tray.

Place oil in a saucepan to 2 inches deep and heat. Fry patties until they turn golden brown. Remove with a slotted spoon and allow to drain on paper towels. Place on a large platter and serve hot.

Potato Pie

Saneeyat Batata
Syria and Lebanon
Serves 6

Once unknown in the Arab world, the potato has become a common and popular food there. This dish is one of many prepared with this vegetable.

3 cups mashed potatoes
2 medium onions, finely chopped
3 cloves garlic, crushed
4 tablespoons butter
3 tablespoons flour
salt and pepper to taste
1 tablespoon finely chopped cilantro
¾ teaspoon cumin
½ teaspoon ground ginger
⅛ teaspoon cayenne

Place all ingredients in a mixing bowl and combine thoroughly. Spread in a well-greased baking dish and bake in an oven preheated to 350°F, for 45 minutes or until top turns light brown. Serve hot as a main course or as a side dish.

Potatoes and Pine Nuts

Batata ma' Snobar
Syria and Lebanon
Serves 4 to 6

To the Middle Eastern Arab, pine nuts are the most desirable of all nuts. As ingredients in appetizers, salads, entrées, and desserts, they are used on a wide scale. The only thing holding back their use on an even larger scale is their price. They are quite expensive— a luxury for many people.

3 cups mashed potatoes, hot
½ cup finely chopped green onions
¼ teaspoon nutmeg
salt and pepper to taste
6 tablespoons olive oil
1 medium onion, finely chopped

2 cloves garlic crushed
½ cup pine nuts

Thoroughly combine potatoes, green onions, nutmeg, salt, pepper, and 3 tablespoons of the olive oil; then spread on a platter and set aside.

Heat remaining oil in a frying pan and sauté onion and garlic over medium heat for 5 minutes. Add pine nuts and stir-fry for another 5 minutes or until nuts begin to brown. Spread frying pan contents evenly over potatoes and serve warm.

POTATO STEW

L'Batata Btskulya
Morocco
Serves 6 to 8

It is said there is no perfect food, but the potato comes close. Relatively easy and cheap to grow, the potato has nourished many. The noble potato is produced worldwide; China, Poland, Russia and the United States are the four largest potato producers in the world.

4 tablespoons olive oil
1 small sweet pepper, finely chopped
1 medium onion, finely chopped
¼ teaspoon cayenne
1 tablespoon ground cumin seeds
½ cup finely chopped fresh cilantro
8 cloves garlic, crushed
6 large potatoes (about 2 pounds), peeled and cut into large pieces
3 cups water
salt to taste
rind from 1 lemon, finely chopped

Heat oil in a saucepan; add sweet pepper and sauté for 5 minutes. Add remaining ingredients and bring to boil. Cover and cook over medium heat for 40 minutes or until potatoes are well done. Serve hot with cooked rice.

Potato and Tomato Pies

Samboosa
Arabian Gulf
Makes 36 pies

Indian samboosas *originally came to the Arabian Gulf by way of Arab dhows plying the seas between India and the Arabian Peninsula. From the eighth to the twelfth centuries, these fine ships would depart from Basra, sailing down the Arabian Gulf to the Indian coast; then to Serendip (Sri Lanka). From this island, the summer monsoons took them across the Bay of Bengal, through the Straits of Malacca to the eastern coast of China.*

Returning, they would take advantage of the southeast monsoon to carry back their precious cargoes of porcelain, silks, spices, and other rare goods for shipment to the Mediterranean markets and beyond. Among the cargo, no doubt, was samboosa.

4 cups shredded raw potatoes
2 medium tomatoes, finely chopped
1 large onion, finely chopped
1 small hot pepper, very finely chopped
2 cloves garlic, crushed
2 tablespoons finely chopped fresh cilantro
salt and pepper to taste
2 tablespoons butter
1 egg, beaten
½ teaspoon cumin
½ teaspoon ground coriander seeds
½ teaspoon ground ginger
1 basic dough (see recipe, p. 11)
oil for deep frying

Prepare filling by thoroughly mixing all ingredients, except dough and cooking oil; then aside.

Form dough into 36 balls and place on floured tray; cover with a damp cloth and allow to stand in a warm place for 30 minutes.

Roll balls into rounds about 3 inches in diameter; then place a heaping tablespoon of the filling in the middle of each round. Fold dough over filling, forming a half-moon, then close by firmly pinching edges together.

Heat oil in a deep fryer and fry *samboosas* over medium heat until they turn golden brown, turning them over once. Drain on paper towels; serve warm.

Note: Samboosas *can be baked in the oven instead of being fried, but they will not be as tasty.*

PUMPKIN KIBBEH

Kibbet Laqteen
Syria and Lebanon
Makes about 12 patties

When Halloween is over and the North American farmers are left with thousands of unsold pumpkins, how happy they would feel if they knew that everyone was waiting to make kibbeh *with pumpkin.*

This recipe is best made with fresh pumpkin because canned pumpkin tends to have too much liquid. If you use fresh pumpkin, remove the seeds and rind; then cut into small pieces and bake in the oven or steam.

2 cups of cooked, mashed pumpkin
1 cup fine *burghul* soaked for 10 minutes in boiling water and drained
salt to taste
½ teaspoon black pepper
½ teaspoon ground coriander seeds
½ teaspoon allspice
½ teaspoon cumin
⅛ teaspoon cayenne
1 medium onion, finely chopped
4 cloves garlic, crushed
1 cup flour
½ cup water
oil for frying

Place all ingredients, except oil, in a food processor and process into a dough that should stick together when squeezed. Form into spheres the size of golf balls. (If the mixture is too soft, add more flour.) Flatten balls into patties.

Pour oil into a saucepan to a depth of 1 inch and heat. Fry patties until they turn golden brown, turning them over once. Drain on paper towels and keep warm until ready to serve.

Note: An alternate way to cook the *kibbeh:* place the mixture in an oiled 9-inch-square baking pan; then pat down and, with a wet knife, cut into 1½-inch to 2-inch squares. Spread a little oil over the top and bake in an oven preheated to 400°F, until golden brown. Serve warm.

RICE AND FAVA BEANS FLAVORED WITH DILL

Aeesh Albajelah
Iraq
Serves 6

Iraq, the Mesopotamia of ancient times, is descended from one of the oldest civilizations in the world. Its rich cuisine includes this tasty treat. Traditionally, aeesh albajelah *is prepared with meat, but without the meat, it still is a mouth-watering dish.*

4 tablespoons butter
1 medium onion, finely chopped
2 cloves garlic, crushed
1 cup rice, rinsed
1½ cups frozen or fresh fava beans
4 tablespoons finely chopped fresh dill
1 teaspoon *ibzar* (Arabian Gulf Spices, see recipe, p. 13)
salt to taste
2½ cups water
4 tablespoons toasted pine nuts

Melt butter in a saucepan and sauté onion over medium heat for 10 minutes. Add garlic and rice and stir-fry for another 3 minutes. Stir in remaining ingredients, except pine nuts, and bring to boil. Cover and cook over medium low heat for 25 minutes; then turn off heat and allow to steam for 30 minutes longer. Place on a serving platter, garnish with pine nuts, and serve.

Rice Flavored with Cardamom

Aeesh Alhaal
Arabian Gulf
Serves 6

Sometimes called "Seeds of Paradise," cardamom is native to India and Sri Lanka where it grows wild. Over 4,000 years ago it was mentioned in the sacred texts of India. It is believed that, 700 years before the birth of Christ, cardamom was grown as an ornamental plant in the gardens of the Babylonian kings.

In later centuries, adventurous Arab traders brought cardamom to the Greek and Roman worlds. In those eras and long after, it was a much-sought-after spice, especially for use as a perfume.

4 tablespoons butter
1½ cups slivered almonds
1 cup rice, rinsed
¼ cup raisins, rinsed
2 ½ cups water
½ teaspoon freshly ground cardamom seeds
½ teaspoon cinnamon
salt to taste
¼ teaspoon nutmeg
⅛ teaspoon cayenne
2 tablespoons finely chopped parsley

Melt butter in a frying pan and sauté almonds until they begin to brown. Add rice and stir-fry for another 3 minutes. Stir in remaining ingredients, except parsley, and bring to boil. Cover and cook over medium low heat for 25 minutes; then turn off heat and allow to steam for 30 minutes. Place on a serving platter, garnish with parsley, and serve.

RICE WITH MUNG BEANS

Al-Momawash Al-Mutabaq
Kuwait
Serves 6

Before petroleum was discovered in the Arabian Gulf, the vast majority of people were poor, either roaming the endless desert with their flocks or sailing the seas to trade or dive for pearls. During these years, this affordable dish flavored with spicy tomato sauce kept the people well fed and healthy.

2 medium onions
4 tablespoons butter
¼ cup mung beans (*maash*), soaked overnight and drained
1 cup rice, rinsed
pinch of saffron
½ teaspoon cinnamon
2 cardamom seeds, crushed
salt and pepper to taste
2¼ cups water
3 tablespoons olive oil
tomato hot sauce (see recipe, p. 21)

Chop and fry one of the onions in butter until light brown; then add mung beans and rice and stir-fry for 3 minutes. Add saffron, cinnamon, cardamom, salt, pepper, and water and bring to boil. Cover and cook over medium low heat for 25 minutes; then turn off heat and allow to steam for another 30 minutes.

In the meantime, slice remaining onion and fry in olive oil until light brown.

Place pilaf on a platter and top with fried onions. Serve immediately with tomato sauce on the side. Each diner adds sauce to taste.

RICE WITH ORZO

Rizz bi ash-Sha'reeya
Syria and Lebanon
Serves 4

Butter, not as healthy as olive oil, is often employed in Arab cooking to give a rich taste to food. However, this dish when prepared with olive oil instead of butter is also quite tasty.

5 tablespoons butter
¼ cup orzo

1 cup rice, rinsed
2 cups boiling water
salt to taste

Melt 4 tablespoons of butter in a frying pan; add orzo and, stirring constantly, sauté until orzo begins to turn light brown. Add rice and stir-fry another 3 minutes. Stir in water and salt and bring to boil. Cover and reduce heat to medium low. Cook for 25 minutes; then turn off heat and allow to steam for 30 minutes. Stir in remaining butter; place on a platter and serve hot.

Note: ¼ cup sesame seeds can be substituted for the orzo.

Rice with Truffles
Aeesh Al-Faqa'a
Arabian Gulf
Serves 4

It is said that truffles, like precious metals, are a treasure the earth conceals within its bosom. The ancient Greeks believed these delectable morsels were planted by thunderbolts striking the earth. The belief, shared by the ancient Greeks and the inhabitants of the Arabian Peninsula, that truffles arrive with storms has a plausible explanation. In the desert, suddenly breaking storms crack the sand and expose the buried truffles. The Arab name for truffles, faqa'a *(to burst or explode), seems to confirm this belief.*

1 cup canned Syrian or Moroccan truffles
4 tablespoons butter
1 medium onion, finely chopped
2 cloves garlic, crushed
1 cup rice
2 cups water
salt and pepper to taste

Drain truffles, wash thoroughly, and chop. Set aside.
Melt butter in a frying pan and sauté onion over medium heat for 10 minutes. Add garlic and rice and stir-fry another 3 minutes.
Add water, truffles, salt, and pepper and bring to boil. Reduce heat to medium low, cover, and cook for 25 minutes. Turn off heat and allow to steam for 30 minutes longer. Serve hot.

SPAGHETTI, TUNISIAN-STYLE

Macaronis Tuniseeya
Tunisia
Serves 8

In the past few centuries, spaghetti was not often found in the Arab kitchen, whereas today it is commonly eaten in many of the Arab countries, especially Libya and Tunisia. According to some modern food writers pasta in the Arab lands has an ancient history. They maintain that pasta was invented in Mesopotamia. From there traders took it eastward to China. From that ancient land, Marco Polo brought this well-known food back to Italy—its modern homeland. This dish may very well be of Italian origin, brought by Italian settlers to Tunisia.

1 pound spaghetti, broken into 2-inch pieces
2 cups finely chopped parsley
½ cup finely chopped fresh basil or 2 tablespoons dried basil
2 cloves garlic, crushed
salt and pepper to taste
4 tablespoons blanched almonds
5 tablespoons olive oil
3 tablespoons butter
1 teaspoon oregano
¼ teaspoon cayenne
½ cup Parmesan cheese

Bring 1 quart water to a boil and add spaghetti. Cover and cook over medium heat for 12 minutes. Drain; then place in a shallow serving bowl and set aside.

While spaghetti is cooking, make a sauce by placing all the remaining ingredients, except cheese, in a blender and blend into a paste. Add the cheese and blend for a moment.

Remove from blender and mix with spaghetti; serve immediately.

Note: Extra sauce can be made and frozen for future use.

Spinach Pies

Fatayar bi Sabanakh
Syria and Lebanon
Makes 24 pies

Sumac, *with its lemony flavor, is a spice favored by Middle Eastern cooks. As a seasoning, it lends a tart taste to salads, curries, sauces, and stuffings. In the eastern Arab countries and adjoining lands, it is also employed extensively along with onions and salt as a savory spice in numerous dishes. Arab gourmet cooks say there is no substitute for this tangy condiment.*

2 pounds frozen pizza dough, thawed, or equivalent amount of homemade bread dough
1 bunch or 1 10-oz package fresh spinach, thoroughly washed and finely chopped
3 medium onions, chopped into small pieces
¼ cup pine nuts
4 tablespoons sumac
1 tablespoon lemon juice
salt and pepper to taste
5 tablespoons olive oil

Divide dough into 24 balls; then cover with damp cloth. Allow to stand for 30 minutes in warm place.

In the meantime, make filling by mixing remaining ingredients, except 3 tablespoons of the olive oil; set aside.

Roll dough into 5-inch rounds, ¼ inch thick. Place 1 heaping tablespoon of the filling on each circle; then bring the edges of the circle together over the filling to form a triangle shape. Close by firmly pinching edges together. Place on well-greased baking sheets and brush generously with remaining olive oil.

Bake in an oven preheated to 400°F, for about 20 minutes or until the pies turn light brown.

Serve hot for lunch or snacks.

STUFFED EGGPLANT

Bathinjan Mihshee
Al-Andalus
Serves 6

During the flowering of their civilization, from the eighth century AD to the thirteenth century, the Arabs were the greatest gourmet cooks in the world. In Al-Andalus or Arab Spain, the cuisine reached the height of perfection. Cookbooks, some of which have come down to our times, were written for the kitchens of the well-to-do. One of these is Fadaalat al-Khiwaan fee Tayyibaat at Ta`aam wa al-Alwaan *written in the thirteenth century by Ibn Razeen at-Tujeebee, an Andalusian Arab from Murcia.*

Even after the passage of more than 700 years, his recipes remain gourmet delights, as this dish will testify.

1 large eggplant, about 2 pounds
salt to taste
2 cups toasted bread, broken into small pieces
4 eggs, beaten
1½ teaspoons *ras el hanout* (see recipe, pp. 14-15)
1 teaspoon ground coriander seeds
6 tablespoons olive oil
4 tablespoons finely chopped fresh mint
4 tablespoons finely chopped fresh cilantro
2 cups water

Cut stem off eggplant and reserve. Core eggplant until a shell about ¼-inch thick remains; set aside.

To make filling: place cored parts from eggplant in a saucepan and add salt to taste. Cover with water and bring to boil. Cover saucepan and cook over medium heat for 15 minutes, stirring a few times. Remove from heat; then stir in bread, eggs, *ras el hanout*, and ground coriander seeds.

Stuff eggplant with filling (if it won't all fit, reserve excess); then close, tying the stem to the eggplant with string. Place in a casserole; then pour remaining ingredients over eggplant, including excess stuffing. Cover with aluminum foil and bake in an oven preheated to 350°F, for 1 hour. Remove aluminum foil and bake for another 15 minutes. Serve hot with sauce from casserole.

STUFFED PEPPERS

Flayfle Mihshee
Palestine and Jordan
Serves 6

In North America, the most common variety of sweet pepper is the bell—so called because of its shape, fat and short like a bell. Mild and sweet, bell peppers are usually harvested green but, left on the plant to ripen, they turn either red or yellow and become sweeter. Shining and brilliant when fresh, they become progressively duller and wrinkled with age. The only type of peppers widely accepted in North America, they are consumed fresh, canned, or dried, and are ideal for pickling or stuffing.

6 large red bell peppers
4 tablespoons butter
1 large onion, finely chopped
2 cloves garlic, crushed
1 small hot pepper, finely chopped
4 cups cooked rice
1 teaspoon oregano
½ teaspoon allspice
salt and pepper to taste
½ cup toasted pine nuts

Cut off stem ends of peppers and remove seeds. Reserve ends. Set aside.

To make filling: melt butter in a frying pan and sauté onion, garlic and hot pepper over medium heat for 8 minutes. Stir in remaining ingredients.

Stuff peppers and replace stem ends. Set upright in a casserole; add 1 cup water. Bake in an oven preheated to 350°F, for 40 minutes or until peppers are done.

Note: Makes a satisfying vegetarian meal when served with a tossed salad.

Stuffed Potato Patties

Kuftat Batata
Arabian Gulf
Makes 24 patties

It is said that King Louis XVI made potatoes popular by wearing potato flowers in his buttonhole. Perhaps he contributed to the potato becoming a basic food, not only in Europe, but throughout the world. In many countries it has become an irreplaceable part of the cuisine.

A dish of Indian origin, kuftat batata *makes a tasty snack or, served with a salad, a tasty meal.*

4 heaping cups mashed potatoes
3 tablespoons flour
salt to taste
2 tablespoons butter
2 medium onions finely chopped
4 cloves garlic, crushed
½ cup pulverized almonds
¼ cup raisins
1½ teaspoons *ibzar* (Arabian Gulf Spices, see recipe, p. 13)
1/8 teaspoon cayenne
½ cup finely chopped fresh cilantro
2 eggs, beaten
1 cup fine bread crumbs
oil for frying

Place potatoes, flour, and salt in a mixing bowl; combine thoroughly. Form into 24 balls and set aside.

For filling: melt butter in a frying pan and sauté onions over medium heat for 10 minutes. Add garlic, almonds, raisins, *ibzar*, cayenne, and cilantro; then stir-fry for 3 minutes. Set aside, allowing mixture to cool.

Place eggs on one plate and bread crumbs on another. Take a potato ball in one hand; then, using finger of other hand, make a well. Place 1 heaping tablespoon of filling in well; then seal and flatten to about ¾-inch thick. Continue until all balls are filled.

Place oil to about 1½ inches deep in a saucepan and heat. Turn patties over in eggs, then in bread crumbs. Fry until golden brown; then drain on paper towels and serve warm.

Swiss Chard Tajin

Mara Silq
Morocco
Serves 6 to 8

Typical of Arab cooking, most of the Moroccan recipes known to the outside world have meat as a main ingredient. The healthier vegetarian ones, like this dish, tend to remain in obscurity, in the homes of the poor.

1 large bunch Swiss chard, washed and chopped
2 medium onions, chopped
2 tablespoons finely chopped fresh cilantro
4 tablespoons olive oil
2 tablespoons lemon juice
½ cup water
1 teaspoon paprika
½ teaspoon ground coriander seeds
salt and pepper to taste
1 cup cooked lentils

Place all ingredients, except lentils, in a saucepan; cook over medium low heat for 30 minutes. Stir in lentils; cover and cook for 10 minutes longer, adding a little water if necessary. Serve hot or cold.

Tamarind Rice

Aeesh Altamar-Hindee
Arabian Gulf
Serves 4

Refrigerated, both the squeezed meaty juice and the paste of tamarind keep for a long time without spoiling.

4 tablespoons olive oil
1 medium onion, finely chopped
2 cloves garlic, crushed
1 cup rice, rinsed
2 cups water
salt and pepper to taste
2 tablespoons tamarind butter (see recipe, p. 20)

Heat oil in a frying pan and sauté onion and garlic over medium heat for 10 minutes. Add rice and stir-fry for another 3 minutes. Stir in remaining ingredients, except tamarind butter, and bring to boil. Cover and cook over medium low heat for 25 minutes. Turn off heat and allow to steam for 30 minutes longer. Stir in tamarind butter. Serve hot.

TOAST WITH ZA'TAR
Khubz Muhammas ma' Za'tar
Palestine and Jordan
Serves 6

In North America, the most important species of sumac, the main component of za'tar, *is the staghorn. Although staghorn sumac fruit is not utilized for food, a pleasant beverage reminiscent of lemonade can be made from its ripe berries. The tree grows wild and is also cultivated for ornamental purposes. In autumn, its brilliantly colored leaves and the reddish cones of its berries beautify many gardens and roadsides. Their vivid colors have inspired bards. The Canadian poet Bliss Carmen wrote:*

> The deep red cones of the sumac
> and the woodbine's crimson sprays
> Have bannered the common roadside
> For the pageant of passing days.

Toast was not common in the Middle East, and this dish was introduced by the immigrants returning from the West to their homeland as a new way of enjoying traditional za'tar. *Eating it, one can contemplate the colorful sumac tree that inspired a poet in a land whose people do not even consume the sumac berries.*

6 slices of bread
4 tablespoons *za'tar* **(Sumac & Thyme Seasoning, see recipe page 19)**
5 tablespoons olive oil

Place bread on a baking sheet and toast under a broiler until barely light brown. Remove and turn over the slices. Sprinkle the *za'tar* evenly over untoasted side of the bread; then sprinkle with oil.

Return to oven and broil for about 3 minutes. Serve immediately.

Note: The North American sumac is not edible; you must purchase the sumac from Middle Eastern food markets or health food stores.

Tomatoes Stuffed with Chickpeas

Tamatim Mihshee bil-Hummus
Palestine and Jordan
Serves 6

Once the most reviled fruit in the vegetable world, tomatoes are now a much sought after garden produce. Among the vegetables grown in North America, they rank second to potatoes in popularity. No other fruit or vegetable is cultivated more widely or has its mass appeal.

12 medium tomatoes, ripe but slightly firm
¼ cup olive oil
2 medium onions, chopped
4 cloves garlic, crushed
¼ cup pine nuts or slivered almonds
½ cup finely chopped fresh cilantro
1 19-oz can chickpeas, drained
2 tablespoons butter
½ teaspoon pepper
½ teaspoon cumin
½ teaspoon allspice
¼ teaspoon cayenne
salt to taste
2 tablespoons olive oil

Cut off tomato tops and scoop out pulp with a spoon. Reserve both the cut tops and pulp.

Heat oil in a frying pan and sauté onions and garlic until they begin to brown. Add pine nuts or slivered almonds and cilantro and stir-fry for 5 minutes. Remove from heat; stir in remaining ingredients, except olive oil. Stuff tomatoes with this mixture; then replace the tops.

Place tomatoes side by side in a casserole. Combine reserved tomato pulp with a little salt and pepper; then pour around tomatoes. Place a little oil on each of the tomatoes; then bake in an oven preheated to 350°F, for 30 minutes or until tomatoes are cooked. Serve hot from casserole with some of the juice spooned on top.

Note: Excellent served with mashed potatoes or cooked rice.

TRUFFLES AND CHICKPEAS

Tajin Terfez
Morocco
Serves 6

Considered by the ancients a supernatural, erotic, and divine food, truffles possess exciting virtues and are unique in the world of fruits and vegetables. Esteemed as a delicacy by many food specialists, this mysterious and rare vegetable is highly valued by almost all who delve into the culinary arts. In his book Lewd Foods, *R. Hendrickson quotes the French gourmet Alexander Dumas Pere. who deemed truffles the "sanctum sanctorum of the gastronomers."*

2 cups canned Moroccan or Syrian truffles
2 cups cooked chickpeas
3 cups water
2 medium onions, finely chopped
4 cloves garlic, crushed
2 tablespoons finely chopped fresh cilantro
4 tablespoons olive oil
1½ teaspoons ground ginger
salt to taste
¼ teaspoon turmeric
⅛ teaspoon cayenne
2 tablespoons lemon juice

Drain truffles, wash thoroughly, and chop. Set aside.

Place all ingredients, except lemon juice and truffles, in a saucepan and bring to boil. Cover and cook over medium heat for 30 minutes. Stir in lemon juice and truffles and cook for 15 minutes longer, adding more water if necessary. Serve immediately.

VEGETABLE CASSEROLE

Tabeekh
Yemen
Serves 6 to 8

During the many centuries when the imam rulers kept Yemen in a medieval state and most of the people poor, only the upper classes could afford meat, eggs, and milk. This forced the masses to develop an alternative cuisine. This tasty dish is an example of their creativity.

3 tablespoons *zhug* (Spicy Relish, see recipe, pp. 18-19)
1 tablespoon *hulbah* (Fenugreek Paste, see recipe, p. 12)
1 pound peeled potatoes, cut into 1-inch cubes
½ pound zucchini, cut into 1-inch cubes
½ pound scraped carrots, cut into ½-inch cubes
½ pound scraped parsnips, cut into ½-inch cubes
2 tablespoons olive oil
1 large onion, finely chopped
4 cloves garlic, crushed
1½ cups water
1 cup stewed tomatoes
salt to taste

Dissolve *zhug* and *hulbah* in ½ cup water.

Place potatoes, zucchini, carrots, and parsnips in a casserole; set aside.

Heat oil in a frying pan and sauté onion and garlic over medium heat for 10 minutes. Stir in water, tomatoes, and salt and bring to boil. Pour over vegetables and cover. Bake in an oven preheated to 350°F, for 1 hour or until vegetables are done. Stir in *zhug–hulbah* mixture and bake for another 10 minutes. Serve hot from casserole.

VEGETABLE STEW

Tajin
Morocco
Serves 8

A vital religious act among all Muslims in the Arab countries is the observance of the month-long fast of Ramadan. From sunrise to sunset, believers deny themselves drink, food, and sexual relations. A 30-day period of penance and forgiveness, it is a time when people renew their community bonds. When the sun sets in Morocco, the fast is broken among the poor with a vegetable hareera *soup; later on, a popular dish, often shared by family and friends, would be this vegetarian* tajin.

4 tablespoons butter
2 medium onions, chopped
3 cloves garlic, crushed
4 tablespoons finely chopped fresh cilantro
1 small hot pepper, finely chopped
3 medium potatoes, peeled and cut into thin slices
2 medium carrots, scraped; then cut into thin rounds
1 19-oz can chickpeas
4 medium tomatoes, chopped
1 teaspoon ginger
1 teaspoon cumin
pinch of saffron
salt and pepper to taste
1 preserved lemon, sliced (see recipe, p. 17)
½ cup pitted green olives

Melt butter in a frying pan and sauté onions, garlic, cilantro, and hot pepper over medium heat for 10 minutes.

Transfer frying pan contents to a casserole; stir in remaining ingredients, except lemon and olives. Cover and place in an oven preheated to 400°F. Bake for 1½ hours or until vegetables are cooked. Spread lemon slices and olives evenly over top; cover and bake for another 10 minutes. Serve hot from casserole.

VEGETABLE STEW WITH VERMICELLI

Dweda bil-Khodhra
Tunisia
Serves 8 to 10

In the town of Tozeur, the center of Tunisia's palm country, my daughter and I dined on this wholesome stew in a restaurant no tourist would think of visiting. As we savored its taste and aroma, I thought of the famous Tunisian poet Abu al-Qasim ash-Shabbi (1909–34). We had visited his resting place on the edge of town a short time before and this bard—who brought about a renaissance in his country's poetry—was still on our mind.

4 tablespoons olive oil
2 medium onions, chopped
4 cloves garlic, crushed
4 tablespoons finely chopped fresh cilantro
2 medium carrots, thinly sliced
2 cups cooked chickpeas
2 cups zucchini, cut into ½-inch cubes
4 tomatoes, finely chopped
1 teaspoon *hreesa* (see recipe, p. 17)
salt and pepper to taste
4 cups water
1 cup vermicelli, broken into small pieces

Heat oil in a saucepan and sauté onions over medium heat for 10 minutes. Add remaining ingredients, except vermicelli and bring to boil. Cover and cook over medium heat for 40 minutes. Stir in vermicelli and cook 20 minutes longer, stirring once in a while and adding more water if necessary. Serve hot with cooked rice.

Vegetarian Couscous

Kesksu
Morocco
Serves 12

Couscous is to North Africa what spaghetti is to Italy, rice to China, and beans to many of the South American countries. Made from semolina and flour, it is almost always on the daily menu of rich and poor alike. Originally called susksoo *in the local dialect of Morocco, it became couscous to the French colonists who took the dish back to France, where it has become very popular.*

2 cups couscous
5 tablespoons butter, melted
4 tablespoons cooking oil
1 large onion, chopped
4 cloves garlic, crushed
½ cup finely chopped fresh cilantro
1 small hot pepper, finely chopped
5 medium tomatoes, chopped
1 19-oz can chickpeas, drained
2 medium carrots, scraped, quartered, and cut into 2-inch long pieces
2 medium parsnips, peeled, quartered, and cut into 2-inch long pieces
2 medium potatoes, peeled and cut into 1-inch cubes
1 very small turnip, peeled and cut into 1-inch cubes
½ cup lentils
¼ cup raisins
1 teaspoon pepper
1 teaspoon ginger
½ teaspoon cinnamon
½ teaspoon allspice
salt to taste
pinch of saffron
6 cups water
1 teaspoon paprika
¼ cup toasted sesame seeds

Note: A couscousière is used in this recipe. If you don't have one, substitute a steamer or a colander set over a saucepan.

Place couscous and butter in a bowl and mix until all kernels are coated. Place in top part of couscousière; then set aside.

In bottom part of couscousière, heat oil; then sauté onion, garlic, cilantro, and hot pepper over medium heat for 10 minutes. Add remaining ingredients, except paprika and sesame seeds, and bring to boil. Fit top part of the couscousière with the couscous, over bottom part; then seal the two together with a narrow piece of cloth soaked in a little flour mixed with water.

Cook over medium heat for 20 minutes, stirring couscous occasionally to make sure no lumps form. At the same time, gradually sprinkle the cup of water over couscous. Cook for 30 minutes more, continuing to stir and add water to the couscous every few minutes. Remove top part of couscousière to make sure vegetables are cooked. If not, cook for a few more minutes.

Mound couscous pyramid-style on a large serving platter, then make a well in the top. Place vegetables with a little of the sauce in well. Sprinkle paprika and sesame seeds over the couscous and serve immediately. Serve remaining sauce in a gravy bowl.

YOGURT WITH CHICKPEAS
Laban ma' Hummus
Palestine and Jordan
Serves 6 to 8

The yogis of ancient India mixed yogurt with honey and called it the "food of the gods." Cleopatra bathed in yogurt to give herself a clear, soft complexion. Genghis Khan fed it to his soldiers to give them courage. One of man's earliest prepared foods, yogurt can claim few equals in culinary folklore.

1 19-oz can chickpeas, with liquid
1 clove garlic, crushed
salt and pepper to taste
2½ cups yogurt
2 cups croutons or pita cut into pieces and well toasted
2 tablespoons butter, melted

Place chickpeas and their liquid in a saucepan and bring to boil.

In the meantime, thoroughly mix garlic, salt, pepper, and yogurt; place in a serving bowl. Pour in boiling chickpeas and stir; then spread croutons or toasted bread over top. Sprinkle with the melted butter and serve immediately.

Note: Makes an excellent breakfast dish.

YOGURT PIES

Fatayar bi Labana
Palestine and Jordan
Makes 12 large pies

In the West it is only recently that yogurt has gained almost universal popularity and become a dietary staple. Catching up with other parts of the world—especially Asia and Eastern Europe—Westerners are recognizing its reputation as a life-extender. Some label it "the miracle milk product," others "a mystery food," while romantics call it "the elixir of life."

1 package dry yeast
½ cup lukewarm water
2 cups flour
¾ teaspoon salt
⅔ cup lukewarm water
2 tablespoons butter, melted
1 beaten egg
2 cups *labana* (Yogurt Cheese, see recipe, p. 22)
2 medium onions, finely chopped
2 tablespoons finely chopped fresh cilantro
½ teaspoon pepper
olive oil

Dissolve yeast in ½ cup lukewarm water and let stand for 10 minutes.

Make a dough by mixing the flour, ¼ teaspoon of the salt, water, yeast solution, butter, and egg; knead well, adding more water or flour if necessary. Cover and allow to rest for an hour.

In the meantime, make filling by thoroughly mixing the remaining ½ teaspoon of salt, yogurt cheese, onions, cilantro, and pepper; set aside.

Form dough into 12 balls; then cover with damp cloth and allow to rest for 30 minutes. Roll balls into 5- to 6-inch rounds; then divide the filling into 12 parts and place on rounds.

Bring the edges of the rounds together over the filling to form triangles. Pinch edges together firmly. Place on well-greased baking sheets.

Bake in an oven preheated to 400°F, for about 15 minutes or until pies turn light brown. Remove from oven; brush tops of pies with olive oil and serve.

ZA'TAR PIES

Manaqeesh
Syria and Lebanon
Makes 12 pies

After immigrants from the West visit their relatives in Syria and Lebanon, they usually return loaded with gifts of za'tar. A mother or a sister will never believe that a relative, living in a faraway land, can ever find za'tar like that made with her own hands.

1 pound frozen pizza dough, thawed, or 1 basic pie dough (see recipe, p. 11)
6 tablespoons *za'tar* (Sumac and Thyme Seasoning, see recipe, p. 19)
½ cup olive oil

Form the dough into 12 balls; then cover with damp cloth and allow to stand for 30 minutes.

In the meantime, mix *za'tar* and oil and set aside.

Flatten dough into ¼-inch-thick rounds; then place on well-greased baking sheets. With your fingers, spread *za'tar*–oil mixture evenly over top of rounds. Bake in an oven preheated to 350°F, for 20 minutes or until edges of pies are well browned.

Note: The pies are at their height of flavor when eaten fresh out of the oven.

ZUCCHINI STEW WITH EGGS

Munazalit Koosa
Syria and Lebanon
Serves 4 to 6

In all Arab countries through the centuries, olive oil has been the most commonly used medium of cooking. Although less expensive vegetable oils have, in our modern age, made inroads into the lands of olives, olive oil is still the most important ingredient used in daily cooking.

½ cup olive oil
2 medium onions, chopped
3 cloves of garlic, crushed
2 medium zucchini, finely chopped
3 medium tomatoes, finely chopped
salt to taste

½ teaspoon pepper
½ teaspoon crushed dried basil
2 eggs

Heat oil in saucepan and sauté onions and garlic until onions begin to brown; then add zucchini and sauté for a few more minutes. Stir in tomatoes, salt, pepper, and basil; then simmer over medium heat for 10 minutes. Break in eggs and stir-fry a few more minutes. Serve hot.

ZUCCHINI AND TOMATO STEW

Al-Ghara bi Tamatim
Morocco
Serves 4 to 6

The first time I had this dish was in the medina *(old city) of Rabat. Clustered around a food stall workers were enjoying this low-cost vegetarian dish, while nearby the aroma of barbecuing meat drew the more affluent.*

4 tablespoons olive oil
2 medium onions, chopped
4 cloves garlic, crushed
2 zucchini (8 to 10 inches long) cut into 1-inch cubes
3 medium tomatoes, finely chopped
1½ cups water
1 teaspoon ginger
1 teaspoon paprika
½ teaspoon ground coriander seeds
salt and pepper to taste

Heat oil in a saucepan and sauté onions and garlic over medium heat for 10 minutes or until they begin to turn light brown. Add remaining ingredients and bring to boil; then cover and cook over medium low heat for 25 minutes. Serve hot or cold.

Pastries & Sweets

I n all but the poorest Arab homes, the table of any self-respecting host is incomplete without trays of pastries. In the Middle East, sweets are served with tiny cups of piping-hot, strong Arabic coffee; in North Africa with refreshing mint tea. Ideally, even the setting for serving pastries is attractively arranged.

Arab pastries are very different from the cakes and pies of the Western world. In the majority of cases, they are made with paper-thin layers of dough filled with nuts, spices, and butter, baked and then then soaked in *qater*, a syrup of sugar or honey. Their delectable, sweet taste has inspired artists through the centuries. Poems have been composed, songs have been sung, and legends born wherever these marvelously delicate pastries have been served. A poet once said: "With our exquisite and luscious sweets, can the beauty of any woman compare?" And another unknown poet on the same topic: "To eat the pastries of the Arabs is to make a person's life serene and happy and free from evil."

The inhabitants of the Iberian Peninsula and Sicily, during the many centuries of Arab rule, became fond of Arab pastries. When the Muslims were expelled from these European lands, the art of making these sweets was retained. Candied fruits and desserts utilizing almonds, egg yolks, honey, and rosewater, which are found in all parts of the Iberian Peninsula, are purely of Arab origin.

In Italy it was the same story. W. Root, in *The Cooking of Italy*, writes that the Italians learned from the Arabs how to concoct the desserts that are now such an important part of their cuisine. He goes on to say that the art of making ice cream and sherbet was introduced by the Arabs, who had learned it from the Chinese. In Italy, as in the Iberian Peninsula, Arabs introduced various sweets based on honey, almond paste, and marzipan as well as sugar. There is no doubt that the desserts of Italy— especially its southern regions—would be much poorer today had the Arabs not left their legacy.

Strange as it may seem, the credit for the preservation of the Arab-introduced sweets should go to the nuns of the Latin-speaking world. No one knows why the nuns, in their numerous medieval convents, kept the Arab recipes for desserts alive. Some historians have theorized that it was the undeniable voluptuousness of these tasty confections that was responsible.

Besides contributing desserts, the Arabs also bequeathed another legacy related to sweets. In traditional Spanish restaurants, as in modern eating places in the Middle East, foreign diners perusing the menus, cannot be blamed if they assume that pastries are unknown. In Spain, as in the Arab East, desserts are served in separate pastry shops. Diners with a sweet tooth must leave the restaurants in quest of dessert—no doubt enhancing their digestion.

The recipes here are but a minuscule sampling of the thousands found throughout the Arab world. There is no doubt that these sweets have the potential to influence the cuisines of the English-speaking world—as they once did in Spain and Italy.

Almond & Sesame Seed Pastry

Samsa

Tunisia

Makes 35 to 40 pieces

Many of the mouth-watering desserts of North Africa have their origin in Al-Andalus, the Arab-created earthly paradise in the Iberian Peninsula. One has to only read Andalusian Ibn Razeen at-Tujeebee's thirteenth-century culinary work to be convinced that the sweets North Africans prepare today had a history in Arab Andalusia.

1½ cups almonds, blanched
1½ cups white sesame seeds
1½ cups clarified butter (see p. 2)
1 1-pound package *baklawa* dough (filo dough)
1 *qater* (Syrup, see recipe, p. 20)

Preheat oven to 350°F. Spread almonds and sesame seeds evenly in a large shallow pan and bake until they turn light brown, stirring occasionally so that they brown evenly. Then pulverize almonds and sesame seeds in a blender; set aside.

In a well-buttered 10 x 15-inch baking pan, place 1 sheet of *baklawa* dough; brush with butter. Continue layering sheets brushed with butter until a third of them are used.

Spread half the almond and sesame seed mixture on the dough layers; then add another third of the dough, sheet by sheet, buttering as before. Spread remaining almond and sesame seed mixture on the stacked dough layers; then cover with the remaining third of the dough, buttering sheet by sheet as before.

Brush top with remaining butter; then with a sharp knife carefully cut into squares or diamond shapes. Bake in oven, preheated to 400°F, for 5 minutes; lower heat to 300°F and bake for approximately 30 minutes longer, or until the sides turn a light shade of brown.

While the *samsa* is baking, prepare *qater* (syrup); then set aside, but keep warm.

Before removing *samsa* from oven, place under broiler for a few moments, rotating pan until top is evenly golden brown. Remove from oven and pour syrup evenly over top of the hot *samsa*. Allow to cool before serving. *Samsa* keeps for a week or so covered, without refrigeration, but it gets harder as time passes. Refrigerated, it could keep for a couple months.

Almond Butter

Amalou
Morocco
Makes about 1½ cups

A Moroccan meal is always preceded by a formal ritual of hand-washing as diners are seated on low pillows around a low table. The food is served on a large communal platter and eaten with the thumb and the first two fingers of the right hand. A piece of fresh crusty bread is used as an aid in scooping and dipping. Nowadays, strangers find it romantic to eat in this fashion.

1 cup blanched and toasted almonds, pulverized
½ cup olive oil
5 tablespoons honey
2 tablespoons pulverized walnuts

Thoroughly combine all ingredients; then serve as a spread on toasted bread for breakfast or as a dessert after a meal.

Almond and Tahini Cookies

Ghuraybat Lawz
Syria and Lebanon
Makes about 40 small cookies

This is a modern version of the traditional ghurayba *made in the Middle East for thousands of years. Perhaps not quite as tasty, they are much more healthful.*

½ cup tahini
½ cup pulverized blanched almonds
1 cup sugar
4 tablespoons butter
2 eggs
1½ teaspoons baking powder
1 teaspoon vanilla
2 cups flour

Place all the ingredients, except flour, in a food processor and process for a few moments. Transfer to a mixing bowl; then add flour, a little at a time, and knead into a dough, adding a little water if necessary. Form into balls about

1-inch in diameter; then place on well-greased baking sheets and flatten to about ¼ inch thick. Bake in an oven preheated to 350°F, for 15 minutes or until cookies turn light brown. Allow to cool; then serve or store.

ARABIAN SHORTBREAD

Ghurayba
Syria and Lebanon
Makes 40 pieces

Children in the eastern Arab world look forward to this delicious shortbread often made by their mothers in the family kitchen.

The Spaniards inherited this delectable treat, which they call polvorones a la Andaluza, *from the Arabs. The ingredients of both versions are basically the same to this day.*

1½ cups butter, softened
1¾ cups confectioner's sugar
1 teaspoon orange-flower water (*mazahar*)
1 egg yolk
3 cups flour
40 blanched almonds

Place butter, 1½ cups of the confectioner's sugar, orange-flower water, and egg yolk in a blender and blend for 1 minute. Transfer to a mixing bowl; then gradually add flour while mixing with fingers, until a smooth dough is formed.

Form dough into 40 balls, a little smaller than walnuts; then place on an ungreased cookie sheet and flatten slightly to about ½-inch thickness. Press an almond on each piece. Bake in an oven preheated to 300°F, for 20 minutes or until bottoms turn light brown. Remove from oven and allow to cool.

Sprinkle with the remaining confectioner's sugar; then serve or store.

Note: The *ghurayba* may feel soft at the end of baking time, but they will harden as they cool.

BAKLAWA

Syria and Lebanon
Makes 35 to 40 pieces

In past ages, Arab pastries reached their height of magnificence in the sumptuous banquets of the wealthy. At any of these feasts, baklawa, *the king of Arab pastry, was always to be found. Made from a paper-thin dough, known in the West as strudel or filo dough, it has stood the test of centuries. This dough, and the shredded version known as* knafa, *form the basis of the many varieties of syrup-soaked sweets of these ancient lands.*

In the Arab East, it used to be said that no young lady would make a good wife unless she knew how to make baklawa *dough. In the* mahajar *(the lands to which Arabs emigrated), my wife was one of the very few who learned this art from her Damascene mother. Fortunately today, not only in the Arab world, but also throughout the Western world, the dough is prepared commercially and young women are spared this ordeal of proving their suitability for marriage. With the commercially produced dough anyone can easily make* baklawa.

2 cups walnuts, chopped
1 cup sugar
2 cups clarified butter, melted (see p. 2)
2 teaspoons cinnamon
1 tablespoon orange-flower water (*mazahar*)
1 1-pound package *baklawa* (filo) dough
1 *qater* (Syrup, see recipe, p. 20)

Combine walnuts, sugar, ¼ cup of the butter, cinnamon, and orange-flower water; set aside.

Butter well a 10 x 15-inch baking pan; set aside.

Remove dough from the package and spread out on a towel. Cover the unused dough with a damp towel or plastic wrap to prevent it from drying out as you work. Take one sheet and place in the baking pan; then brush with butter. Keep repeating the procedure until half the dough is used. Place walnut mixture over buttered layers, spreading evenly.

Take a sheet of dough, spread it over walnut mixture and brush with butter; continue until remainder of the dough is used.

Heat remaining butter and pour it evenly over dough. With a sharp knife, carefully cut into approximately 2-inch squares or diamonds. Bake in an oven preheated to 400°F, for 5 minutes; then lower the heat to 300°F and bake 30 minutes longer, or until the sides turn light brown.

While *baklawa* is baking, prepare *qater* (syrup); then set aside, but keep warm.

When sides of *baklawa* turn light brown, place the pan under broiler, turning frequently, until top of *baklawa* turns evenly golden brown. Remove from oven; then spoon syrup over each piece. Allow to cool before serving.

BARLEY PUDDING
Muhallabiat Shi'eer
Iraqi Kurdistan
Serves 4 to 6

Some historians believe that the oldest civilization in the world evolved in Iraq, between the Tigris and Euphrates rivers. From this ancient land, it spread both east to India and China and west to the Mediterranean region. There is no doubt that much of ancient Greece's knowledge was inherited from Egypt and the civilizations of Mesopotamia. Hence, the foods of Iraq have a venerable history.

½ cup barley, washed
4 cups milk
¼ teaspoon salt
¾ cup brown sugar
⅓ cup butter
2 eggs, separated
grated rind of 1 orange
1 orange, separated into segments
1 teaspoon cinnamon
¼ cup confectioner's sugar

Place barley in a saucepan, cover with water, and bring to boil. Cook over medium heat for 20 minutes. Stir in milk, salt, brown sugar, and butter; again bring to boil, stirring until the sugar is dissolved. Lower heat and simmer until barley is cooked; then remove from heat and cool slightly.

Beat egg yolks until thick and creamy in appearance; then add orange rind and stir into barley mixture.

Beat egg whites until stiff; then fold gently into mixture. Pour into a well-buttered baking dish; then decorate with the orange segments. Sprinkle cinnamon over top; then bake in an oven preheated to 350°F, for about 20 minutes. Sprinkle with confectioner's sugar and serve hot.

BREAD OF THE PALACE

'Aysh as-Saraaya
Syria and Lebanon
Serves 8

With a long culinary history stretching back thousands of years, the desserts of the Middle East are among the most delicious in the world. Some are still prepared the way they were when the armies of the famous Syrian Queen Zenobia defeated the legions of Rome; others have evolved under the many influences brought through the centuries by merchants and conquerors who came to the Greater Syria area. Some desserts were further developed in North America and Europe by the emigrants from those regions.

One of these is 'Aysh as-Saraaya—a dessert, as its name implies, once made in palaces where there was time and staff enough to devote to its long and complicated preparation. The distinctive, crusty bread was made from scratch; even the cream is concocted by a special method. My daughter, Leila, who lives in Allentown, Pennsylvania, simplified this recipe to fit into the rushed life of our modern age.

8 slices white bread, crusts removed and toasted
2 cups half-and-half cream
8 slices white bread, crusts removed, cut into tiny pieces
2 tablespoons sugar
2 tablespoons orange-flower water (*mazahar*)
1 *qater* (Syrup, see recipe p. 20)
4 tablespoons crushed pistachio nuts

Place toasted bread in a 9 x 13-inch pan; set aside.

Place cream, bread pieces, sugar, and *mazahar* in a saucepan; then, stirring constantly, bring to boil. Continue stirring over medium heat until mixture thickens; then keep warm over very low heat.

Prepare syrup and allow to cool.

Pour syrup over toast in pan; then spread cream mixture evenly over top. Sprinkle pistachios over top; then refrigerate for at least 12 hours. Cut into 8 pieces and serve.

BURGHUL DESSERT

Hilwat ad-Daqeeq
Yemen
Serves 4 to 6

In Yemen, which the Romans called Arabia Felix (Happy Arabia), for sourness, lemon is always used—never vinegar—and for desserts, honey is the favored sweetener.

1 cup coarse *burghul*
½ teaspoon salt
4½ cups water
1 teaspoon cinnamon
¼ teaspoon crushed cloves
½ cup honey

Place *burghul,* salt, and water in a saucepan and bring to boil. Cover and cook over medium heat for 30 minutes or until *burghul* is well cooked. Stir in remaining ingredients and serve hot.

BURGHUL AND PINEAPPLE PUDDING

Burghul wa Annanas
Syria and Lebanon
Serves 8 to 10

Unexcelled as a nourishing grain, burghul *has more food energy than corn meal; more iron than rice; less fat than uncooked wheat; six times more calcium than corn meal and three more than rice; and more vitamins than barley, corn meal, or rice.*

1 cup fine *burghul*
1 19-oz can crushed pineapple
1½ cups milk
½ cup brown sugar
2 eggs, beaten
4 tablespoons butter
1 teaspoon vanilla
½ teaspoon cinnamon

Soak *burghul* in warm water for 15 minutes; then drain in a strainer, by pressing out as much water as possible.

Place *burghul* and remaining ingredients in a casserole and combine thoroughly. Bake uncovered in an oven preheated to 350°F, for 40 minutes or until top turns golden brown. Serve hot from casserole.

CANDIED EGGPLANTS

Bathinjan Ma'aqqad
Syria and Lebanon
Serves 6 to 12

Eggplants are usually eaten as a savory vegetable, but here they are prepared as a dessert that is strangely delightful.

1 dozen tiny eggplants, about 3 inches long, washed and stemmed
2 cups sugar
2½ cups water
½ teaspoon whole cloves
2 teaspoons orange-flower water (*mazaha*r)
3 tablespoons lemon juice

Place eggplants in a pot, cover with water and bring to boil. Cook for 3 to 5 minutes over medium heat; then remove and drain. Set aside.

In the meantime, place sugar, water, and cloves in a pot. Stirring constantly, bring to boil over medium heat and stir until sugar melts. Add eggplants and cook for 20 minutes over low heat. Stir in the orange blossom water and lemon juice; then cook for another 5 minutes. Remove from heat and allow to cool. Serve with or without the cooking syrup.

CAROB PUDDING

Muhallabiat Kharoob
Syria and Lebanon
Serves 6

Known as "Saint-John's-bread," "honey locusts," or "locust-beans," carob beans are, according to legend, the "locusts" eaten in the wilderness by John the Baptist. Before the Arabs introduced them into Europe as a common food, carobs were indeed called "locusts" by the Europeans.

A. Ward, in the Encyclopedia of Food, *states that the name locust bean arose because the carob pod resembles a large locust. The name in turn gave birth to the notion that the pods were the locusts eaten by John the Baptist in the wilderness. Ward goes on to say that the locusts St. John consumed were actually not carob pods but the insect, which is still much relished as a food in a number of the world's desert areas.*

2½ cups milk
2 tablespoons sugar
4 tablespoons cornstarch
½ cup shredded coconut
½ cup carob chips
4 tablespoons butter
½ teaspoon almond extract

Place milk, sugar, and cornstarch in a saucepan and mix thoroughly. Stirring constantly, cook over medium low heat until mixture thickens. Add remaining ingredients; stirring constantly, cook for about 3 minutes. Place in serving cups and chill before serving.

COCONUT SQUARES
Hilwat Koko
Morocco
Makes 16 squares

Coconuts entered the Arab kitchen on an appreciable scale only in this century. Making up for lost time, this tropical delicacy is fast becoming a favorite among the Arabs. Today, many of the dishes that include coconut, such as this fudge, grace the tables of Arabs from the Atlantic to the Arabian Gulf.

2 cups grated coconut
¾ cup half-and-half cream
1½ cups sugar
3 tablespoons butter
3 tablespoons lemon rind

Place coconut, cream, and sugar in a saucepan and bring to boil. Turn heat to low and simmer until a soft ball is formed when a small amount is dropped into cold water, about 234°F on a candy thermometer. Stir in butter and lemon rind; allow to cool to room temperature. Place in a blender and blend until thick and glossy. Pour into an 8 x 8-inch buttered pan and chill; then cut into 2-inch squares and serve.

CROISSANTS

Tisharaq al-Aryan
Algeria
Makes about 24

The long French occupation of Algeria led to the introduction of a good number of French dishes. Among them is this great morning treat that has become the main breakfast dish throughout North Africa.

Ironically, the croissant was first prepared as an anti-Muslim token. It was invented by the Austrians in the seventeenth century during the Ottoman siege of Vienna. The Turks were digging underground passages by night to break through the city walls when Austrian bakers, working at their underground ovens, heard the noise and raised the alarm that saved the city.

A pastry, formed like the crescent on the Turkish flag, was created to commemorate the victory over the Ottomans. At the time, the eating of this pastry was a figurative gesture of consuming the Muslim crescent. Eventually the French adopted the croissant and perfected its buttery taste and light flaky texture, while its political symbolism faded away.

3 egg yolks
1 cup milk
4 cups flour
1½ cups sugar
4 teaspoons baking powder
grated peel of 2 oranges (zest)
grated peel of 2 lemons (zest)
½ cup clarified butter (see p. 2)
½ cup oil
1 teaspoon vanilla
1 cup pulverized almonds
1 teaspoon orange-flower water (*mazahar*)
1 teaspoon cinnamon
1 cup coarsely chopped or slivered almonds

Beat two of the egg yolks well, then mix with milk and set aside.

In a large bowl place flour, 1 cup of the sugar, baking powder, orange and lemon zest, butter, and oil; then rub well with hands. Add vanilla and yolk–milk mixture and combine thoroughly to make a dough, adding a little flour or water if necessary. Let stand for 15 minutes.

In the meantime, make a filling by mixing the remaining ½ cup of sugar, pulverized almonds, orange-flower water, and cinnamon; set aside.

Roll dough ⅛-inch thick; then cut into triangles the size of pie wedges. Place filling in center of the triangle; then roll up from bottom. Continue until all triangles are rolled. Place on well-greased baking sheets with the point down, curving them into crescents.

Beat remaining egg yolk and brush it on the croissants. Sprinkle with chopped or slivered almonds. Bake in an oven preheated to 350°F, for 15 to 20 minutes or until croissants turn light brown. Serve hot.

DATE AND ALMOND COOKIES

Tamar bil-Lawz Mitabukeen
Morocco
Makes about 3 dozen cookies

In the villas of the rich or in the huts of the poor, Moroccan hospitality knows no bounds. As a guest you are treated as one of the family. The best of what the host can afford, be it plain couscous or a roasted lamb, is offered with courtesy and charm. After the meal is over, mint tea and sweets are usually offered. From among these sweets, tamar bi-lawz mitabukeen *is often served.*

⅓ cup butter
1 cup sugar
2 eggs
1½ cups flour
½ cup cream
1 teaspoon vanilla
1 teaspoon baking powder
¼ teaspoon baking soda
1 cup finely chopped dates
1 cup pulverized almonds
½ teaspoon salt

Place all ingredients in a food processor and process into a soft paste, adding a little water if necessary. To form cookies, drop heaping tablespoons onto well-greased baking trays, placing them about 1 inch apart. Bake in an oven preheated to 350°F, for 10 minutes or until cookies turn golden brown.

DATES WITH BANANAS

Tamar wa Mawz
Palestine and Jordan
Serves 6 to 8

To the Arabs, the date palm has a personality with human qualities. They might well have a point for, like human beings, if its head is severed, it will die. A frond once cut will not grow again, and its crown is covered with thick foliage, like the hair on a human head.

1 cup whipping cream
1 tablespoon sugar
1 cup whole dates, pitted and thinly sliced lengthwise
3 large bananas, sliced in half lengthwise, then sliced into ½-inch half-rounds
1 teaspoon cinnamon

In a bowl, combine cream and sugar; then whip until stiff. Add dates and bananas and toss gently. Place in 6 to 8 serving dishes; then sprinkle with cinnamon. Chill for 30 minutes; then serve.

DATES IN BUTTER SAUCE

Ar-Rangina
Saudi Arabia
Serves 4 to 6

To thrive, the date palm needs a hot, dry climate with no rain but water for its roots. It is said this majestic tree needs its head in the sun and its feet in water, or, as the Arab proverb puts it: "its feet in heaven but its head in hell." Under ideal conditions, the tree usually grows from 20 to 30 feet tall. Its life span is 100 years, although it has been known, in some instances, to reach the age of 200.

When a date palm is about five years old, it begins to bear fruit and continues until it dies of old age. The palm has no branches, but the leaves of a mature tree are from 20 to 30 feet long. There are male and female trees and, to bear fruit, the female trees must be fertilized. In the wild, this function is performed by the wind. When palms are commercially cultivated, they are pollinated artificially by human hand. There are perhaps several thousand species that bear fruit, ranging from the size of a tiny plum to that of a large orange.

¾ pound whole dates, pitted
¾ cup butter

⅔ cup flour
2 teaspoons cinnamon
3 teaspoons confectioner's sugar

Arrange dates on 4 to 6 small serving plates; then set aside.

Heat butter over medium heat until it begins to sizzle; then add flour and cinnamon. Cook, stirring constantly, for no more than 3 minutes or until a soft paste sauce is formed. Pour sauce over dates and allow to cool; then sprinkle with confectioner's sugar and serve.

DATE CAKE

Ka'ak Tamar
Iraq
Makes about 40 pieces

A single date palm, when full grown, will produce up to 300 pounds of fruit annually, hanging in great bunches that weigh from 18 to 30 pounds each. The dates need at least six months to mature. They develop in four stages: kimiri, *the green stage;* khalal, *when they turn yellowish with a red tinge;* rutub, *the first stage of ripeness; and* tamar, *fully ripe. In the last stage, dates are light brown, plump, and glossy with a sweet pulp.*

¾ cup butter, melted
1 cup sugar
3 eggs
1½ teaspoons vanilla
1 teaspoon cinnamon
½ teaspoon salt
1 cup flour
1½ teaspoons baking powder
1½ cups finely chopped dates
1 cup coarsely chopped or broken walnuts
½ cup chopped blanched almonds

Place butter, sugar, eggs, vanilla, cinnamon, and salt in a mixing bowl and combine thoroughly. Sift in flour and baking powder and mix thoroughly, adding a little water if necessary. Add dates, walnuts, and almonds and mix well; then place in an 9 x 13-inch greased baking pan. Bake in an oven preheated to 350°F, for 30 minutes or until cake turns golden brown. Cut into squares; then allow to cool before serving.

Date Cookies

Klaycha at-Tamr
Iraq
Makes about 45 pieces

Dates are one of the world's most complete foods. They contain carbohydrates; fat; protein; vitamins A, B, D, and G; and the minerals iron, magnesium, potassium, phosphorus, calcium, and copper. Their sugars are not acid forming and they have enough fiber to provide needed roughage. To the bedouins of the Arabian Peninsula, dates are truly a miracle food. It is no wonder they call them the "bread of the desert."

From the early days of civilization, humans have ascribed medicinal qualities to dates. The bedouins maintain that a diet of dates can cure any ailment, from a simple cold to impotence. Many firmly believe that dates cure the diseases of the lung and chest, steady the blood pressure, and clear the intestines, thus helping to keep away cancer of the bowel. There may be some merit to these claims, since the Arabs who eat dates on a daily basis do not suffer from high blood pressure or many of the common digestive ailments of the West.

In addition to the fruit, which is much valued as a food, the date palm yields products that are of great economic importance. Its fiber is utilized for ropes and mats; its wood for building material and furniture; its leaves for roofs, baskets, and hats; and the stones of the fruit are crushed for animal food. The sap, called the "drink of life" by the early inhabitants of the Middle East, is made into sugar, vinegar, or alcoholic drinks, and the tree acts as an umbrella for other fruits and vegetables growing in its shade. It is said that there are at least 800 uses for the date palm and its by-products.

2 cups flour
1 teaspoon baking powder
½ teaspoon ground cardamom
½ teaspoon salt
¾ cup butter, melted
1 cup sugar
3 eggs, beaten
1 cup chopped dates
1 cup chopped walnuts

Sift together flour, baking powder, cardamom, and salt; set aside.

Thoroughly combine butter, sugar, and eggs; then gradually stir in dry ingredients until a soft dough is formed, adding a little water if necessary. Stir in dates and walnuts; then place heaping teaspoons of the dough an inch apart on an ungreased baking sheet. Place in an oven preheated to 350°F and bake for 15 minutes or until cookies turn golden brown. Remove and allow to cool before serving.

DATE CRESCENTS

Aqras Tamar
Syria and Lebanon
Makes about 36 pieces

In the Arab lands there is a common belief that the venerated palm is the oldest cultivated fruit tree in the world. In its native homeland, the Arabian Peninsula, the inhabitants have no doubt that it was first grown in paradise. According to Muslim belief, the archangel Gabriel told Adam in the garden of Eden: "Thou art created from the same substance as this palm tree which henceforth shall nourish you."

1¼ cups butter, melted
2 eggs
½ cup milk
½ teaspoon salt
1½ teaspoons vanilla
3 cups flour
2 teaspoons baking powder
1 cup finely chopped dates
¾ cup blanched almonds, ground
¼ cup sugar
½ teaspoon cinnamon
pinch of nutmeg
pinch of ground cloves
½ cup confectioner's sugar

Combine 1 cup of the butter, eggs, milk, salt, and vanilla in a bowl; set aside.

Sift together flour and baking powder; then gradually knead into butter–egg mixture until dough is formed, adding a little water if necessary. Form into spheres the size of golf balls; then allow to rest, covered with a cloth, for 1 hour.

In the meantime, make a filling by thoroughly mixing remaining ingredients, including the remaining ¼ cup of butter, but not the confectioner's sugar.

Roll out balls to 3- to 4-inch rounds; then place 1 heaping teaspoon filling in the center of each round. Fold dough over to cover filling; then pinch edges together to seal, in the process forming them into crescent shapes.

Place on greased baking trays; then bake in an oven preheated to 350°F, for 20 minutes or until crescents turn golden brown. Remove from oven and allow to cool. Place on a serving platter, sprinkle with confectioner's sugar, and serve.

Date Fruit Cup

Khshoof al-Balah
Egypt
Serves 6

Perhaps at the beginning of the Pharaonic era, the cultivation of date palms spread to the valley of the Nile. Paintings found in the tombs of the Pharaohs show that this stately tree was known in that ancient land at least since the time hieroglyphics were invented.

In later centuries, Phoenician traders carried the date palm from the Fertile Crescent and Egypt to North Africa and Spain. In Spain the date palm was not cultivated on a large scale, until after the Arabs occupied the Iberian Peninsula in 711 AD. In the Alicante province on the eastern coast of Spain, palm orchards first established by the Arabs are still flourishing today.

4 cups water
2 cups dates, pitted
⅓ cup sugar
¼ cup raisins
6 whole cloves
2 tablespoons lemon juice
½ cup whipping cream

Place water in a saucepan and bring to boil; then add dates and cook for 5 minutes. Remove dates with a slotted spoon (reserve the cooking water in the saucepan); allow to cool. Peel the dates, then set aside.

Bring reserved water to a boil; add sugar and stir until sugar dissolves. Stir in raisins, cloves, and dates and cook for 15 minutes over medium heat. Add lemon juice and cook for another 5 minutes. Remove from heat and allow to cool.

Place in fruit cups. Whip cream and spoon over the dates before serving.

DATE JAM
Maraba Tamar
Palestine and Jordan
Makes about 1 quart

The stately palm, which some people call "the tree of paradise," has had religious significance since the dawn of history. The ancient Mesopotamian religions regarded it as a sacred plant, and this reverence was passed on to later religions and civilizations. In the Old Testament, the story of Genesis mentions it as the "tree of life," and the Book of Psalms records that the "righteous shall flourish like a palm tree." Even today among Christians, its leaves are used in the Easter celebration of Palm Sunday.

1½ cups water
2 cups sugar
10 whole cloves
2 cups finely chopped dates
3 tablespoons lemon juice
¼ cup blanched almonds, finely chopped
¼ cup walnuts, finely chopped

Place water in a saucepan and bring to boil. Add sugar and cloves and, stirring constantly, bring water to boil again. Stir in dates; then turn heat to low. Cook for about 10 minutes or until a paste is formed. Add lemon juice, almonds, and walnuts and cook for a few more minutes. Remove from heat and allow to cool; then place in a glass jar and store.

DATE AND NUT PIE

Hilwat Tamar
Iraq
Serves 6 to 8

Even though most European languages derive their words for date from the Greek daktylos (finger), Hilda Simon in her excellent book, The Date Palm: Bread of the Desert, *suggests that the name could have come from the Arabic* daqlan *(seedling). Others have indicated that the Greek* daktylos *is derived from the Arabic* daql, *a type of date. The Arabic origin of this historic tree makes it quite certain that* daqlan *or* daql *passed through Greek and Latin to become the name for dates in the European languages. Portuguese is an exception. The Arabic name for ripe dates,* tamar *became* tâmara, *the Portuguese name for dates.*

½ cup coarsely chopped blanched almonds
½ cup coarsely chopped walnuts
¼ cup sugar
½ cup butter
1 cup half-and-half cream
1 pound dates, finely chopped
½ teaspoon cinnamon
1 tablespoon orange-flower water (*mazahar*)
2 tablespoons sesame seeds, toasted

Combine almonds, walnuts, and sugar and set aside.

Melt butter in a frying pan; stir in cream, dates, cinnamon, and *mazahar*. Cook over low heat until dates become soft, stirring once in a while to make sure the dates do not stick. Add a little more cream if necessary. Stir in nut mixture and cook for another 3 minutes.

Spread evenly in a pie pan; then bake in an oven preheated to 300°F, for 15 minutes. Remove from oven; then sprinkle with sesame seeds. Allow to cool; then cut into thin wedges.

Deep-Fried Sweet Balls

'Awamee
Syria and Lebanon
Makes about 3 dozen pieces

As a child growing up on an isolated prairie farm, I often watched my mother make this simple dish. Even today, the mouth-watering taste of these syrupy balls charms me.

2 cups flour
4 tablespoons cornstarch
½ teaspoon salt
1 package dry yeast, dissolved in ¼ cup warm water
2 cups warm water
1 *qater* (Syrup, see recipe, p. 20)
2 cups cooking oil

Combine flour, cornstarch, and salt in a mixing bowl; then pour in yeast and mix well. Add water and stir until mixture is the consistency of pancake batter, adding more water if necessary. Cover and set aside for 1 hour.

In the meantime, prepare syrup; then set aside, keeping warm.

Heat oil in a saucepan; then drop 1 tablespoon of batter into hot oil. Cook over medium heat until *'awamee* turns golden brown; then remove with a slotted spoon and place on paper towels to drain. Dip *'awamee* balls into warm syrup; then remove and arrange on a serving platter. Continue until all the batter is used.

Fig Jam

Teen Ma'aqqad
Syria and Lebanon
Makes about a quart

Originating in western Asia, figs are one of man's most ancient foods. In the Bible, Adam used the fig leaf to restore his dignity and Buddha is said to have received his revelations under a fig tree. In the Mediterranean countries, since the times of ancient Greece and the Roman empire, figs have always been greatly valued. Today, figs are grown extensively in California, Greece, Italy, Portugal, Spain, Lebanon, and Syria, but the best figs come from Smyrna in Turkey.

1 pound dried figs
1 cup sugar
1 cup cold water
1 teaspoon fennel seeds, ground
6 cloves
½ cup pine nuts
1 tablespoon sesame seeds
1 tablespoon lemon juice

Grind figs in a food processor or meat grinder. Then place figs, sugar, water, fennel, and cloves in a saucepan and bring to boil. Cover and cook over medium heat for 20 minutes or until jam consistency is reached, stirring every few minutes during last 15 minutes. Remove and stir in pine nuts, sesame seeds, and lemon juice. Allow to cool before use.

Note: Store in sterilized containers. Excellent when spread on buttered toast or pita bread.

Fruit Dessert

Halawah bil-Fawaaki
Libya
Serves 8

In North Africa, honey is used much more than in the Middle East. During Ramadan, the enticing sweets are enhanced by being soaked in a honey syrup or having honey as a main ingredient. In that part of the world, people have long believed that honey is a healthy food.

Not just in North Africa, but throughout the Mediterranean basin, honey has long been known to have beneficial effects on humans. It was prescribed by ancient doctors for a number of ailments.

Honey is the only natural sweet that is not manufactured by human beings. An instant energy-building food, it contains seven B vitamins, amino acids, enzymes, and a number of beneficial minerals.

2 large plums, diced
1 large apple, peeled, cored, and diced
2 medium peaches, diced
1 cup diced cantaloupe
¼ cup raisins
2 tablespoons lemon juice
½ cup honey, melted
3 tablespoons butter, melted
1 teaspoon cinnamon
½ cup couscous
2 tablespoons crushed pistachios

Combine plums, apple, peaches, cantaloupe, raisins, lemon juice, and honey in a saucepan; then cover and cook over low heat for 10 minutes. Add butter, cinnamon and couscous. Cook over low heat, stirring often, until couscous is done.

Transfer to a serving bowl and allow to cool for 1 hour. Sprinkle with pistachios just before serving.

Gazelle's Ankles

Ka'ab Ghazaal
Algeria
Makes approximately 36 pieces

In Algeria and Morocco, this picturesquely named sweet is the dessert par excellence. No feast would be complete without this sweet, served with mint tea after a meal.

2 cups flour
½ cup clarified butter (see p. 2)
¼ cup olive oil
½ cup water
2 teaspoons orange-flower water (*mazahar*)
½ cup finely ground blanched almonds
¼ cup sugar
½ teaspoon cinnamon
½ *qater* recipe (Syrup, see recipe, p. 20)
¼ cup confectioner's sugar

Place flour, butter, and oil in a bowl and rub together until crumbly. Add water and 1 teaspoon of the orange-flower water; then knead into smooth dough, adding more flour or water if necessary. Cover with a cloth and set aside for 30 minutes.

In the meantime, prepare filling by mixing almonds, sugar, cinnamon, and remainder of orange-flower water.

Form dough into walnut-size balls, then cover with a damp cloth. Remove one ball at a time and roll into very thin round. Place 1 heaping teaspoon of filling in center of round and fold over to form a half-circle. Pinch the edges closed; then trim with a pastry wheel and mold into a crescent shape.

Repeat until all balls are used, placing the crescents on ungreased cookie sheets. Bake on middle rack of an oven preheated to 350°F, for 15 to 20 minutes or until *ka'ab ghazaal* begin to turn golden brown.

In the meantime, prepare syrup; then set aside, keeping warm.

Place 2 or 3 hot *ka'ab ghazaal* at a time in syrup for a few moments; then remove and place on a serving platter. Sprinkle with confectioner's sugar and serve.

HONEY PIE

Bint as-Sahan
Yemen
Makes two pies

In Yemen, on special occasions in the homes of the affluent, bint as-sahn *is always served as a first course; at other times it is eaten during the meal. However, it makes an excellent dessert.*

4 cups flour
½ teaspoon salt
1 package yeast, dissolved in ½ cup of warm water
5 eggs, beaten
2 tablespoons milk
1 cup butter, melted
1 cup honey

Thoroughly mix flour and salt in a mixing bowl; then make a well in the middle. In a separate bowl, combine yeast, eggs, and milk. Then pour into the flour. Knead into dough, adding more milk or flour if necessary. Cover and allow to stand in warm place for one hour.

Form into 12 balls and place on a floured surface; cover with damp cloth and allow to stand for 30 minutes. Roll balls into rounds the size of a pie plate; set aside.

Place a round in pie plate; then brush with butter. Add five more rounds, brushing each with butter. In a second pie plate, repeat with the other six rounds.

Mix remaining butter with honey; then brush generously.

Bake in an oven preheated to 350°F, for 25 minutes or until the tops turn golden brown. Remove from oven; immediately pour half the remaining butter–honey mixture over tops of both pies. Allow to stand for 10 minutes; then cut into wedges. Serve with the remaining butter–honey mixture on the side for diners to add according to taste.

HONEY-DIPPED PASTRY

Bariwaat
Morocco
Makes approximately 40 pieces

In the eastern Arab lands, honey is rarely used in pastries. In contrast, in Morocco, and generally throughout North Africa, this bee product is extensively used in the preparation of sweets. The tradition of using honey to create mouth-watering desserts was brought to North Africa by the Arabs expelled from the Iberian Peninsula.

1 cup blanched almonds
½ cup sugar
½ teaspoon cinnamon
1 tablespoon butter, melted
1 egg
1 package filo dough
2 cups cooking oil
2 tablespoons orange-flower water (*mazahar*)
2 cups honey

Place almonds and sugar in a blender and blend until the almonds are coarsely ground. Transfer to a bowl, stir in cinnamon and butter, and set aside.

In a separate bowl, beat egg and set aside.

Place orange-flower water and honey in a saucepan and heat thoroughly. Reduce heat to very low.

Cut each filo sheet in two, lengthwise. Place 1 tablespoon of almond mixture near the right hand bottom corner of each half-sheet. Fold half-sheet in half lengthwise over the filling. Then fold over corners to make a triangle.

Using a pastry brush or your hand, paint each *bariwaat* with egg, especially at the openings to seal them.

Heat oil in a frying pan until it sizzles; then lower heat and place *bariwaat* in oil. Fry until *bariwaat* turns light brown.

Remove *bariwaat* from oil with a slotted spoon and place in honey for ten seconds. Remove *bariwaat* from honey and place in a strainer, allowing excess honey to drain back into the saucepan.

Lemon Sherbet

Ya'sama
Syria and Lebanon

It is said that Haroon ar-Rasheed, the Abbasid Caliph made famous in the Thousand and One Nights, *would have runners bring ice from the mountains of Lebanon so that he could enjoy a cooling dish during Baghdad's hot summers. Today we can relish a modern version of that ancient dish. Its English name, sherbet, is derived from the Arabic* sharbat *(drink).*

¾ cup lemon juice
1 cup honey
2½ cups water
rind of one lemon

Place all ingredients in a blender and liquefy. Pour into ice-cube trays and freeze. Serve frozen on hot summer days.

MILK COOKIES
Ka'ak bil-Haleeb
Syria and Lebanon
Makes 24 cookies

Ka'ak bil-haleeb! Ka'ak bil-haleeb! *Are cries heard daily as young men carrying huge trays of milk cookies walk the streets of eastern Arab cities. Children learn early that these street vendors sell a delightful treat and, as they grow up, many retain a love for these cookies all through their adult lives.*

2 tablespoons sugar
2 packages yeast
½ cup warm water
4 cups flour
2 teaspoons ground anise seeds
2 teaspoons *mahlab* (see p. 3)
½ teaspoon salt
½ cup clarified butter (see p. 2)
1 cup sugar
1 cup lukewarm milk
⅔ cup whipping cream
⅔ cup confectioner's sugar
4 tablespoons butter
2 teaspoons orange-flower water (*mazahar*)

Dissolve 2 tablespoons of sugar and the yeast in ½ cup of warm water and allow to stand for 10 minutes.

In a mixing bowl, thoroughly combine flour, anise, *mahlab*, and salt; then add clarified butter and sugar and knead well. Add milk and yeast mixture; then knead into a smooth dough, adding a little water or flour if necessary. Form into a ball and coat with oil.

Cover and allow to rest in warm place for 2 hours.

Form into spheres the size of golf balls; then place on greased baking sheets and flatten to about ¼ inch thick. Allow to rest for 15 minutes.

In the meantime, prepare a glaze by heating whipping cream over medium heat until hot, but not boiling. Add confectioner's sugar, butter, and orange-flower water (*mazahar*). Stir constantly over low heat until mixture thickens slightly; then set aside, keeping hot.

Bake cookies in an oven preheated to 325°F, for 20 minutes or until cookies turn golden brown. Allow to cool; then brush heavily with glaze mixture and serve.

ORANGE DESSERT

Litcheen bil-Karfah Uskar
Morocco
Serves 4

Morocco's exotic markets offer a cornucopia of foods from around the world—a dizzying array of fascinating herbs and spices along with succulent fresh fruits and vegetables. A rich selection of edibles through the centuries has resulted in a cuisine that is among the most palatable in the world.

4 medium oranges, peeled
1 teaspoon orange-flower water (*mazahar*)
2 tablespoons sugar
½ teaspoon cinnamon
¼ teaspoon nutmeg
pinch of ground cloves

    Slice oranges thinly; place slices cartwheel fashion on a serving platter. Sprinkle with orange-flower water, then with sugar.

    Combine remaining ingredients and sprinkle on orange slices. Chill in a refrigerator for an hour; then serve.

POMEGRANATE AND ALMOND DELIGHT

Rumman bi Lawz
Iraq
Serves 6

"Wonderful to look at, appetizing in flavor, delicious in taste, with a juice refreshing on a hot summer day" is how a northern European tourist visiting the Middle East once described the pomegranate. The people of southwestern Asia, the original home of this fruit, cannot but wholly agree. There is nothing more longingly remembered by a thirsty traveler crossing the burning desert lands than a cool invigorating drink made from the fluid of the pomegranate.

In their mythology, the Greeks believed that the liquid of the pomegranate sprang from the blood of the god of wine and revelry, and thereafter became the drink of the gods. A number of historians have hypothesized that Eve gave Adam not an apple as stated in the Bible, but a pomegranate. In later centuries, Solomon sang of an "orchard of pomegranates." Many people in the eastern lands came to believe that the juice of this historic fruit would purge a person of envy and hatred.

seeds from 4 medium pomegranates
1 cup slivered almonds
4 tablespoons liquid honey
2 teaspoons orange-flower water (*mazahar*)

Thoroughly mix all ingredients until the honey coats pomegranate seeds and almonds; then place in a serving bowl. Chill before serving.

POMEGRANATE AND CHEESE DESSERT

Rumman Bjiben
Morocco
Serves 4

Westerners, as a whole, have not yet learned to appreciate the joys of pomegranates. Perhaps the difficulty of getting at the ovules is part of the reason this marvelous fruit is not widely popular. The pomegranate's color, tangy-sweet taste, and glittering appearance may eventually make it as popular in the West as in the East.

seeds of 4 pomegranates
4 tablespoons grated mild cheese
½ cup honey
½ teaspoon cinnamon

Place all ingredients in a bowl and mix thoroughly. Place in small dessert cups and serve.

POMEGRANATE JELLY

Hilwat ar-Rumman
Syria and Lebanon
Serves 6

Depending on size, a pomegranate may contain from 60 to 100 calories, with no fatty acids. In addition, the fruit contains carbohydrates, iron, protein, and vitamins B and C.

5 tablespoons pomegranate concentrate (*dibs rumman*)
4 cups warm water
½ cup sugar
2 packages unflavored gelatin
2 tablespoons lemon juice
whipping cream
2 tablespoons chopped walnuts

In a saucepan, dissolve pomegranate concentrate in water. Add sugar and, stirring constantly, bring to boil. Remove from heat and stir in gelatin and lemon juice. Place in serving cups and chill to set gelatin.

Serve, topped with whipped cream and walnuts.

Pomegranate and Pistachio Dessert

Rumman bi Fustuq
Syria and Lebanon
Serves 6

To remove the seeds of the pomegranate, roll and press the fruit on a hard surface; then remove the stem and surrounding pulp. Then lightly score the outer skin with a sharp knife from top to bottom at 1-inch intervals. Now the fruit can be easily broken into pieces and the seeds removed.

seeds from 5 medium pomegranates
1 cup finely chopped pistachios
6 tablespoons honey
1 teaspoon almond extract

Thoroughly combine all ingredients until honey coats all pomegranate seeds and pistachios. Place in a serving bowl, chill, and then serve.

Pudding

Muhallabiyya
Egypt
Serves 6 to 8

Throughout the Middle East, muhallabiyya *is one of the most common desserts served in both homes and public eating places. Simple to prepare and with a silky texture, it can be enjoyed as a light snack in the afternoon or late evening.*

⅓ cup cornstarch
4 cups milk
6 tablespoons raisins
⅓ cup sugar
1 teaspoon vanilla extract
1 teaspoon cinnamon
2 tablespoons finely chopped walnuts

In a bowl, dissolve the cornstarch in 1 cup of the milk; set aside.
Place remaining 3 cups of milk, raisins, and sugar in a saucepan. Bring to boil over medium heat, stirring until sugar dissolves. Reduce heat to low; then add dissolved cornstarch and, stirring constantly, simmer for about 10 minutes, or until mixture is thick enough to heavily coat a spoon. Stir in vanilla; then pour

mixture into small individual dessert bowls. Sprinkle with cinnamon; then scatter the walnuts decoratively on top.

Refrigerate for at least 2 hours before serving.

Rice Pudding

Rizz bil-Haleeb
Iraq
Serves 8

Rizz bil-haleeb is a dessert common throughout the eastern Arab world. It is prepared in a variety of ways. This Iraqi version is somewhat spicier than other recipes.

2½ cups water
½ cup rice, rinsed
2 cups milk
1 cup sugar
1 teaspoon cinnamon
½ teaspoon nutmeg
1 cup raisins
1 teaspoon vanilla

Place water and rice in a saucepan and bring to boil. Cover and cook over medium heat for 10 minutes.

In the meantime, combine remaining ingredients, except vanilla. Add to rice and, stirring constantly, bring to boil. Reduce heat to low and, stirring occasionally, cook for 20 minutes or until rice is well done. Stir in vanilla; then place in serving dishes.

Chill before serving.

SEMOLINA WITH HONEY

Lââssida
Morocco
Serves 6 to 8

If a new bride in Morocco wants to please her husband, the first morning after their wedding she will cook him lââssida *swimming with honey. This dish is also traditionally prepared on* Eid al-Mawlad *(the Prophet's birthday).*

¾ cup semolina
3 cups cold water
4 tablespoons butter
salt to taste
1 tablespoons orange-flower water (*mazahar*)
½ cup honey

Place semolina and water in a saucepan and, stirring constantly, bring to boil. Stir in 2 tablespoons of the butter and salt. Then stirring constantly to ensure that semolina does not stick to the bottom of saucepan, cook over medium low heat for about 10 minutes or until semolina is cooked, adding more water if necessary.

In a small saucepan, combine remaining butter, orange-flower water, and honey and heat. Transfer to a serving bowl and set aside.

Pour semolina into a serving bowl and spoon half the honey mixture over top. Serve hot, allowing diners to add remaining honey mixture to taste.

SEMOLINA MUFFINS

Khanfaroosh
Arabian Gulf
Makes 12 medium size muffins

A traditional dish in the Gulf region of the Arabian Peninsula, khanfaroosh *were originally prepared with rice flour. However, this sweet can be made with semolina or any other type of flour.*

1½ cups semolina
1 cup sugar
2 teaspoons baking powder
½ teaspoon ground cardamom seeds
3 eggs, beaten
½ cup rose water (*maward*)
1 teaspoon vanilla
2 tablespoons melted butter

Combine semolina, sugar, baking powder, and cardamom in a mixing bowl; make a well in the middle.

Mix remaining ingredients and pour into dry ingredients.

Knead into a soft dough. If batter is too wet or dry add a little flour or water; then cover and allow to stand for 30 minutes.

Place in greased muffin tins and bake in an oven preheated to 350°F, for 20 minutes or until muffins turn golden brown.

Note: Khanfaroosh are more tasty if they are deep fried. A little more flour should be added to the batter if they are to be fried. Then, place spoonfuls of batter in sizzling oil until golden brown.

SEMOLINA PUDDING

Maamuneeya
Syria and Lebanon
Serves 8

At the western end of the Silk Road from the Far East and the northern end of the Frankincense Road from southern Arabia, Aleppo has a long and venerable history in the world of eatable delights. Echoes of the exotic spices and foods carried on these routes are to be found in the cuisine of Aleppo—a rich kitchen, developed through the centuries. This dish, a specialty of that city, testifies to its renowned culinary history.

4 tablespoons butter
1 cup semolina
1 cup milk
1 cup sugar
water
½ cup whipping cream
3 tablespoons crushed pistachios

Melt butter in a saucepan and stir-fry semolina until it turns light brown. Stir in milk and sugar and stir over medium heat for 10 minutes or until the semolina is cooked, adding a little water at a time to ensure the end product is a soft paste.

Place on a platter. Whip cream, then spread evenly over *Maamuneeya*. Sprinkle with pistachios and serve warm.

SESAME COOKIES

Baraazak
Syria and Lebanon
Makes about 40 cookies

A specialty of Damascus, barazak *have been peddled in the streets of that city for centuries. I remember the first time I visited Damascus, at the beginning of the 1960s, I was captivated by their taste and I have enjoyed them ever since.*

¾ cup sesame seeds
½ cup honey
½ cup coarsely chopped pistachios
2 eggs
1½ cups butter
1½ cups sugar
2½ cups flour
2 cups wheat hearts or semolina
2 teaspoons baking powder
½ teaspoon salt

Place sesame seeds, honey, and pistachios in separate bowls and set aside.

Place eggs, butter, and sugar in a food processor and process into paste. Transfer to a mixing bowl; then add flour, wheat hearts or semolina, baking powder, and salt. Knead into a dough, adding a little water if necessary.

Form into spheres the size of golf balls. Dip balls, one at a time, into the pistachios and flatten with fingers on a greased baking sheet. Continue until all the balls are used; then brush each cookie with honey and sprinkle with the sesame seeds.

Bake in an oven preheated to 350°F, for 15 minutes or until the cookies turn golden brown. Remove and allow to cool before serving.

SHREDDED DOUGH CHEESE CAKE
Knafa bil-Jiban
Syria and Lebanon
Serves 8 to 10

In the Middle East, knafa bil-jiban *is a traditional breakfast dish. It also makes an excellent dessert.* Knafa *dough is available in Middle Eastern grocery stores.*

1 1-pound package *knafa* dough
1 cup clarified butter (see p. 2)
1 pound ricotta cheese, stirred
1 teaspoon orange-flower water (*mazahar*)
1 *qater* (Syrup, see recipe, p. 20)
¼ cup crushed pistachios or crushed blanched almonds

Thaw the dough if frozen; then mix it with butter and place in a baking pan. Place pan over very low heat; then gently rub dough with hands for about 15 minutes, ensuring that every part of the dough is moist. Divide dough into two portions; spread and pat down one portion of dough into a well-buttered 9 x 13-inch baking pan that is 2 inches deep.

Combine cheese and orange-flower water; then spread on dough in the pan. Spread the other portion of dough on top.

Bake in an oven preheated to 300°F, for 20 minutes or until surface of dough becomes golden brown. If surface is not golden brown in 20 minutes, place pan under broiler, turning until the top of *knafa* is evenly browned.

In the meantime, prepare syrup using only half the sugar listed in the recipe. Remove *knafa* from the oven and, while still hot, pour syrup evenly over top. Garnish with pistachios or almonds; then cut into 8 pieces and serve hot.

STUFFED DATES

Tamar Mihshee
Iraq
Serves 8–12

From Spain, the Conquistadors brought the date palm to the Americas. As a food crop, however, it did not thrive until this century, and then in only a few locations in North and South America.

In the early 1900s, the date tree was brought to the United States from North Africa and planted on a commercial basis. The Algerian deglet noor *was the first type cultivated on a large scale, and still is the most important variety grown in the United States. Today, the Coachella Valley in California is the heart of a prosperous date industry.*

Despite the spread of its propagation to many lands, the Arab lands are still the date tree's main cultivator. Iraq, Saudi Arabia, the United Arab Emirates, and a number of other Arab countries account for most of the world's date supply.

1 pound whole dates, pitted
½ cup coarsely chopped walnuts
¾ cup half-and-half cream
⅔ cup sugar
1 tablespoon orange-flower water (*mazahar*)
4 tablespoons cocoa
1 cup shredded coconut, spread in a shallow dish

Slit dates along one side; then stuff with walnuts. Press closed and set aside.

Place cream in a small pan and bring to boil. Add sugar and stir over medium heat until sugar melts. Add orange-flower water and cocoa and, stirring constantly, cook over medium heat for about 5 minutes. Remove from heat and allow to cool.

Dip dates in the cocoa syrup; then roll them in coconut and place on a serving tray.

STUFFED PANCAKES

Qatayif
Syria and Lebanon
Makes about 28 pancakes

Qatayif *are the pancakes of the Middle East. Usually eaten for breakfast, they are also excellent as dessert and, served with coffee and tea, make tasty snacks.*

A. J. Arberry, in his book Aspects of Islamic Civilization, *quotes the Arab poet Mahmood ibn al-Husayn Kushaajim when describing* Qatayif:

> When, my friends, the pang of hunger grows
> I have *katayif*, like soft folios;
> As flow of lambent honey brimming white
> So amidst other dainties it is bright,
> And, having drunk of almond-essence deep,
> With oil it glitters, wherein it doth seep.
> Rose-water floats thereon, like flooding sea,
> Bubble on bubble swimming fragrantly;
> A foliated book laid fold on fold—
> Afflicted hearts rejoice when they behold;
> But when divided, like the spoils of war,
> All have their heart's desire, and sated are.

Batter
2 cups flour
1½ teaspoons baking powder
½ teaspoon salt
2 cups milk
2 eggs, beaten
1 cup butter, melted
1 *qater* (Syrup, see recipe, p. 20)

Sift dry ingredients together into a large mixing bowl. Add milk and eggs and mix thoroughly until smooth. Add 2 tablespoons of the melted butter and mix again. Cover and allow to rest for a few hours. In the meantime, prepare syrup and keep warm. Make either of the following fillings.

Cheese Filling
2 cups ricotta cheese
¾ cup sugar
1 teaspoon cinnamon
2 teaspoons orange-flower water *(mazahar)*

Walnut Filling
2 cups chopped walnuts
¾ cup sugar
1 teaspoon cinnamon

Combine filling ingredients and set aside.

Heat a pancake griddle and grease with shortening or butter. Pour about 2 tablespoons of batter to make pancakes about 3 inches wide. (A griddle usually has room for 4 pancakes at one time). Cook pancakes on one side only; remove and place on paper towels.

Place about 2 teaspoons of filling on each pancake; then fold over to make a half-moon shape. Press edges firmly closed; then place in a baking pan. Repeat procedure until all batter used.

Pour remaining melted butter over the pancakes; then place in an oven preheated to 375°F and bake for 10 to 15 minutes. Remove from oven. Dip in syrup; then drain in a strainer and allow to cool before serving.

SUGARED DATES

Hilwat Tamar
Morocco
Serves 8-12

The inhabitants of the oases in the Arabian desert and the Sahara of North Africa value the graceful palm above all other trees as a symbol of wealth and prestige. For thousands of years it has been the foundation of life for the dwellers of these arid lands. The climate in these countries is ideal for its cultivation, and its fruit is easily preserved. When ripe and dried, dates do not spoil. It is as if this valuable fruit was tailor-made for the desert lands.

1 pound dates, pitted
½ cup blanched almonds
¾ cup sugar
2 tablespoons butter
1 teaspoon orange-flower water (*mazahar*)
pinch of nutmeg

Slit each date along one side and set aside.

Place almonds in a shallow baking pan and lightly brown in oven. Remove and allow to cool; then grind finely.

Make filling by thoroughly mixing almonds, ¼ cup of the sugar, butter, orange-flower water, and nutmeg. Stuff each date with about 1 teaspoon of filling; then close and roll in remaining ½ cup of sugar. Place on a serving dish and serve as candies or for dessert.

Tunisian Date Cookies

Makroodh
Makes about 25 cookies

In North Africa, dates with a bowl of milk are offered to a visitor as a symbol of hospitality.

2½ cups semolina flour
1 cup butter, melted
1½ teaspoons vanilla
2 eggs, beaten
½ teaspoon salt
½ cup finely chopped dates
1 cup honey
½ cup water
1 tablespoon orange-flower water (*mazahar*)
2 cups oil
2 tablespoons confectioner's sugar

Combine semolina, butter, vanilla, eggs, and salt; knead to make a smooth dough, adding a little water if necessary. Shape dough into cylinders about 2½ inches long and one inch in diameter. Hold a cylinder in palm of hand and make a small trench. Place about ½ teaspoon of dates in trench; then close and pat into a rectangular cookie. Repeat with remaining cylinders. Allow to rest for one hour.

In the meantime, make syrup. In a saucepan place honey, water, and *mazahar*, and, stirring constantly, bring to boil. Set aside, but keep warm over low heat.

Heat oil in a saucepan; then fry the *makroodhs* over medium heat until they turn golden brown, adding more oil if necessary.

Dip hot *makroodhs* in honey syrup, then drain and allow to cool. Sprinkle with confectioner's sugar and serve.

Tunisian Doughnuts

Yo-yo

Makes approximately 2 dozen small doughnuts

Yo-yos are no doubt an adaptation of the western doughnut but the Tunisians have added a touch of their own to give it a North African character. Sold in little stalls in Tunisian cities, these donuts are enjoyed by people thronging the streets.

3 eggs
2¼ cups oil
¼ cup orange juice
2 tablespoons finely chopped fresh coconut
1¼ cups sugar
2½ cups flour
1½ teaspoons baking soda
2 cups water
2 tablespoons lemon juice
1 cup honey

Place eggs, ¼ cup of the oil, orange juice, 1 tablespoon of the coconut, and ¼ cup of the sugar in a blender; blend until smooth.

Transfer to a bowl; then sift in flour and baking soda. Knead until the mixture is a soft dough, adding a little water if necessary. Cover bowl; then set aside to rest for at least 1 hour.

In the meantime make syrup: place remaining sugar, water, and lemon juice in a saucepan. Stirring constantly, boil over high heat until sugar dissolves. Reduce heat to low; then add honey and the remaining 1 tablespoon of coconut. Simmer for 10 minutes; then turn heat to very low to keep the syrup warm.

Place remaining oil in a small saucepan and heat until oil is moderately hot.

Form dough into walnut-size balls; then flatten slightly. Hold a flattened ball in palm of one hand and punch a hole through center with floured index finger of other hand. Deep fry, a few at a time, for about 5 minutes, turning them over with a slotted spoon until they turn golden brown on both sides. Transfer to paper towels to drain. With tongs, pick up the *yo-yos* and dip into warm syrup. Serve at once.

Yogurt Cake

Kaykat al-Laban
Iraq
Serves 12

Eaten alone or used as an ingredient in other foods, yogurt's subtle and exciting taste is enjoyed by more people than any other dairy product made from milk. In addition, it is a health food par excellence.

1½ cups yogurt
½ cup butter, melted
½ cup whipping cream
4 eggs, beaten
1 cup sugar
2 cups flour
2½ teaspoons baking powder
½ teaspoon salt
½ cup honey
½ cup water
3 tablespoons lemon juice

Thoroughly combine yogurt, butter, cream, eggs and sugar; set aside.

Sift flour, baking powder, and salt into the yogurt mixture; then stir. Place in a well-greased 7 x 11-inch baking pan and let stand for an hour.

Bake in an oven preheated to 300°F, for about 1 hour or until wooden skewer inserted into center of cake comes out clean.

In the meantime, to make syrup: Place honey and water in a pot and bring to boil. Boil for about 5 minutes over medium heat, stirring a few times; then stir in lemon juice. Remove from heat and set aside.

Remove cake from oven and allow to cool; then invert onto a serving plate. Spoon the syrup evenly over cake; serve warm.

WHEATHEART CAKES

Nammoora
Syria and Lebanon
Makes about 35 pieces

Also called hareesat al-lawz *when almonds are used, this sweet is very common throughout the Middle East.*

2 pounds cream of wheat cereal
1½ cups yogurt
1½ cups whipping cream
1 cup shredded coconut
4 teaspoons baking powder
2½ cups sugar
¾ cup water
2 tablespoons lemon juice
1 tablespoon orange-flower (*mazahar*) or rose-blossom water (*maward*)
1 cup melted butter

Place cream of wheat, yogurt, whipping cream, coconut, baking powder, and ½ cup of the sugar in a mixing bowl and mix thoroughly. Pour batter into a well-greased 10 x 15-inch baking pan. Bake for 30 minutes in an oven preheated to 350°F.

In the meantime make syrup: Place the remaining 2 cups of sugar and water in a saucepan. Bring to boil over medium heat, stirring constantly. Turn heat to low; then stir in lemon juice and simmer for another 10 minutes. Turn heat to very low and stir in orange-flower or rose-blossom water. Keep warm.

Before removing cake from oven, brown evenly for a few minutes under the broiler; then cut into 2-inch squares. Spoon melted butter over cake and allow it to soak in. After a few minutes, pour the warm syrup evenly over the top. Allow to cool before serving.

DRINKS

In the Arab world in past centuries, sherbets, lemonade, coffee, tea, and similar non-alcoholic drinks were the common beverages. Today, even though they are still common throughout the Arab lands, Western-style drinks are slowly edging them out. Of course, this applies mostly to cold drinks; coffee and tea are still very popular at all levels of society.

Perhaps the most common ancient drink still found in every Arab country is a licorice root beverage, sold by street vendors everywhere. Almost every tourist is impressed by these colorfully dressed vendors clinking their cups and crying out, *'Irq as-soos, 'irq as-soos!*

Alcoholic drinks have been in the past and remain today traditional among the Christian and Jewish Arab communities, especially in Egypt, Lebanon, Syria, Tunisia, and Morocco. Muslims generally avoid alcohol, although lapses do occur.

Coffee and tea in all their forms are drinks par excellence among the Arabs. In the Arab East, coffee rules supreme. A traditional sign of hospitality, it is the first offering to guests. A gift from the Arabian Peninsula to the world, coffee has been for centuries and still is associated with the exotic lure of Arabia. Its Arab origin is attested to by the languages of the world, most of which derive their name for coffee from the Arabic *qahwa*.

In North Africa, mint tea plays a role similar to that of coffee in the eastern Arab lands. A few minutes after a stranger enters a North African home, a glass of piping hot mint tea is offered. Refreshing, tasty, and diffusing an inviting aroma, it is also a great ending for a festive meal. Visitors may in time forget their adventures in the North African world, but never the lure of freshly brewed mint tea.

ALMOND MILK

'Aseer al-Lawz
Morocco
Serves 8

A drink similar to this is horchata, *for which the Valencia region in Spain is famous. The Spanish Moors invented this rich beverage and when the Arabs were expelled from the Iberian Peninsula, they took the drink with them. Today, in Morocco, an affluent host highly honors his guest when he serves this drink.*

1 cup pulverized blanched almonds
4 cups warm water
4 cups milk
½ cup sugar
4 tablespoons lemon juice
1 tablespoon orange-flower water (*mahazar*)

Place almonds and water in a blender; then liquefy for 3 minutes. Strain through thin cloth; then place in a pitcher and stir in remaining ingredients.
Chill; then stir before serving.

ANISEED TEA

Shai Yaansoon
Arabian Gulf
Serves 4

Since the Middle Ages, aniseed tea has been sipped by nursing mothers to increase milk production. It has mild estrogenic effects, which explains the use of this plant in folk medicine to increase milk production, facilitate birth, and increase libido. In addition, its appears to ease colic and flatulence.

4 cups water
4 teaspoons tea
2 teaspoons ground aniseed
sugar to taste

Boil water; then while water is boiling, place remaining ingredients in a teapot.
Place boiling water in teapot; then stir. Allow to steep for 5 minutes; then serve immediately.

ARABIC COFFEE

Qahwa 'Arabiyya
Syria and Lebanon
Serves 8

Coffee was introduced into Europe from Arabia via Turkey. The drinking of coffee is a very important activity in the eastern Arab world. Men spend hours during the long summer evenings, and whenever they can during the day, sitting in cafés, sipping cups of coffee.

Business negotiations and bargaining in the marketplace never take place without coffee. At home, it is served as soon as visitors arrive, always freshly brewed and usually from freshly roasted and pulverized coffee beans.

In the eastern Arab countries, especially in the rural areas, an elaborate ritual has evolved, rivaling the Japanese tea ceremony in its intricacies, beauty of utensils, and decorative arrangement. Amid colorful rugs, tapestries, cushions, and silver-inlaid copper coffee appliances, the host begins the ceremony by saying bismillah *(in the name of God). He then begins to roast the green beans in an iron ladle over a charcoal fire, all the while pursuing a lively conversation with his guests. After the coffee is roasted to the host's taste, he pulverizes the roasted beans, moving his mortar and pestle to a musical beat. The fine powdered coffee is then allowed to stand for a few minutes—an act that apparently retains the aroma and flavor. During this interval, the host boils water in a large brass or copper Middle Eastern coffee pot* (ibreeq) *while at the same time burning incense. All the ingredients are then placed in a similar, but smaller, pot and brewed. The brewed coffee, without the sediment, is then transferred into a small brass serving pot.*

2 heaping tablespoons pulverized coffee
1 tablespoons sugar
2 cups water
1 cardamom seed, crushed

Place coffee, sugar, and water in a pot and bring to boil. When froth begins to rise, remove from heat and stir. Stir in cardamom and heat again until froth rises; then remove from heat and allow to settle for a minute. Use Arab coffee cups. Spoon a little froth into each cup, pour in coffee, and serve hot.

Note: Pulverized Arab coffee can be purchased from most Middle Eastern grocery stores. To enjoy Arabic coffee to the utmost, it should be served in small Arab coffee cups (which are smaller than demi-tasses). Sugar may be omitted, if desired, and the coffee served bitter or with an artificial sweetener.

ARABIC COFFEE, KUWAITI-STYLE

Qahwa Kuwayteeya
Serves about 8

This bitter coffee is served not only in Kuwait, but by many bedouin tribes in the northern part of the Arabian Peninsula.

2 cups water
4 heaping tablespoons of pulverized coffee
6 cardamom seeds, crushed

Place all ingredients in an *ibreeq* and bring to boil. Turn heat to very low and simmer for 15 minutes. Fill each Arab coffee cup about a third full and serve. Two more servings of coffee should be offered to each guest.

ARABIC COFFEE, SAUDI ARABIAN-STYLE

Qahwa Sa'udeeya
Serves about 8

The first time I had this coffee was in the Saudi Arabian section of the Arab pavilion of Caravan, a festival held in Toronto every year at the end of June. I enjoyed it so much that it is now often brewed in our home.

Even though this recipe is simple to prepare, its authenticity can be enjoyed if the coffee beans are roasted fresh. To roast, place the green coffee beans in a thick frying pan and stir-fry constantly over high heat until the beans barely begin to brown. Remove the beans from the heat and grind them in a coffee grinder for just a few seconds, or pound them coarsely with a mortar and pestle.

2½ cups water
¼ cup very coarsely ground, partially roasted coffee
1 teaspoon pulverized cardamom seeds

Place water in saucepan and bring to boil. Remove from heat and add coffee. Return to heat; then brew over medium heat for 10 minutes. Pour slowly into an *ibreeq,* making sure the grounds remain in the first pot. Add cardamom; then boil for 3 minutes. Serve in Arab coffee cups, about a third of cup at a time.

ARABIC COFFEE, YEMENI-STYLE

Qahwat Qisher
Yemen
Serves about 8

Strange as it may seem, in the land where coffee was first drunk, it is not brewed from the beans but from the husks and served strong and very sweet with ginger. Outside of Yemen one is not likely to find qisher, *ground coffee husks, but powdered coffee beans can be substituted.*

2 cups water
10 tablespoons pulverized coffee husks (*qisher*) or 4 tablespoons
    pulverized coffee
1 tablespoon sugar
1 teaspoon ground ginger

Place all ingredients in a pot and bring to boil. Allow to boil for 1 minute; then serve in Arab coffee cups.

CARDAMOM TEA

Shai bil-Haal
Arabian Gulf
Serves 4 to 6

In the Arabian Peninsula, where cardamom is used extensively, many believe that this spice makes an effective deodorizer. For neutralizing the smell of garlic and freshening the breath, a few cardamom pods are slowly chewed, allowing the flavor to linger in the mouth. At times, a cardamom pod is combined with a few fennel seeds and a clove to create a more effective breath freshener. Sipping on this spicy tea has a similar effect.

3 cups water
1 teaspoon black tea
1 small cinnamon stick
4 cardamom seeds, whole but cracked
½ teaspoon fennel seeds
1 cup milk
1 tablespoon sugar

Place water, tea, cinnamon stick, cardamom, and fennel seeds in a pot and bring to boil. Cover and simmer over medium heat for 10 minutes. Stir in milk and sugar; then bring to boil again before serving.

CAROB DRINK

Mashroob Kharroob
Syria and Lebanon
Serves 4

The ancient Egyptians used a paste made from carob to bind their mummies. The carob fruit was eaten on a small scale in the Greek and Roman worlds. It was only when the Arabs carried the carob from its home in the Middle East to the Iberian Peninsula that it became widely known in Europe. The name carob is derived from the Arabic kharroob.

4 tablespoons carob powder
1 cup boiling water
2½ cups hot milk
4 tablespoons sugar
1 teaspoon vanilla

Dissolve carob flour in boiling water; then add remaining ingredients and mix thoroughly. Serve warm or chilled, but always stir before serving.

Note: Carob drinks, already prepared, are sold in health food stores, and carob powder is usually available as well.

CINNAMON TEA

Shai Qirfah
Kuwait
Serves 4

Cinnamon is a spice favored by the Middle Eastern Arabs. It is mainly the countries along the Arabian Gulf, however, that make it into a tea.

4 cups water
4 cinnamon sticks, each about 4 inches long
2 teaspoons sugar

Place water and cinnamon in a pot and bring to boil. Brew over medium heat for 20 minutes; then remove cinnamon sticks. Stir in sugar; then boil for a minute before serving.

GINGER TEA

Shai Zanjabeel
Yemen
Serves 4

In the past, ginger was not only used in foods but also as a medicine. It was an ingredient in home remedies for external applications such as compresses and in medical preparations for internal use. According to R. Landry in The Gentle Art of Flavoring, *ginger is included in the pharmacopoeia of the Arabs.*

King Henry VIII of England believed that it could cure the plague, and the Indians have long made a paste which they believe keeps away scurvy. For generations, herbalists have maintained that it fortifies the chest and have prescribed ginger tea for colds. This invigorating, full-bodied, and healthy drink might serve such a purpose.

2 tablespoons fresh ginger root, grated
2 tablespoons honey
1 very small cinnamon stick
4 cloves
5 cups water

Place all ingredients in a pot and bring to boil; then cover and simmer over medium low heat for 40 minutes. Strain into cups and serve.

GINGER TEA WITH MILK

Az-Zanjabeel ma' Al-Haleeb
Arabian Gulf
Serves 6 to 8

In the Arabian Gulf countries this tea is often served as a remedy for colds and sore throats—though the healthy have been known to enjoy it as well.

4 cups milk
1 tablespoon ginger powder
⅛ teaspoon ground cloves
2 tablespoons honey

Place milk, ginger, and cloves in a pot. Bring to boil, stirring constantly. Reduce heat to medium low; then simmer for 8 to 10 minutes, stirring once in a while. Stir in honey and serve piping hot in demi-tasse cups.

GRAPE DRINK

'Aseer 'Inab
Morocco
Makes 1 quart

In the past, most Arabs ate grapes fresh from the vineyard or dried as raisins. Only in this century has grape juice become popular as a drink. In the Moroccan town of Chauen, founded by the Muslims expelled from Spain, however, a fermented grape drink called samit *has been made for some 500 years.*

This recipe is grape juice with a Middle Eastern touch of spice.

1 quart grape juice
2 tablespoons sugar
1 teaspoon cinnamon
2 tablespoons orange-flower water (*mazahar*)

Thoroughly combine all ingredients; then refrigerate. Stir and serve.

LEMONADE

Lamoonadha
Palestine and Jordan
Serves 4

The consumption of lemons is recommended as a preventive measure against respiratory ailments such as bronchitis, the common cold, pneumonia, flu, and other conditions associated with fevers. Pleasant tasting, lemons are a delightful medicine to take, as this drink will testify.

3 cups water
½ cup lemon juice
4 tablespoons sugar
1 tablespoon orange-flower water (*mazahar*)

Thoroughly combine all ingredients. Serve with ice cubes.

LEMON TEA

Shai bil-Laymoon
Kuwait
Serves 6

Besides containing vitamins A and B, lemons are loaded with vitamin C. One lemon provides nearly 80 percent of a person's daily requirement of this vitamin. Researchers have established that the large concentration of vitamins in lemons acts as a mild antiseptic and disinfectant, destroying bacteria in cuts; relieving insect bites and irritations caused by poison ivy or oak; easing skin diseases such as acne, boils, eczema; and curing scurvy.

6 cups water
2 unpeeled lemons, washed and quartered
5 tablespoons sugar
1 tablespoon orange-flower water (**mazahar**)

Place water and lemons in a pot and bring to boil. Cover and simmer over medium heat for 20 minutes. Strain into a teapot; then stir in sugar and *mazahar*, and serve.

MINT TEA

Atay bi Na'na'
North Africa
Serves 4

The preparation of atay *is considered an art by the Moroccans. It is traditionally served in a richly engraved silver pot, and poured from a great height into ornamented glasses. Atay is Morocco's most popular drink, consumed at all times of day by all types of people. Whether served in a humble café, an elegant restaurant, or in the home, this drink is the refreshment most loved by the Moroccans and the other peoples of North Africa.*

boiling water
1½ tablespoons green tea
½ cup of fresh mint leaves with stalks (dried mint leaves are not as good, but can be used if fresh mint is not available)
4 tablespoons granulated sugar

Rinse out a three-cup metal teapot with hot water; then add tea. Pour in

½ cup boiling water and swish around in the pot quickly. Discard the water, but make sure not to throw away tea. This rinse removes the bitterness from tea.

Stuff mint leaves with their stalks into the pot; then add sugar. Fill the pot with boiling water. Let steep for 5 minutes, checking occasionally to make sure mint does not rise above water. Push it down with a spoon if necessary. Stir and taste, adding more sugar, if desired, before serving.

Note: Traditionally, this tea is served in small glasses set in silver holders, but demitasse cups or standard cups will do.

For second helpings, leave mint and tea in pot; add a teaspoon of tea, several mint leaves, and some more sugar. Fill again with boiling water. When mint rises to surface, the tea is ready. Stir and taste for sugar; then serve. The same process can be repeated for a third pot. In Morocco, custom requires that three helpings be offered and three helpings be accepted.

If green tea is not available, use an Indian tea. You may also serve the tea Western style by omitting the sugar, allowing each person to add sugar to his or her own cup to taste.

ORANGE JUICE DRINK
Litcheen Awasahr
Morocco
Makes 1 quart

The popular orange contains a large amount of vitamin C as well as small amounts of minerals and other nutrients.

Morocco is one of the top producers of oranges in the world, and orange juice is, not surprisingly, a common drink among the population. The mixture of cinnamon and orange-flower water lend this drink an absolutely unique flavor.

1 quart orange juice
4 tablespoons sugar
1 teaspoon cinnamon
2 tablespoons orange-flower water (*mazahar*)

Thoroughly combine all ingredients; then refrigerate. Stir and serve.

POMEGRANATE DRINK

Sharab Dibs Rumman
Syria and Lebanon
Serves 4 to 6

In North America, grenadine syrup, made from pomegranates, is employed mostly as a base for drinks. It usually contains artificial flavoring. Dibs rumman, in contrast, is a pure product made by boiling pomegranate juice until it becomes thick and turns brownish. Grenadine syrup is not an appropriate substitute for dibs rumman.

1 quart water
½ cup pomegranate concentrate (*dibs rumman*)
1 tablespoon rose water (*maward*)
sugar to taste

Thoroughly combine all ingredients. Serve at once with ice cubes. The drink can also be chilled in a refrigerator; stir before serving.

TAMARIND DRINK

Sharab Tamar Hindi
Arabian Gulf
Serves 6

In addition to its culinary uses, tamarind is valued for its medicinal benefits, especially for the intestines. Containing carbohydrates, calcium, fat, iron, phosphorus, protein and vitamins A, B, and C, it has been on the herbalist's cure list for centuries. In the past, this drink was prescribed to bring down fevers; as a diuretic; and for bilious disorders, jaundice, and catarrh.

4 tablespoons tamarind paste
½ cup sugar
6 cups water
1 tablespoon orange-flower water (*mahazar*)

Place tamarind, sugar, and water in a pot; then stirring a few times, bring to boil. Turn heat to low and allow to simmer for 5 minutes. Remove from heat and allow to cool.

Stir in orange-flower water and, if desired, some ice cubes just before serving.

Note: Drink can be refrigerated and ice cubes added to individual servings.

YOGURT DRINK

'Aryaan
Iraq
Serves 6

A very refreshing drink during the hot summer months.

2 cups yogurt
4 cups water
½ teaspoon salt

   Thoroughly combine all ingredients; then refrigerate for at least two hours. Stir just before serving.

BIBLIOGRAPHY

Arberry, Arthur John. *Aspects of Islamic Civilization*. London: George Allen & Unwin, Ltd, 1964.

Hendrickson, Robert. *Lewd Foods*. Radnor, PA: Chilton Book Co., 1974.

Landry, Robert. *The Gentle Art of Flavoring: A Guide to Good Cooking*. New York: Abelard-Schuman, 1970.

Nefzawi, Shaykh, 'Umar Abu Muhammad. *The Perfumed Garden*. Trans. Sir Richard Burton. New Jersey: Castle Books, 1964.

Nelson, Nina. *Tunisia*. London: Batsford Ltd, 1974.

Nelson, Kay Shaw. *Yogurt Cookery*. New York: Robert B. Luce, 1972.

Roden, Claudia. *A Book of Middle Eastern Food*. New York: Knopf, 1972.

Root, Waverly. *The Cooking of Italy*. New York: Time-Life Books, 1968.

Root, Waverly. *Food: An Authoritative and Visual History and Dictionary of the Foods of the World*. New York: Simon and Schuster, 1980.

Simon, Hilda. *The Date Palm: Bread of the Desert*. New York: Dodd Mead, 1978.

Spencer, Colin. *The Vegetable Book*. New York: Rizzoli, 1996.

Thoreau, Henry David. *Walden*. New York: Oxford University Press, 1997.

Ward, Artemas. *The Encyclopedia of Food*. New York: Baker and Taylor, 1929.

Weiss, E.A. Castor, *Sesame and Safflower*. New York: Barnes and Noble, 1971.

Wolfert, Paula. *Couscous and Other Good Food from Morocco*. New York: Harper and Row, 1973.

Zayani, Afnan R. *A Taste of the Arabian Gulf*. Bahrain: Government Press, Ministry of Information, 1988.

Morocco Guidebook (Knopf Guides). Trans. Wendy Allatson. New York: Knopf, 1994.

Medieval Sources and Texts

al-Baghdadi, Muhammad Ibn al-Karim. *Kitab al-Tabikh* (The book of cooking). Beirut: Dar al-Kitab al-Jadid, 1964.

al-Ghafiqi, Abu Ja'far Ahmad ibn Muhammad. *al-Adwiyah al-Mufradah* (The book of simple drugs). Ed. Gregorius Abu'l-Farag. Trans. Max Meyerhof. Cairo: 1932–40.

Ibn al-'Adim, Kamal al-Din 'Umar ibn Ahmad. *al-Wuslah ilá al-Habib fi wasf al-*

Tayyibat wa at-Tib (The connection to the beloved in the description of pleasures and medicine). Ed. Sulayma Mahjub. Aleppo: University of Aleppo, 1986–1988.

Ibn Baitar, Abu Muhammad 'Abdallah Ibn Ahmad Ibn Muhammad. *Kitab Jami'li Mufradat al-Adwiyah wa al-Aghdiya* (A compendium of different drugs and foodstuffs). Baghdad: Maktabat al-Muthanná.

Ibn Rustah, Abi 'Ali Ahmad ibn 'Umar. *al-Mujallad al-Sabi' min Kitab al-A'laq al-Nafisah* (The seventh volume from the book of precious objects). Baghdad: Maktabat al-Muthanná.

al-Tujeebee, 'Ali ibn Muhammad Ibn Razeen. *Fadaalat al-Khiwaan fee Tayyibaat at-Ta'aam wa al-Alwaan: Surah min Fann al-Tabkh fi al-Andalus wa-al-Maghrib fi Bidayat 'Asr Bani Marin* (Making the best of the remains from the dining table made into the tastiest and most colorful of foods: a chapter from the art of cooking in Andalusia and Morocco at the beginning of the age of the Banu Marin). Ed. Mohamed B. A. Benchekroun. Beirut: Dar al-Gharb al-Islami, 1984.

al-Warraq, Abu Muhammad al Muzaffar ibn Nasr ibn Sayyar. *Kitab al-Tabikh wa Asl al-Aghdiya al-Ma'kulat.* (The book of cookery and the origin of nourishing foodstuffs). Eds. Kaj Ohrnberg and Sahban Mroueh. Studia Orientalia Vol. 60.

Where to Find Ingredients

California

Al-Jibani Halal Market
23385 Golden Springs Drive
Diamond Bar, CA 91765
(909) 861-3865

Avocado Food Market
852 Avocado Avenue
El Cajon, CA 92020
(619) 588-1773

Fresno Deli
2450 E. Gettysburg Avenue
Fresno, CA 93726
(559) 225-7906

Levant International
9421 Alondra Boulevard
Bellflower, CA 90706
(562) 920-0623

Marhaba Supermarket
10932 East Imperial Highway
Norwalk, CA 90650
(562) 868-2272

Middle East Food
26 Washington Street
Santa Clara, CA 95050
(408) 248-5112

Near East Foods
4595 El Canjon Boulevard
San Diego, CA 92115
(619) 284-6361

Samiramis Importing Company
2990 Mission Street
San Francisco, CA 94110
(415) 824-6555

Sweis International Market
6809 Hazeltine Avenue
Van Nuys, CA 91405
(818) 785-8193

Colorado

Middle East Market
2254 South Colorado Boulevard
Denver, CO 80222
(303) 756-4580

Connecticut

Nouzaim Middle Eastern Bakery
1650 East Main Street
Waterbury, CT 06705
(203) 756-0044

Florida

Ali Market
5361 North Dixie Street
Fort Lauderdale, FL 33311
(954) 428-3739

Damascus Mid East Food
5721 Hollywood Boulevard
Hollywood, FL 33021
(954) 962-4552

Illinois

Holy Land Grocery
4806-4808 North Kedzie Avenue
Chicago, IL 60625
(312) 588-3306

Maryland

Yekta Deli
1488 Rockville Pike
Rockville, MD 20800
(301) 984-1190

Massachusetts

Near East Baking Company
5268 Washington Street
West Roxbury, MA 02132
(617) 327-0217

Syrian Grocery
270 Shawmut Avenue
Boston, MA 02118
(617) 426-1458

Minnesota

Sinbad Café and Market
2528 Nicollet Avenue South
Minneapolis, MN 55404
(612) 871-6505

New Jersey

Al-Khayyam
7723 Bergenline Avenue
North Bergen, NJ 07047
(201) 869-9825

Fattal's Syrian Bakery
975 Main Street
Paterson, NJ 07503
(973) 742-7125

M & N Market, Inc.
28-01 Kennedy Boulevard
Jersey City, NJ 07306
(201) 963-8683

Nouri's Syrian Bakery
999 Main Street
Paterson, NJ 07503
(800) 356-6874

New York

Oriental Pastry and Grocery
170-172 Atlantic Avenue
Brooklyn, NY 11201
(718) 875-7687

The Family Store
69-05 3rd Avenue
Brooklyn, NY 11209
(718) 748-0207

Sahadi Importing Co.
187 Atlantic Avenue
Brooklyn, NY 11201
(718) 624-4550
(800) SAHADI-1

North Carolina

Nur Deli
28 Hillsborough Street
Raleigh, NC 27606
(919) 832-6255

Ohio

Gus's Middle Eastern Bakery
308 East South Street
Akron, OH 44311
(330) 253-4505

Sinbad Food Imports
2620 North High Street
Columbus, OH 43202
(614) 263-2370

Oklahoma

Mediterranean Imports
36-27 North MacArthur Boulevard
Oklahoma City, OK 73122
(405) 810-9494

Pennsylvania

Salim's Middle Eastern Food Store
47-05 Center Avenue
Pittsburgh, PA 15213
(412) 621-8110

Texas

Droubi's Bakery and Grocery
7333 Hillcroft Boulevard
Houston, TX 77081
(713) 988-5897

Phoenicia Bakery and Deli
2912 South Lamar Boulevard
Austin, TX 78704
(512) 447-4444

Worldwide Foods
1907 Greenville Avenue
Dallas, TX 75206
(214) 824-8860

Virginia

Halalco
108 East Fairfax Street
Falls Church, VA 22046
(703) 532-3202
Mediterranean Bakery
352 South Picket Street
Alexandria, VA 22304
(703) 751-1702

Canada

Byblos Food, Inc.
2667 Islington Avenue
Rexdale, Ontario
Canada M9V 2X6

Samiramis Arabic Supermarket
977 Albion Road
Toronto, Ontario
M9V 1A6

Town and Country
3355 Hurontario Street #8
Mississauga, Ontario
Canada L5A 2H3

Marché Adonis
9590 Boul. de l'Acadie
Montréal, Quebec
Canada H4N 1L8

Supermarché Al-Challal, Inc.
475 Côte-Vertu
Saint-Laurent, Quebec
Canada H4L 1X7

Provisions Byblos
175 Côte-Vertu
Saint-Laurent, Quebec
Canada H4N 1C8

Richard Suidan, Inc.
705 Boul. Cure-Labelle
Laval, Quebec
Canada H7V 2T9

Mid-East Food Centre
1010 Belfast Road
Ottawa, Ontario
Canada K1G 4A2

Lockwood Farm Market
699 Wilkins Street
London, Ontario
Canada N6C 5C8

Phoenicia Foods Ltd.
2594 Agricola
Halifax, Nova Scotia
Canada B3K 4C6

Jasmine Hallal Meats
Deli and Mediterranean Produce, Ltd.
4413 Main Street
Vancouver, British Columbia
Canada V5V 3R2

Mediterranean Speciality Foods
2768 Kingsway Street
Vancouver, British Columbia
Canada V5R 5H4

On the Web

To order ingredients online, visit
www.cafearabica.com

INDEX

Index   327

INDEX OF RECIPES AND INGREDIENTS IN ARABIC

F

Falaafil 194
Falaafil Yamanee 195
Falfal bil-Labid 10
Fasoolya ma' Futr 169
Fasoolya ma' Rizz 170
Fatayar 'Adas 211
Fatayar Bayd wa Banadoora 152
Fatayar bi Labana 245
Fatayar bi Sabanakh 231
Fatayar Kurath 206
Fatayar Za'tar ma' Jiban 218
Fattat Hummus 188
Fattoosh 101
Fattoot 147
Flayfle Mihshee 233
fool 3
Fool biz-Zayt 154-155
Fool Fass 196
Fool ma' Laban 112-113
Fool ma' Tomatim 198-199
Fool Mudammas 198
Fool Nabed 69
Fooliyya 197
fulful ahmar 2
fulful hiloo 4

G

ghar 2
Ghurayba 253
Ghuraybat Lawz 252-253

H

haal 2
habb al-fulful 4
Halawah bil-Fawaaki 271
Hamid Msyiar 17
hareesa, hreesa, harisa 3, 17
Hareera 78
Hareera Karawiya 61 *Hareera Kuskus* 67
Hareera Marrakashee 76
Hareesat al-Lawz See *Nammoora* 293
Harrak bi Isba'hu 208
Hasa al-Hummus 70
Hasa al-Khadar 88-89
Hasa Fasoolya 60
Hasa Laban Barida 66
Hasa Laban ma' Rizz 70-71

Hasa Laban ma' Tamata 66
Hasa Sabanakh ma' Laban 84
Hasa Tamata ma' Hummus 87
Hilwat ad-Daqeeq 257
Hilwat ar-Rumman 279
Hilwat Koko 259
Hilwat Tamar (Iraq) 268
Hilwat Tamar (Morocco) 289
Hlalem 88
hulbah 3, 12
hummus 2, 3
Hummus bi Dibs Rumman 32
Hummus bi Taheena 32-33, 34
Hummus bi Taheena Filasteeniya 30-31
Hummus bi Tamar Hindi 34
Hummus Habb 30
Hummus ma' Loobya 181

I

ibreeq 5
ibzar 3, 13
Ijwaz 163
ikleel al-jabal 4

J

jawz at-teeb 3
Jazar Fass 199
Jazar ma' Laban 177

K

Ka'ab Ghazaal 272
Ka'ak bil-Haleeb 276
Ka'ak Tamar 263
Kabab An-Nikhi 182
kama, kamaieh 3
Kama ma' Bayd 153
kammoon 2
karawya 2
Kaykat al-Laban 292
Kesksu 243
Khanfaroosh 283
Khissoo 105
Khiyar bi Laban 109
Khiyar Maqlee 200
khoolinjaan 3
Khshoof al-Balah 266
Khubz 'Arabee 9
Khubz Muhammas ma' Za'tar 237